Hector's Story

From school slates to computers

The life story of a boy growing up in the beautiful village of Mellon Udrigle in the North West Highlands of Scotland in the 1930s, through to manhood and the turmoil of war, going away to sea in the mid-20th century, and finally into industrial management.

Cover illustration by Ian Van Hinsbergh

Hector's Story

From school slates to computers

Hector Grant

Wordworks Ltd
Gairloch, UK

First published in 2009 by Wordworks Ltd
for Hector Grant (hectorgrant@rocketmail.com)

Second impression 2010

British Library Cataloguing in Publication Data
A catalogue record for this book is available from the British Library

ISBN 978-0-9564657-0-2

Typeset by Wordworks Ltd
wordworks@gairloch.co.uk

Contents

Preface

I have been thinking for a long time that I ought to record my childhood memories for posterity. Each generation I am sure, believes its time to have been unique, but I honestly believe that my time and place – the 30s and 40s in a small North West Highland village – might justifiably lay some claim to uniqueness. Anne knows the place very well, but only from the mid-50s. Alasdair and Lisa also know and love it well, but again only from the 60s. Kim has known it from the mid-80s, our grandchildren, Calum, Niall and Rohan are now getting to know the place by going there on holidays, and I hope that they will also get to love it.

The boys are the most compelling reason for getting this short period of history recorded, as I feel that when I have gone there will be nobody left who is able to tell them about a way of life that has gone forever. Alasdair and Lisa have always impressed upon me the need to record in some way the anecdotes and memories from this time, which they have listened to many times. For this encouragement I thank them, although by the time I have finished I might be thinking of some other word besides thanks.

The story as I tell it will be as true as my memory serves me. The places and the people are real, but the sequence of events will not always be chronologically correct.

Hector Grant
Heswall, May 2009

Family Trees

Thank you to David Grant and Margaret Hood for providing the family tree information used as the basis of the diagrams appearing on the following four pages.

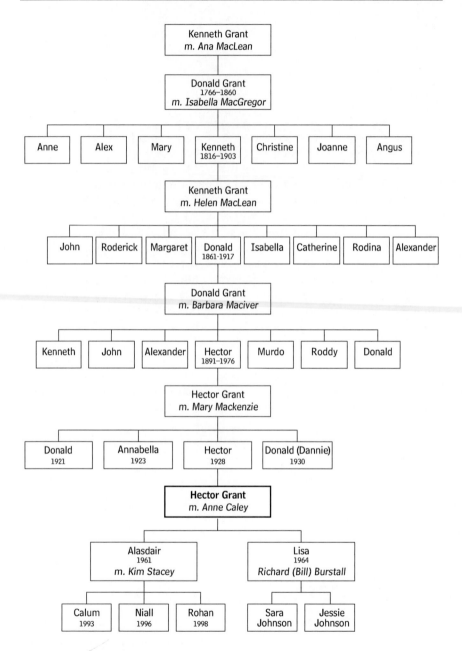

Figure 1: Grant family tree

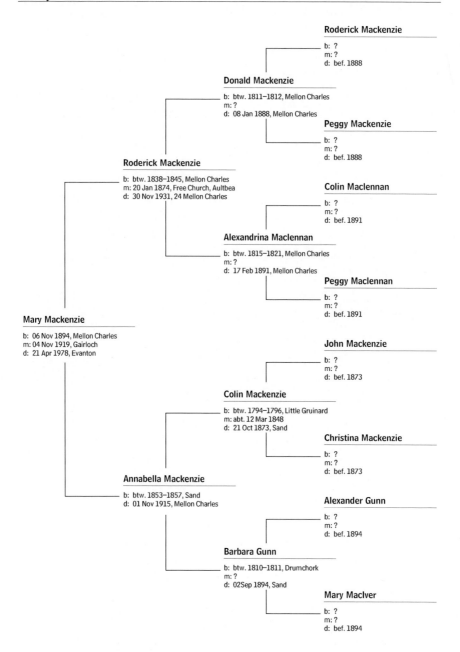

Roderick Mackenzie

b: ?
m: ?
d: bef. 1888

Donald Mackenzie

b: btw. 1811–1812, Mellon Charles
m: ?
d: 08 Jan 1888, Mellon Charles

Peggy Mackenzie

b: ?
m: ?
d: bef. 1888

Roderick Mackenzie

b: btw. 1838–1845, Mellon Charles
m: 20 Jan 1874, Free Church, Aultbea
d: 30 Nov 1931, 24 Mellon Charles

Colin Maclennan

b: ?
m: ?
d: bef. 1891

Alexandrina Maclennan

b: btw. 1815–1821, Mellon Charles
m: ?
d: 17 Feb 1891, Mellon Charles

Peggy Maclennan

b: ?
m: ?
d: bef. 1891

Mary Mackenzie

b: 06 Nov 1894, Mellon Charles
m: 04 Nov 1919, Gairloch
d: 21 Apr 1978, Evanton

John Mackenzie

b: ?
m: ?
d: bef. 1873

Colin Mackenzie

b: btw. 1794–1796, Little Gruinard
m: abt. 12 Mar 1848
d: 21 Oct 1873, Sand

Christina Mackenzie

b: ?
m: ?
d: bef. 1873

Annabella Mackenzie

b: btw. 1853–1857, Sand
d: 01 Nov 1915, Mellon Charles

Alexander Gunn

b: ?
m: ?
d: bef. 1894

Barbara Gunn

b: btw. 1810–1811, Drumchork
m: ?
d: 02Sep 1894, Sand

Mary MacIver

b: ?
m: ?
d: bef. 1894

Figure 2: Pedigree tree for Mary Mackenzie

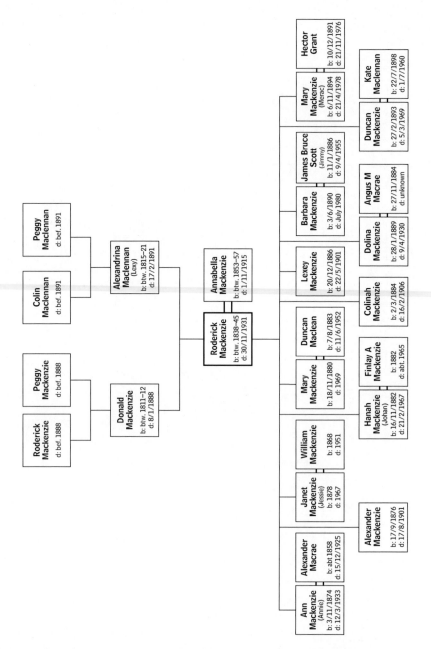

Figure 3: Hourglass tree of Roderick Mackenzie

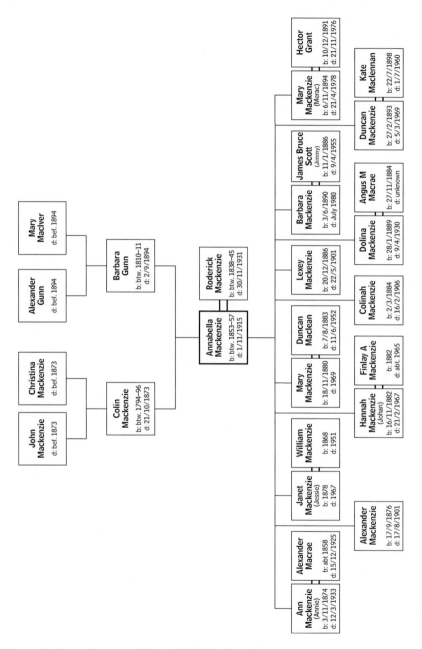

Figure 4: Hourglass tree of Annabella Mackenzie

Chapter 1

Pre-school Years

I was born at 2.30 a.m. on the 16th of February 1928 at No.18 Mellon
Udrigle, a little crofting village of, at that time, only six croft houses and a
schoolhouse which also served the adjoining village, which at that time
had eight croft houses. These two villages, Mellon Udrigle and Opinan,
stand at the Northern end of the peninsula of Rubha Mor in the parish of
Gairloch in Wester Ross. The name Mellon I believe to be a corruption of
the Gaelic word for hill, *meall*, and Udrigle is almost certainly of Norse
origin. There is plenty of evidence in local place names of Norsemen
visiting the area.

In crofting areas the general rule is that the croft house stands on the
croft. However in Mellon Udrigle there was a departure from this general
rule in that three of the six houses stood on common land in fairly close
proximity to each other, the other three being on their respective crofts.
This made for a real closeness of community between these three neigh-
bouring houses, although it must be said that there was a very strong
sense of community in the village as a whole. This was not always true of
the adjoining village of Opinan, where a certain amount of feuding took
place. As a child I was well aware that some families there had not spoken
to some other families for many years and that attitudes towards these
families by the people from Mellon Udrigle differed according to which
faction they belonged to. When I was very young I never questioned this
state of affairs and it was only as I got older that I began to wonder why
people could not get on amicably in such a small community. I think I was
influenced by my own parents, who always seemed to be on friendly
terms with everyone.

That is the community that I was born into, and as to the place itself I
think it is the most beautiful on Earth, but I accept that I might be preju-
diced. In fact it is not as beautiful as it was when I was a child. The mountains are still there and the sea is the same, but what is missing is the
cultivation of the fields. In those far off days every square foot of arable land
had crops growing in it and the pastures were green and filled with wild
flowers. If you think that is nostalgic nonsense let me illustrate the point by
explaining the difference between crofting then and crofting now as I see it.

A croft consists of about ten acres of mixed arable and pastureland. In addition there is access to open hill on a common basis, where all the crofters share several square miles. Each croft supports about three cows and between fifty and a hundred sheep. Most crofters would have one horse, usually a tough little Highland pony. The crops grown would be potatoes, turnips and swedes, oats, barley and a hay crop which would be a mixture of rye grass and clover, and these would be grown in a strictly adhered to and traditional rotation. The part of the croft given over to pasture because it was less fertile was so well grazed by the cows that it usually looked lush and green. Any rushes that grew were always cut and used for thatching, so the general appearance of the place was neat, tidy and well cared for. In addition, the area around the houses was fenced off to keep out cattle and sheep for all except the winter months so that the green in front of the houses, which stretched right down to the shore, was always clean.

Today it is quite a different story. Nobody now keep cows, so no land is tilled except possibly for the occasional small plot of potatoes. The land is no longer drained properly, so rushes have taken over from sweet meadow grass, and sheep are allowed to wander everywhere even down on to the sands when the midges drive them there to seek some respite close to the sea.

There are many other great differences between then and now, as you will be able to judge for yourselves as the story of my childhood unfolds.

When I was born I became the third child in the household. Donald, my older brother is nearly seven years older than me, and Anna, my sister is nearly five years older than I am. The family was complete two years and five months later when my younger brother Danny was born. It is said that no adult has a memory of anything that happened before they were three years old, but I would dispute this as there are two very clear memories that I hold of events that took place when I was just two and a half years old. My very earliest memory is of the day that Danny was born, although not for that reason. (Sorry Danny, but I was totally indifferent to your birth.) No, it was something much more exciting that captured my attention.

I had been left in the charge of some of the older girls in the place. There is a photograph in existence of me being carried around on the green by Betty Maciver who would have been about thirteen years old then. This was the day that our next door neighbours, the Macleans, decided to kill a pig. The method used in those days was to stick a knife in one of the pig's arteries and let it run around until it bled to death. You must realize that this was very much a self-sufficient society and that DIY extended into areas that would be hard to imagine today. Be that as it may the sight of this poor pig running around with blood pouring out of it is still imprinted indelibly on my mind. I do not believe that it was intended that the pig should be allowed to run around among the children at play. I think it

Me, feeling neglected on
the day Danny was born

must have escaped from its pen. I have had this incident confirmed although I always thought it strange that a pig would be killed on 9th July in the days when the only method of preserving meat was by salting. It was more usual to kill animals in late autumn and winter, when the meat would keep fresh for much longer, so less of it would need to be salted.

My other early memory is of the day that my brother Danny was christened. I don't know what the date was, but judging by what normally happened in those days it would have been within the first couple of months of life. Infant mortality at that time was still fairly high, and it was considered prudent and very desirable to be baptised at an early age.

The schoolhouse in small remote villages like ours doubled up as village hall, prayer meeting house, grazing committee meeting house or any other extra-curricular activities that it might be required for. The church that we belonged to was at Aultbea, a distance of six miles. That would be no problem today, but in 1930 when hardly anyone had a car it was six miles too far with a little baby. In these circumstances, the minister, who was one of the few people who owned a car, came to us. The people who came to the christening service, which would have been just about all the inhabitants of the village, managed somehow to squeeze into the children's double-seater desks and a long low form that sat against one of the side walls. That is where I had been parked on the form next to Kenny

Maclean, our next door neighbour, a widower and father of seven children ranging in age at that time from nine to late twenties. I have a very clear memory of seeing my baby brother wrapped in a white shawl in our mother's arms up in front of everyone and in the belief that I might be getting bored with the proceedings, Kenny Maclean leaning across and whispering in my ear and asking me whose little boy I was. I have no recollection of my reply although I was told later that I had said something like "what about being your own". Maybe I was feeling neglected that day.

Strangely, although the two episodes referred to above and dating from the time when I was just around two and a half years old are very clear in my mind the next year and ahalf is a blank. However, there are some incidents from my pre-school days that might be worth recording. There are no incidents that stand out in my memory other than those I have already mentioned, so these will be stories about myself that were told to me in later life by my parents and others.

I was reputed to have been a great wanderer, and if not watched would wander off and then fall asleep in the oddest of places. I had got completely lost on one occasion, and, in despair, our mother went to the school and asked if all the children would join in a search. This they did, and I was eventually found fast asleep in a rabbit burrow.

Family group (left to right) my brother Donald, my Aunt Mary,
my brother Danny, my mother, me, my sister Anna with cat

There was another occasion when I was left in the sole charge of my older brother Donald. He, and his best friend, Kenalick Maclean, wanted to go away somewhere to play, and being concerned not to lose me, tied a rope 20 yards long round my waist with the other end tied to the barn. Our father came home earlier than expected and found me there, quite happily playing on my own on the end of a tether. I don't believe the boys got into any trouble over it, as I think our father was quite appreciative of their inventiveness.

There was another story that our father was rather fond of relating, and about which I have a vague memory. I was about three and a half years old and staying at my grandmother's house. The house next door had many sons, and one of them, Harry Macrae, was home from university at the time. He was a piper and decided to clean out his bagpipes. The insides of the pipes are made up of a lot of tubes connected to a rubber bag, and he must have wanted a piece of string to pull a cleaning wad through. In any case the story goes that he had asked me to go in to the house and get this piece of string. I came out saying that I could not find it, to which he replied that my eyes must be in the back of my head as the string was on the hall table. I am supposed to have replied that if my eyes were in the back of my head I would have seen the string on my way out of the door. I do remember that after cleaning the pipes he poured warm syrup through the tubes. This was supposed to make the music sweeter, but I think it just made the mouthpiece sweeter to the taste.

We loved going to stay at our grandmother's house. I have memories of being tucked up in bed by her and having lullabies sung to me, which must be from my pre-school days. Our Uncle John (Shonochan) always seemed to be there. There was a little shop quite near to Grannie's house, which was owned by an elderly couple and their son. I don't know what time they went to bed, but they never seemed to get up before 2 p.m. Shonochan would give Danny and I a halfpenny with which to buy sweets at the shop and we would spend the early part of the day waiting impatiently for smoke to appear from the shopkeeper's house. The shop was just a room at one end of the house. A halfpenny does not seem very much with which to buy sweets, but in 1933 or 1934 I can remember getting about 12 inches of liquorice cut from a roll for this amount.

I have a hazy recollection of my 4th birthday when Roddy Maciver, father of Ian and Norma Maciver, gave me four pennies. Birthdays were not celebrated by the exchange of cards and presents as they are now. I think we were always aware of the day when it was our birthday and probably wished each other many happy returns, but that was about the extent of our celebrations. That was almost entirely a product of the area where we lived and to a much lesser extent a product of the times.

Chapter 2

Early School Years

My next clear memory is of the day that I started school. This was at the Easter term after my 4th birthday when I was only four years and two months old. The only reason I started then, instead of at the age of five as was normal, was because my best friend, Murdo Urquhart, who was nine months older than me had started then. I must have been feeling lonely having lost my playmate, and my mother pleaded with the teacher to take me into school. This she did on a full-time basis although I did not go on to the register officially until I was five.

In our home the language spoken was Gaelic and I am told that when I started school I had only a very rudimentary knowledge of English. I don't remember this and it bears out the belief that this is the time to learn foreign languages as I am told that I was speaking English after a couple of weeks as well as any other four year old. It was not a very big school, and I can still visualize the certificate that hung on the back of the classroom door, and which read *"This school is certified for 22 pupils"*. At the time that I started I think there would have been fourteen children in the school of whom only five were boys. My older brother Donald, Kenalick Maclean, the youngest of the Maclean family from next door, and Willie Macpherson from Opinan being the big boys, and Murdo and I being the infants. The girls would have been my sister Anna, Alice and Jessie Maciver, three Macpherson girls and three Macaskill girls.

There was only one teacher, at that time a Miss Macalister and she had the difficult task of teaching all the different age groups in one room. This was quite common and the teachers were well adapted to the system. I don't think there was a strict adherence to keeping everyone in his or her particular year. As the youngest at that time I always seemed to be taught among children who were older than me and this went on for the whole of my school life. I believe this to have been of benefit to me.

The fourteen who were at the school when I started was the highest number attained in all my time there. The numbers fluctuated up and down over the years, going up in the summer and autumn when the children of relatives of the local inhabitants came for summer holidays and stayed on for extended periods, and going down again in winter. There was a general downward trend, however, and the nadir was reached in 1939 when we were down to four – three boys and one girl.

There was Murdo and myself in one class, with Danny and Mary Macaskill in a lower class. When you consider all the effort being put into reducing class sizes these days this must have been an ideal situation with about as close to one-to-one tuition as you could get.

It might have had disadvantages in the acquisition of so-called living skills but I never felt that I had lost anything by it, however I will let others be the judges of that. I think it probably made us gentler towards, and more courteous to, females as, being in a three-to-one majority. there was never any need to prove our masculinity.

Needless to say, these thoughts did not exercise our minds very much then. We just got on with living, and what a happy contented life it was. To try and recapture the flavour of the time I will start by describing our house, as it was when I can first remember it clearly.

The house had a small entrance hall with a room off to each side and a scullery at the back. Stairs led up from the hall to a landing with two bedrooms off and a third smaller bedroom accessed through one of the others. This was fairly typical of the croft houses of the region. The room to the left was the kitchen/living room and had a stone flag floor. When I was about eight years old the flags were removed to be replaced by what was thought then to be a proper floor. The cooking was done on an open fire until a black cast iron stove was installed at the same time as the 'proper' floor was put in.

There was quite an art to cooking on an open fire, and, although it was then the norm, I am amazed now at the great variety of delicious meals our mother used to produce. The fuel used was peat, which was cut and dried on the open moor. That is another story in itself, which I will tell later.

The open fire was set on the hearth with a raised area to each side and which were linked across the front by four horizontal bars. If I remember correctly, the top bar had a small metal grid attached to it on which the teapot stood. It was always felt necessary to place the teapot close to the fire to help the infusion. The habit still persists in that part of the world if nowhere else as I have seen people turn the electric hob on low to infuse the tea.

All the cooking pots and pans had to have hooped handles to enable them to be hung from a hook. There was a metal bar fixed horizontally about four feet up the chimney from which hung a flat iron bar with about five holes in it. These were at about four inch centres and would have a double ended hook placed in them. The pot that was being used at the time would hang from the lower hook, while the top hook would be placed in one of the holes. As you can imagine this allowed the pot to be suspended at five different heights above the fire to regulate the cooking heat. Was this the precursor of the term *"Regulo 1 to 9"* used today in gas cooking? An interesting thought.

The raised areas at each side of the fire were used to keep food hot in the pots, as only one dish at a time could be cooked. I believe you could simmer on them by edging the pot over the fire a short distance. Pot roasts were the order of the day as there was no oven. Pancakes, scones and oatcakes were baked on a griddle. A form of large shallow cake was baked in what must have been a square metal pan. The frying pan was of heavy cast iron with the customary hooped handle and was quite deep, but being circular, could not have been used for the cake.

Baking took place just about every day, with oatcakes one day, pancakes the next, and scones on the third day. There would also be the occasional cake. Strangely, the baking of bread was never undertaken, even when ovens became common. I suppose the traditional way of doing things had been laid down at the time when everyone had open fires, and traditions die hard in remote rural areas.

There was a large meal chest in the scullery, which was subdivided for flour and oatmeal. One third was for flour and two thirds for oatmeal. Oatmeal was bought by the bol, and flour by the half bol. A bol, as far as I can remember, was 140 pounds. I cannot verify this in any dictionary. Was it related in some way to the bushel, which is a dry measure of eight gallons?

You might wonder why there was twice as much oatmeal as there was of flour. The reason was that the staple diet for breakfast was brose, which took a lot of meal, as well of course as the regular baking of oatcakes. Brose was made by putting three heaped dessert spoons of meal in a bowl and adding a good pinch of salt and a dessert spoon of sugar. Into this was poured sufficient boiling water to make a sloppy mixture, stirring all the time. It was usually taken with milk, but in winter, when there were times when milk was in short supply, it would be taken with syrup or treacle

Because the quantity of meal taken in brose was so much greater than would be taken in porridge, where the meal is cooked, it sustained one for a long time. We each prepared our own brose, from quite an early age. Our mother kept an eagle eye open while this was going on, as some of us would use more sugar than necessary if not watched.

In describing the house I find that I have spent all the time in the kitchen, which in reality is the place where most of our time was spent, except maybe in bed. It was after all the kitchen/living room.

Another important room in the house was the scullery. This room was the equivalent to the utility room of today even though it had far fewer pieces of equipment and hardly any gadgets. There was no bathroom in the house and the chemical toilet was outside. There was in fact no running water in the house, all water being carried in pails from the well.

These pails were placed on a low shelf in the scullery with a dipper beside them. All the washing up was done in the scullery as well as the preparation of food and vegetables. It was a very small room and you can imagine the pushing and shoving that would be going on there in the mornings as we all tried to get to the meal chest to make our brose before going off to school.

The scullery was also used by all the family to wash ourselves. This would be done standing in a wooden tub for a full wash down. When we were quite young we used to get bathed in a tin bath in front of the fire. Danny and I always seemed to be having our hair washed by our older brother Donald, who seemed to take great delight in rinsing our hair with jugs of cold water. I suppose the truth of the matter was that he had used up all the hot water in washing our hair.

As I mentioned before there was no running water in the house. The well that we got our water from, which was shared with the Macleans from next door, was about a quarter of a mile away and it was the job of the older children to fetch the water. In fact I seem to remember that the task of fetching water started at quite a young age. I think we would have been given a small tin pail until we were old enough to carry the two-gallon pails. You will notice that I keep referring to pails and not buckets. We always knew them as such, and the Gaelic word for them was much the same.

The pails that were used for carrying and holding drinking/cooking water were white enamelled and of something over two gallons capacity. Similar pails were used for milking cows. For all other uses, galvanized metal buckets were used.

To save endless trips to the well, use was made of the plentiful rainfall. Not all houses had a water butt, maybe because their wells were nearer to the houses, but ours certainly did.

I can clearly remember a water butt being installed, probably as a replacement. It was a large wooden barrel that had held lard. My father must have got it from the local merchant and to remove all traces of the lard he set a fire to the inside of it. This actually charred the whole of the inside. This was then scraped off and after several changes of water and having a tap fitted it gave sterling service for many years.

If there was not enough water in the water butt we would carry water up from the burn for washing clothes etc. It was lovely and soft and you hardly needed any soap. More later about big wash days.

Chapter 3

A One-room Schoolhouse

So it is back to school. I think it was so different from anything that could be experienced anywhere in the modern world today that it is worth while trying to explain the system.

As I said earlier, there was only one classroom and one teacher. Pupils were grouped according to ability rather than age for full class lessons such as mental arithmetic, or poetry reading.

In most cases work was set according to the ability of the pupil, so it virtually amounted to individual tuition. I seem to remember that, for mental arithmetic, everyone in the school stood in a row at the front of the classroom and the teacher asked the questions one by one. It was not a case of whoever knew the answer giving it. This would allow the teacher to adjust the level of difficulty according to age.

All rough work was done on a slate with a slate pencil and not with pencil and paper. The slate was very smooth, and if I remember correctly was about the size of an A4 sheet of paper and set in a wooden frame. It was very economical as you just wiped the slate after that particular piece of work was finished. I seem to remember that I had the same slate for the whole of my school life.

Homework was always set and must have been fairly similar to current practices. The one thing that was very different was the punishment meted out for errors in our work. Don't forget that at this time corporal punishment was the norm in all schools. Although the cane may have been used in some parts of Scotland, in the Highlands it was the tawse. The tawse was a thick leather strap, which would have anything from two to five fingers at the end. It was always administered to the palm of the hand. So as to leave no excuses about being unable to write due to the pain, it was always given on the left hand. The exception to the rule was Danny who was strapped on the right hand, as he was left-handed.

I don't think we got punished for mistakes in homework, as there would be such strong temptation to cheat in order to avoid punishment. I cannot remember how it worked for most lessons, but I remember exactly how it worked for spelling mistakes. You got one stroke on your non-writing hand for every spelling error. In spite of all the apparent evidence to the contrary today I still think it was an extremely effective way of improving spelling.

What I can say without any fear of contradiction is that it had no ill effects whatsoever and that we bore no malice towards the perpetrator of this arcane punishment. Indeed, as we grew up and were able to relate to these teachers as adults, we were always on very friendly terms with them. It is quite possible of course that the teachers did not like what they had to do, but had to adhere to the system as laid down by the authorities. It was quite painful, particularly on a cold winters day. My friend Murdo claimed to have a potion that toughened the hands, and we pretended to believe him. He also claimed to have a substance that repaired cracked slates. This was nothing more than sand that he picked up on his way to school, but we must have got some pleasure in pretending that we believed him.

The school curriculum was not very different to what it would have been anywhere else at that time. We did have a Gaelic period, but it was only one period per week. Maths was taught as three separate subjects: Arithmetic, Algebra and Geometry.

History covered the period from about the 9th century up until the end of the Great War. There was a fairly strong bias towards Scottish history. For instance Robert the Bruce was a hero whereas Edward I was a villain.

The rest of the world was not ignored however, and I believe we got a very thorough grounding in world history. We had to learn and memorize long lists of dates and had to be able to name every monarch in correct rotation in England and Scotland from Alfred the Great to the present time. We also had to state the dates on which they ascended to the throne and the dates of their deaths. Lots of other dates had to be memorized, such as battles and any other important events. I am sure it would be argued today that this method of teaching was of debatable value. I have a theory that the capacity of the brain to absorb knowledge is infinite and that the more you exercise it the more readily it absorbs new knowledge. It is also very useful when you are playing Trivial Pursuits.

The teaching of geography was also quite different. The dictionary definition of geography is the science of Earth's form, physical features, climate, population, etc. Nowadays the emphasis seems to be on the last two, and while we did not ignore them I think we probably did emphasize the first two.

All the principal rivers in the British Isles with their respective lengths had to be learnt. The position of every county with the county capital and the main manufacture and/or activity of every large town or city in the British Isles. One exercise that I remember was being given a blank map of Scotland or England where only the outline of the country was shown. We then had to trace in every county, every large town, and every river. I must admit that this produced some very weird maps.

It is debatable if this form of teaching was any better than current methods, but at least it gave you a great sense of where you were at any given time. I find that I can visualize the world in my mind's eye, and while I might not be able to pinpoint every given place, I would, if given a few clues, make a fair stab at it.

We had no musical instruments in the school, but valiant attempts were made to teach us to sing unaccompanied. This must have given the teacher a lot of wry amusement. I think that most of the singing would have been together as a group. We did practice the scales with the aid of a tuning fork. The scales were printed on oiled cloth, which would be hung on the blackboard.

Poetry had quite an important place in the curriculum, as I seem to remember doing a lot of poetry reading. We also had to memorize quite a lot of poems, and stand up before the rest of the school and recite them.

I remember clearly the trouble that I had with a particular poem. It was not because I could not remember the words, but because I could not say them for laughing. I had something of a reputation as a giggler, and could not stop myself from laughing, sometimes at the most inopportune moments. The poem on this day was Young Lochinvar. I have forgotten most of the poem now but I do remember the offending line. It was *"Oh, young Lochinvar has come out of the West, and through all the wild border his steed was the best."* My friend Murdo stood up before me to give his rendition and gave it as *"Oh, young Lochinvar has **jumped** out of the West."* This does not seem much of a cause for great hilarity, but when my turn came I just could not get past that line without bursting into laughter. The teacher was very patient or maybe sadistic because she made me persevere, but it was to no avail and in the end I had to turn my back on the class and face the wall. I managed somehow to get it done but the rest of the pupils had great fun watching the back of my neck getting redder by the minute as I tried valiantly to suppress my laughter.

We were taught to knit at school. This may have been a wartime innovation, as I seem to remember that the only knitting that we did was comforts for servicemen. This included socks, gloves, mittens, scarves and balaclava helmets. The best part of this was that we got some time off school to go up into the hills to gather loose wool that sheep would have left stuck to heather etc. Most of the knitting had to be done as homework, in addition to the normal workload. I remember Danny knitting a scarf and being told it had to be a certain length by Monday morning. He spent the weekend knitting a few rows and then tying the scarf to the doorknob and pulling on it. I think he eventually got it to the required length but it must have been so narrow as to serve well as a necktie.

There seems to have been quite a lot of laughter around at school and elsewhere. Looking back now over all those years, I had a happy childhood and I am sure that I was happy at school as well. I was no different from anyone else in that Friday was the best day and that I looked forward as much as anyone else to the holidays. In fact I remember that Danny and I used to pin up a sheet of paper on our bedroom wall on the day that school re-opened after the holidays. with the number of days until the next holiday, and we would then cross one off each night.

When I was ten years old the schoolhouse got a major re-furbishment. As far as the inside was concerned this just amounted to a complete paint job in nice bright pastel shades. The great excitement for us was the introduction of running water and flush toilets. Up to this time we only had outside chemical toilets. The new ones were still outside but had been smartened up. There was a urinal for the boys—all three of us—and if I remember correctly it was outside the girls toilet, but with no door to it.

There was no septic tank, a situation that would not be allowed to prevail today. The sewage pipes were laid down towards the sea and terminated in a long cast iron pipe that extended well out over the sea. One of our games used to be to put some paper down the pan and flush it, and then run down to see if we could beat the said paper to the sea.

When I was about seven or eight years old, the teacher's accommodation in the schoolhouse was let out during the summer holidays to an English family called Ogilvy.

The house was an integral part of the schoolhouse, or more correctly the classroom was an integral part of the house, but with no connecting door. It was rather a fine building of pink granite, the house having two entertaining rooms and three bedrooms. It is now a good substantial dwelling, with the classroom and the space above it being incorporated into the house. It had, like so many small village schools, closed the year after I left.

The English family that came to the schoolhouse during the summer holidays must have been rather wealthy as they had a chauffeur, and a governess for their younger daughter. They also employed a cook and a housemaid locally. They did not live in, nor did the chauffeur, who lodged at the Macleans' house.

They must have come to stay in the schoolhouse every summer until 1939 and may well have been there when war broke out. If not they must have come back soon after that, probably in late September. Mr Ogilvy did not come back, and in fact was never seen again at Mellon Udrigle. Mrs Ogilvy had been married before, when her name had been Sewell. The older daughter Antonia was called Sewell. I don't remember whether she had been divorced or widowed.

Antonia was about my age and Maryanne was about six years younger. At this time I suppose they would have been considered to be wartime evacuees. The governess came back with them and stayed for some time and taught Maryanne. It was not long before she met a young naval lieutenant who must have been stationed at the naval base in Aultbea and they were married soon after. She left at this point, and Maryanne joined the rest of us at school, Antonia having been there from the beginning.

When the governess got married our teacher decided that the children should make something as a present for her. Alice Maciver, who of course, had left school long before this time, was fairly artistic, and was commissioned to do a drawing of the school. This was then traced on to some white cloth and all of the children helped to embroider it and frame it. I know she loved the school so I wonder how long she cherished the picture for. If I remember correctly she had become a Mrs Gradwell.

I owe my ability to swim, such as it is, to Antonia. It must have been during one of the earlier years as I am sure that I was swimming well before my 11th birthday. We spent all our spare time playing on the sands and in and out of the water all day long, especially during the summer holidays. In those days the summer holidays ran from about 9th July until about 1st September.

The regular beachcombers would have been Murdo, Danny and I, but any other holidaymakers who happened to be around at the time would join us. The most regular of these would have been Mary and Sadie Macrae, granddaughters of Kenny Maclean. They came every summer for the whole of the holidays. Sometimes they would arrive before our school broke up, and they would then join us at school. There always seemed to be enough spare capacity to take other pupils in.

The Macleods' house at the back of ours also had its share of summer grandchildren, some of whom joined our school from time to time. I particularly remember boys from the island of Lewis who spent a whole summer there. They were grandsons of Alexander Macleod who lived in the house behind ours. At least two of those boys spent some time at our school.

When I first started at school there were, as far as I can remember, fourteen pupils in the school, and the numbers fluctuated between that, and a minimum of four. The trend was generally downwards. We did get a few evacuees at the beginning of the war in 1939: the Ogilvy girls I mentioned earlier, and two other girls from Glasgow, who stayed with the Macivers. I believe they were relations of the Macivers.

The minimum of four must have been reached at the very early part of the war after the Ogilvy girls left and before the other evacuees arrived and before the younger Macaskill girl started school. I seem to remember that when I left school there were about six pupils left, the only boy being Danny. Murdo had left in the summer of 1941 and I left at the Easter of 1942.

Fourteen was the normal age for leaving school if one was not going on to higher education in those far off days. Going on to higher education meant going to boarding school in Dingwall which cost more money than could easily be afforded by most families. The only grant was a £20 bursary, which I had qualified for by passing an entrance examination.

There were two main examinations in the whole of our time at school. The first was the 11+, or the qualifying examination as it was known to us. Passing this examination enabled one to move to the higher divisions which took three more years. I cannot remember what happened to pupils who did not pass, but clearly they would have stayed on at school, as there was nowhere else to go. They probably did the same lessons as those that had passed, but with lower expectations.

The other examination was taken towards the end of school life and was called the Scottish Leaving Certificate. You were assessed on class work and by examination on all the subjects that you had taken. I had ten of those certificates in the usual range of subjects. Earlier, I mentioned an entrance examination for High School, which was taken at the age of twelve. We knew it as the Bursary examination. I took this examination so as to keep company with a girl who was taking it for the purpose of going on to higher education. We both passed with high marks. The girl, Ina Macpherson, went on to Dingwall, but we lost touch after that as the family moved away from the area.

I have lost touch with all the children with whom I had spent most of my school life except for my brother Danny and Murdo Urquhart. It may be of interest to note, in the context of our form of schooling, and the fact that we each left school at age 14, what course our careers took.

I did not follow Murdo's career closely, but I do know that he became a farm manager and possibly an estate manager at one time. Danny, having spent some time at sea, joined the Glasgow Police and attained the rank of Detective Superintendent. I also went to sea, gaining my Master's Foreign Going Certificate and a Mersey Pilots Licence. I subsequently came ashore and reached a reasonably high position in industrial management.

For Danny and I, to my certain knowledge, this meant the burning of a lot of midnight oil while we studied, and frequent returns to college, but I do believe the basis had been well laid at Mellon Udrigle Public School.

I mentioned earlier in this chapter that the three main beachcombers were Murdo, Danny and myself. Well, that is not strictly true as there was a fourth member of the gang called Bute. Bute was Murdo's faithful dog that accompanied him wherever he went. She was a Border collie and used to come to school with him in the morning and lie outside the schoolhouse door until playtimes when she would join us in the playground. I remember coming back to school once after the long summer holidays, and we all had to write an essay on what we had done during the holidays. Some things in education don't change, do they? Murdo started his essay with the memorable words *"Hector, Danny, Bute and I found a nest on the sands"*. I think that places the dog well and truly at the heart of the gang.

Danny and me with our dog Nelly

Chapter 4

Work on the Croft

I made some reference in an earlier chapter to peat as a fuel. It was in fact the only fuel used by all the households in Mellon and Opinan. The only place that used coal as a fuel was the school.

Most of the peat was cut on the open moor, although we did have one peat bank on the croft. The amount of peat cut each year would be about 300 linear yards to a width of approximately 30 inches and to a similar depth. The first part of the job was to remove the tough heather turf to the depth of a spade. This would be done in March, well in advance of the actual peat cutting. It was easier to do it then, before the new spring growth took place.

It would be left then until about the middle of April. You then had to remove a further few inches of the dry crust, until you had a good, level and soft, workable platform. The cutting of the peats was performed with a special peat knife and required a lot of skill in its efficient use. Each peat when first cut, and still very wet, measured about 3 inches by 5 inches and about 21 inches long. When dry they would probably have decreased to half that size. Assuming all the preparation work already done, a good day's work would be, say, 50 to 60 yards of bank cut.

As children we took no part in the peat cutting until we were about 14 years old. Maybe we would do some of the removal of the dry crust with a spade. Our real usefulness came a little later. After the peats had lain on the ground, well spread out, for a couple of weeks, they would have dried to a certain extent, and at this time they were lifted and stood on end in groups of about ten and leaning against each other. This was a job that was considered suitable for quite young children.

Peats stood like that for a further four weeks, depending on the weather. When they were completely dried out they were stacked up and the stacks were covered over by the turf that had been stripped off in March. If you had a large enough storage shed they could be taken home instead of being stacked. Our peat store was an upturned boat resting on a six-foot high wall built to the contours of the boat. We generally had about a month's supply stored there, as well as other things, including a lot of kindling wood.

The peats were brought home by horse and cart. We would first fill

My mother milking a cow

about 30 large hessian sacks and carry those to a point that was accessible to the horse and cart. A good load for our highland pony would be 15 bags. Daily usage would be about one large bag on average for the year. The calorific value of peat varied according to its colour. The darker the colour the more heat they gave out. We tried to keep the hardest and blackest peats for winter use.

There was always a lot of work to be done on a croft and children were expected to help, and indeed did so without question, as that was the norm. When I was about twelve years old I used to get up about 6.30 a.m. during the lambing season and walk all the way round the area known as Rubha Beg looking for any newborn lambs. All the sheep belonging to the Macleods, the Macleans, and us ran together on the hill and they were looked after on a co-operative basis. Whoever saw the lamb first marked it up to indicate which household it belonged to. This was done by cutting the ears in a particular way. Our mark was having the two ears slit lengthways and a "v" cut out of the lower side of the right ear. Each house had their own distinctive mark and these marks all had names. You had to carry a very sharp knife with you so as to do the job with the least suffering to the lambs. It had to be done when they were newly born, as it would be rather difficult to catch them once they were a couple of days old. This is why I did it before going to school. Fortunately school did not start until

10 a.m. Our father worked at the salmon fishing station from late February to mid-August with a very early start in the morning; otherwise he would have taken care of the lambing.

We also helped with milking the cows, but only in the evening. In the summer the cows were herded on to fenced-off areas of pasture on the croft until about midday, after which they were let out on to the hill. This was because there was not enough good pasture to keep them on all day, every day. We had to go and find them on the hill in the evening and herd them home, as they would never come home on their own. Each of the three houses had their cows on their own fields and, in spite of being let out on to the hill at different times they always got together once out there.

If there were a lot of children around, as there would be at the summer holidays, we would all go off together and we thought of this as a happy social event. At other times, when we had to do it on our own, it was considered a chore.

In those far-off days all the work on the croft was done either by hand or with horses. As two horses were required for ploughing, the only way to get it done was by linking up with another crofter who had a similar-sized horse and to do each others work in turn. The alternative was to hire the services of someone who had two horses of his own and who made his living by hiring out his services.

Our father tended to use the latter system most of the time, as he did not have the time to do his own ploughing. The man who seemed to do most of our ploughing was Findlay McLennan, who always had two big strong horses. He used to do ploughing all over the district, to distances of up to eight or nine miles. As the working day was from 8 a.m. to 6 p.m. he would have to get up at 4 a.m. to feed the horses so that he could leave at 6 a.m. to be on site for an 8 a.m. start. He would then have to walk home with the horses after the day's work, and by the time he got them fed and bedded down for the night it would be 9 p.m. If I remember correctly, his charge for a day's ploughing was £2 at a time when the average weekly wage for a labourer was probably about £4. As the ploughing season lasted no more than six weeks, he did not make a fortune.

The planting of potatoes was done differently from the system used universally now. The plot of land to be planted was liberally manured, and instead of then making drills, it was just ploughed in the normal way with the potatoes being planted in every third furrow. We used to plant about eight or ten bags – about half a ton. It took four people to do the planting without causing any interruption to the horses. I remember one particular time that the said Findlay came to our croft to plant a small field of four or five bags of potatoes, and Danny and I were the only ones available to do the planting. We were probably only about ten and twelve years old respectively but very fit, as we needed to be. Findlay had the horses almost at a gallop to try and beat us, but he never caught us, although we had the horses breathing down our backs at times. It was years later before he told us that he had just done it for his own amusement, but I think the joke rebounded on him a little.

By the time that I was about 15 and Danny was 13, we did quite a lot of our own ploughing. I think we used the horse belonging to the Macaskills that was about the same size as our own horse. Because of the difficulty of handling the plough and guiding the horses, we adopted the method of having one person leading the horses while the other person just handled the plough.

The next job on the croft that was considered very suitable for children was the weeding of the potatoes. A scraper was first pulled between the drills by a single horse, but this only cleared the weeds from between the drills. We then cleared all the weeds from between each individual plant by hand. Some weeks after that a drill plough would be run between each drill to earth them up. It was then just a question of waiting until they were ready for lifting.

The busiest time on the croft was in the autumn. First the hay had to be cut using a hand scythe. As children we probably started to do this at the age of twelve, but would not be allowed to sharpen the scythe for another year or two. This meant that we could use a scythe only when there was an adult with us, as it had to be sharpened every five to ten minutes. I remember Danny getting a very bad cut on his wrist when he was about fourteen, while sharpening his scythe. He just jumped on his bike and cycled to Aultbea to have it stitched by the doctor. The doctor, who explained that the effort of cycling speeded up his heart, which caused him to lose rather a lot of blood, told him off.

After cutting, the hay had to be dried. This was achieved by turning it over regularly, and scattering it thinly on the ground. Eventually it would be made into small coils, which then would be consolidated into larger coils. When it had dried and matured properly it would be made into a large stack, or carted home and stacked in the barn.

By the time the hay was all secured, it was time to start cutting the oats and barley. This had to be cut with a scythe, but then had to be bundled into sheaves immediately after cutting. These were then made into stooks, which had twelve sheaves in each. The sheaves were stood on end, grain end up and six on each side leaning against each other. They remained like that for two or three weeks, after which they would be made into stacks. Each stack would have about 400 sheaves in it. There was a fair amount of skill required in making a good stack that would stand the rigours of a long winter.

The next harvesting job was lifting the potatoes. This like everything else was done by hand. Well not exactly by hand as a garden fork was used to turn the potato drill, and then the potatoes were lifted by hand. As quite young children we would do the lifting while our father or mother used the fork. By the time we were twelve years old we would be doing the whole job.

The potatoes were stored outside on a raised bed. They were first covered by thin sections of turf and then a deep layer of soil. Enough potatoes would be stored in the barn to last the winter. The outside clamp would be opened up in the early spring and sorted through, choosing about half a ton of the correct-sized potatoes for seed and the rest brought in to last until the next harvest.

The final harvest job was the lifting of the turnips. This could be quite late in the year and was a miserable job if the frost had arrived by the time we had to do them. The method was to pull each one out individually by its top and, while holding it by the left hand, slash off the root with a heavy and sharp cleaver, then slash through the top as close to the turnip as possible, taking care to miss one's fingers. As the tops were usually wet and very cold your hands would be quite numb so that you could chop off a few fingers without noticing. Working gloves had not been heard of in those days, or certainly not by us.

Work on the croft did not finish with the end of the harvest, of course. Cattle still had to be fed and cleaned out and all the food prepared for them. Oats and hay had to be brought from the stacks to the barn. Peats had to be brought home and a hundred and one other little jobs. The days, however, were very short, especially around midwinter and it was indeed an easier time.

Chapter 5

The Community

When I was young we thought of the area that we lived in as comprising Mellon Udrigle and all the villages from there to Aultbea and beyond to the end of the road in Mellon Charles. As children we did not as a rule travel beyond those bounds. I do remember once being taken with Danny by the chauffeur for the Ogilvies to Poolewe for tea. I think it was probably the first time we had ever been to Poolewe, and it was definitely the first time we had been to a café. We called them tea-rooms in those days. I think I would have been about eight or nine years old.

The parish of Gairloch, of which we were part, also included Poolewe and all the villages along the road to Cove, Gairloch itself, and all the villages along the roads to Badachro and Melvaig respectively. The total population of the parish of Gairloch in 1936 was 1800. At a rough guess I think that the population of what I have defined as our area would be about 500.

This is now where one of the greatest differences between life in a rural area and in an urban area will be illustrated. In an urban area you would have many thousands of people living within a mile or two of your home, but how many of them would you know well? As children you would know all your own classmates well, and probably be on nodding terms with most of the pupils at the school. You would also know your friends' parents and other family friends. Adults also would have a fairly large circle of friends and acquaintances and they would know their immediate neighbours.

I think we could agree that a good knowledge of 5% of the people living in what you consider as your area would be quite generous.

When you compare that with a rural area you get a completely different picture. I can only relate with authority what happened in my area, but I believe it to have been true of most rural areas at that time. I accept that it is quite different now.

When I was a child, even I knew all 500 people who lived in our area. Or at the very least I knew their names and where they lived. As an adult you would have an extensive knowledge of everyone. You would know who was married to whom, how many children they had, what jobs they had, how much they earned. Maybe not their birthdays, but definitely their ages. If anybody was ill a daily bulletin was issued on his or her condition, or so it seemed. I find it difficult now to imagine how all this information was disseminated, in an age when the only telephones would have been in the shops and the Post Offices

One of the conduits for passing on information was the postman. There were three postmen covering our area. One of them worked out of the Aultbea Post Office and two out of the Laide Post Office. One of those actually went beyond what I have called our area, as he did Sand, Coast and on to Gruinard. The two who worked from Laide obviously met daily and exchanged all the local gossip.

Doors were never locked during my childhood. I don't think we had a key. Doors wouldn't even be shut, unless the wind or rain was blowing in. The result of this was that the postman would come right in to the house to deliver the mail. There may not have been any mail – there was less junk mail in those days – but he would call anyway as he usually brought the paper. At the same time as delivering the mail/paper he would pass on all the local news. As he did this at every house he must have taken a long time to complete his round.

The local shops all sent vans around the countryside on different days of the week. As there were three shops in Aultbea, another in Laide, and a butchers in Mellon Charles, most days of the week were covered by a van. This was another good source of information. In pre-war days the butcher was my own cousin, Roddy Macrae. His day for the Mellon Udrigle round was Monday and he used to time his arrival at our house at precisely 1 p.m. and have his lunch with us. We always enjoyed his visits as he was great fun and always made a fuss of us as children.

In addition to the shops just mentioned there were some other smaller ones. The one that I mentioned earlier near to our Grandmother's house did not open until the afternoon. One in Sand actually did a van round after the war. There was an other shop in Udrigle that did a local round with a horse and trap. That one closed at the beginning of the war with the advent of ration books ,as the lady who ran it could not be bothered with all the attendant bureaucracy. While it existed it was very convenient, being our nearest shop, a mere two miles. I would often be sent there on my bicycle when I was quite young. The lady whose shop it was did not have enough customers to require her to stay in the shop so we would have to go to the house. That was Udrigle House, which has since been restored, although all the beautiful panelling has been lost. It was in this house as a young boy that I first saw a grandfather clock

I mentioned in Chapter 1 that I had got four pennies on my fourth birthday from Roddy Maciver. What I had not told you then was that he drove the horse and trap for the lady from the Udrigle shop, who was known to us as Katie Udrigle. It was a small trap, and with two people in it I don't know how they fitted in any groceries. I do remember that we always got our tea from her, and it was always Liptons tea in a silver foil packet. I am sure that she carried the full range of groceries, such as it was in those days. What did it consist of? There would be bread, sugar, tea, and butter in the winter, cooking fats, the occasional bottle of sauce, salt and pepper. I am sure there would have been more than that, but we did produce so much of our own that these basics would have sufficed.

Eggs were used to partially pay for groceries and were accepted by all the vans as far as I can remember. Katie Udrigle certainly accepted them, as I can remember the large basket of eggs that sat on the floor of the trap. I think the going rate would have been one penny for an egg. There was always a surplus of eggs during the summer months so it was a useful source of revenue with a very convenient means of disposal.

Talking about the price of eggs reminds me of a story that I was told recently while visiting Lisa at Rubha Riabhach. I think it must have been culled from the Ullapool museum. In the early part of the 20th century there was a village store and a church in Scoraig, which was a two-mile walk from Rubha Riabhach. Apparently there was a woman in Rubha Riabhach who used to walk to the store in Scoraig with one egg on a Saturday, which she would sell for one penny. She would then do the same walk on Sunday to church and put her penny in the collection.

Our hens had their house near the shore and as a result they used to go on to the beach and scrabble amongst the rotten seaweed. This gave the eggs a very distinctive taste, which was not to our liking. Flora Maclean from next door also had hens and sold surplus eggs, but her hens did not go on to the beach, so our mother used to swap enough eggs for our own consumption with her, and she sold our seaweed-tasting eggs along with her own. I often wondered what people must have thought about these strange-tasting eggs. At least they would not have been bought locally as everyone had their own hens. I think they must have gone to the market town of Dingwall.

On the subject of surpluses, not all the eggs were sold. A large red crock would be filled with eggs, which were then preserved in isinglass. I don't remember how this was done, although I believe the eggs must have been immersed in the isinglass. The crock would have held about five or six dozen eggs.

A lot of the produce would likewise be preserved. Another large crock would be filled with sliced beetroot and preserved in vinegar. Butter would be salted down, and cheese made from the surplus milk. We always had a lot of rhubarb in the garden, and jam would be made from it as well as eating it fresh. When it was the right time for picking gooseberries, our mother used to visit her sister at Lochmaree for a few days and always came back with a large bag full of gooseberries. We would all sit round the table then with scissors and top and tail the berries. Most of these were then made in to jam.

Crofting is really only a form of subsistence farming where just about everything that is produced is for consumption by the family. The only cash crops were eggs as described above, milk to campers during the summer, all bull calves, which would number anything from one to three, most of the wether lambs and all the wool from the sheep.

We had only three breeding/milking cows, hence the number of calves would always be three. It was outside our control as to how many of them would be bull calves. The heifer calves were generally kept to renew the herd. Of the wether lambs, two or three would be kept back from sale to be fattened up for slaughter, usually as two year olds. Sometimes a fleece or two would be kept back and our mother would send this off to the woollen mills to be turned into knitting wool. She knitted all the jumpers and socks for the whole family.

Many of the crofts would have had more than three cows and therefore provide a greater income, although still not enough to raise a family on. Every family would have at least one member earning a wage, although very often for only a part of the year. Where all the children were still of school age, the wage earner would invariably be the father.

The work that would be available locally in pre-1939 days would be rather limited. Work in shops and hotels was usually reserved for women. Maybe a few van driving jobs, working on the roads for the County Council and as mentioned earlier there were three postmen. The seasonal work would include acting as gillies for hunting lodges and hotels. In the stag- hunting season the gillies would often take their own horses with them, and of course this was another source of income.

Other employment in the area was provided by the commercial fishing of salmon at sea. Our father was the foreman at the Laide salmon fishing station, and as I also worked there for one season I think this could be the subject of a chapter on its own.

There was another cash crop that I did not mention – rabbit skins – and how that came about is a little story in itself.

Our older brother Donald kept a ferret from as far back as I can remember, and I believe he must have had an obsession with hunting rabbits. Rabbits were not as abundant in Mellon Udrigle in those days as they are now, and the hunting of them required greater skill than it would do nowadays. The landscape was quite different as well. What we now know as Alice and Jessie's field was grass all the way down to the fence on top of the dune leading to the beach, with just a few rabbit burrows.

Donald had made a lot of nets of fine twine with a curtain ring at each end and string running through the outer meshes and the rings. This in turn was attached to a peg that was driven in to the ground and the net spread over the escape hole. When all the holes were covered thus, the ferret would be sent underground.

A lot of patience was required as it sometimes took two hours for the ferret to frighten the rabbits so that they bolted out of their burrows and into the waiting nets. In those days a good catch would be only about four rabbits. When Danny and I were little boys Donald would let us accompany him occasionally, but he made us stand motionless and without uttering a sound. The theory was that the rabbits would prefer to be caught by the ferret than to escape to the outside world where human beings were waiting for them.

Needless to say, rabbit was on the menu very often, but we never got tired of it. It was usually cooked in a rich brown sauce with plenty of carrots, turnips and onions. Occasionally our mother would cook it using a jugged hare recipe, which was particularly delicious.

The skins would be dried and stored until a travelling man would come around and buy them, very cheaply if I remember correctly. These travelling men would have been tinkers, I think. We always had tinkers coming around in those days, and indeed as far as some commodities were concerned they were the only source of supply. At least they were the easiest source for things like needles, buttons and cotton – all the things you would get at haberdashers, only there were no haberdashers within easy reach. They also made and sold various articles in tin: mugs and pails of various sizes, etc. I suppose this is why they were called tinkers.

There were regular families of tinkers visiting the area in those days. They would set up their camps on the north side of the road between Laide and Aultbea near where the viewpoint is located now. The tents always seemed to be of brown canvas, and they would have a stovepipe sticking out of the top. Two or three families would arrive at the same time and stay for a week or two. I suppose that this was just one of their stops in their circuit of the Highlands.

I can remember the names of only two of these families, Macmillan and Stewart. While staying in the area they would travel around on foot, calling at every house in the place, trying to sell their wares. I seem to remember them being very persistent in their sales methods, and were not above invoking gypsy curses to further their aims.

In those days people did not lock their doors, but when the tinkers were around greater care was taken about leaving stuff lying about. Some of them had a reputation for being light-fingered. They also had a reputation for heavy drinking and fighting among themselves.

I remember Alexander Macleod who lived in the house behind ours telling a story about a fight that he had witnessed. Alexander was a cattle drover and a master mason, so he moved around the country quite a lot. He must have been born around 1860 so we are probably talking about something that happened in the 19th century. His only means of getting about was on foot, and he was walking back home from Gairloch one night when he came to the tinkers' camp. He was invited to stop and have a cup of tea, and being weary from his long walk he accepted. It was fairly obvious that some heavy drinking had been going on and very soon a fierce argument broke out between two of the men. The one who started the argument was a well-known troublemaker but was also much smaller and was clearly going to come off much worse in the fight. Seeing this, his wife removed her coat, rolled up her sleeves, and exclaiming, "Would that God would help the wives of weak men!" knocked the bigger man sense-less with a mighty blow to the jaw. The exclamation sounded better in Gaelic, but you get the idea.

Tinkers stopped coming during the war, and indeed I don't think they ever came back again. Most of them were assimilated into the general population at this time. The younger ones would have been conscripted and would have found a different life. They would have no desire to go back to the old ways.

No other event in my lifetime brought about such a change in attitudes and lifestyles as World War II had done. Before the war a lot of the young people, male and female, went away to work as waiters, porters and bar staff at hotels all over the Highlands. I remember being told by one of these men who had served in the army throughout the war that he could never demean himself by doing that kind of work again. I think this attitude must have been shared by many at this time. It is strange that what had been seen as an honourable calling should now be so despised. Since then the greater exposure to the international scene has given the service industry a higher profile and a greater cachet.

Not all the changes were for the best. Full employment and greater prosperity did have a somewhat corrosive effect on the sense of commu-nity that had prevailed before. I suppose this is true of all places and maybe it is more in the perception rather than the actual, and the percep-tion may just be the product of our advancing years. What gives us the right to say that our time was better than the present? When people used to talk about the good old days, our father always retorted that the good days were now. For all of his life, or at least for all the years that I knew him, he always believed that the moment in time which was then the present was the good time. I believe that to be the mark of the true optimist.

In those far-off days before television and other easy forms of entertainment, people had to make their own amusements. I think conversation came more easily to people then than it does now. I have very clear memories of the whole family sitting round the table at meal times and the conversation flowing even if the wine was not. In fact very little drinking took place in the home. A bottle of whisky would be bought at Hogmanay and what was left lasted for the rest of the year.

Visiting each other's houses particularly in wintertime was very common. Some houses were more popular than others. I don't recall my own parents doing any visiting, but our house always seemed to be full of visitors. As children I don't think we went to bed very early, and we loved it when we had visitors. We would sit quietly on the floor by our father's armchair listening to the wide-ranging conversations and stories of olden times that would be told by the adults.

When I refer to 'we' as children, it is usually just Danny and me that I refer to. Donald and Anna, being much older than us, would be away doing their own things. Donald used to spend a lot of time at the Macleans' house with his best friend Kenalick. Anna used to spend a lot of time with Alice and Jessie Maciver.

Our mother, who was a great baker, would have trays of home-baked scones, pancakes and cake with home-made jam set up for everyone. I wonder if it was the suppers, rather than the visitors, that we enjoyed so much?

I spoke in a previous chapter about Findlay McLennan. He lived with his aged father in Opinan in what was the last thatched house in Opinan or Mellon Udrigle. The father hardly ever went out of the house in all the years that I knew him. He was always neatly dressed with highly polished boots and sat by a big open fire enveloped in tobacco smoke. As boys, we would go along to visit him when we knew Findlay was not there, as he then felt less inhibited about telling us some very tall tales.

The *Ross Shire Journal*, which was, and still is, the local paper for the area, used to print a column every week with a story from 50 years ago to the day. Findlay's father used to read this and then relate to us these happenings as if they were current news. I don't know whether he really had not realized his error, or was trying to have fun at our expense. Whichever it was, we played along with the deception, and had a good laugh afterwards.

The thatched house that they lived in only had two rooms and a bed recess off the kitchen. The front door opened on to a lobby. To the left there was a door which led in to the master bedroom which was used by Findlay. To the right the door led to the kitchen/living room. Off one corner of this room there was a recess which was just large enough to take a bed. This would be the space at the back equivalent to the lobby at the front. The father slept in this bed.

I remember one time when he was very ill and confined to bed. As it was the busy time of year, in the spring, Findlay could not stay at home to look after him, so he had passed word around that anyone passing should go in and give him a drink. He was so weak that he could not lift his head off the pillow, so Findlay had jammed an old teapot down the side of the pillow with its spout within reach of his mouth. We used to call in occasionally and top up the old teapot.

The doctor used to call regularly and got a great surprise one day to find the old man sitting by the fire puffing away at a pipeful of his favourite black twist tobacco. I think he was even more surprised to find that he had cooked for himself a meal of salt herrings and potatoes, which he had thoroughly enjoyed. He was a tough old man, and lived for many more years.

Chapter 6

Fishing for Fun and for Food

One of the greatest joys of being brought up in Mellon Udrigle, which I have not even mentioned before now, was going out in our father's boat, fishing and sailing. The boat, registration UL17 and called Mina, was a lovely sailing fishing boat of 16 feet overall length and with four oars. The rowing positions were: two in the centre, which could be one or two rowers, one bow and one stroke.

When Danny and I were quite small we learned to row by sitting on either side of our father on the central rowing thwart while he plied the two oars. We soon graduated from there to the bow and stroke positions.

When we were younger our fishing trips were mostly for fun. We used to troll for lythe and mackerel. It was not always entirely for fun. We used to eat the fish of course, but it was also being caught and salted down to be used later as bait in lobster pots.

Our father had been a lobster fisherman for as far back as I can remember. In fact one of my very early memories was of a creel of lobsters in the house preparatory to being boxed up and making the very distinctive sound that lobsters make after they have been removed from the sea. It is a sound made up of water draining out of them and the movement of the carapace against their neighbour.

Lobster fishing in those far-off days was quite different from what we know and see nowadays. When fishing with a relatively small sailing/rowing boat you could handle only about 40 pots at most. They would all be set singly, not in fleets, and set very close inshore. Production per pot would be as much as four times the present day production, and a reasonable living could be made.

All the pots were home-made and this was a constant ongoing job as worn-out ones were always being replaced as well as being lost in storms. The base was made of wood, and the frame on which the net was spread was made of branches of Alder. The nets were often made in the long winter evenings by the fire.

The old men from before my time used to say that it took a whole day to make a lobster pot from scratch. That would include going out into the woods to collect the Alder and might even have included beachcombing for wood to make the base. Of course nobody would go about the job in that way. As I said before, nets would be made in the winter evenings, and when going to the woods one would collect as much as was easily available, and not just enough for one pot. The wooden base would be recycled more than once with some minor repairs.

The art of making lobster pots was learnt by us when we were quite young, starting with making the base, which was straightforward carpentry. The more difficult part was the bending of the bows into the correct shape. Even more difficult was fitting of the net and making the entry doors. This was in the days before nylon ropes. We used manila or sisal which was not buoyant and had to have corks lashed to it every six feet, otherwise it would lie on the sea bed and get tangled up in the seaweed.

Because of the materials they were made from, the pots were buoyant as distinct from the metal-framed pots in use today. This meant that we had to lash a reasonably heavy flat stone in the bottom. The bait holder was placed between this stone and the top of the pot.

As boys, we thought that the making of the pots was great fun, but I suspect it was the anticipation of what it was leading up to that caused the real joy. I have thought a lot about the pleasure I get out of catching fish and lobsters. I get no joy out of killing anything. Quite the contrary in fact as I find as I get older that I hate having to kill anything. Nevertheless I still get the same surge of joyous anticipation that I always did when pulling in a net, or hauling in a lobster pot. I believe it goes right back to the time when man lived entirely by hunting and that this instinct has stayed with us beneath our veneer of sophistication.

We never thought about it then, of course, but just got on with the job. It was our living after all, but it also happened to be something that we enjoyed doing very much. It took two men to operate a boat of this size successfully, so before we were old enough to act as crew our father always took someone on as a share fisherman. When I was old enough I became the second hand, followed a couple of years later by Danny. I suppose we must have done a season with the three of us before I left home to go away to sea.

Having three of us meant that we could be more ambitious and work more pots, and go further in search of more lobsters. We used to go round Greenstone Point and as far as Slaggan. This was fine if there was a nice breeze so that we could sail, but it was a very long way if you had to row all the way there and back.

Winds between south and west were best for us, and they were the most common directions in that part of the world. North winds, if strong enough, usually brought heavy ground swells with them, which often resulted in the loss of a lot of gear. East wind was also very unpopular as it made boarding the boat at the moorings very difficult.

The rock at which we had the boat moored on an off-lying mooring had wide steps over which the seas washed at anything above half tide, and it faced east. When boarding in these conditions one person handled the mooring rope and allowed the boat to come in stern first with the outhaul taking the strain so that at any time she could be pulled out quickly. The other person stood by for a smaller wave and just leapt on to the stern of the boat, usually landing on his knees, or sometimes in the water, but hanging on to the gunwale and hauling himself on board. He would then be hauled out a safe distance from the rocks, release the painter from the mooring, and with oars manoeuvre the boat back in again stern first to let the next person make the leap. This would be repeated again if there were three of us.

One of the other clear memories connected with wind is of coming back to the moorings from the West in a force six or seven Southerly blow. If there were only two of us we would sail up, taking a long starboard tack past Carraig Mhor, then a port tack home. However, when there were three of us our father would usually decide that sailing took too much time and that we should row the last half-mile to the mooring. We would sail up to the point that lies directly North of the mooring then lower the sail and mast. We would then row as far as the last little inlet before being exposed to the full force of the wind. From there to the mooring it was a hard slog right in to the teeth of the wind, the first part of it being along a cliff face and only an oar's length off. Limpets grew on this cliff, and as progress was very slow, our father encouraged us now and then by exclaiming that we had passed another limpet. It was very hard work, but we enjoyed the challenge.

In similar conditions, but when there were only two of us, we would sail back to the moorings. This, quite often, had some heart-stopping moments. In Southerly wind, the first starboard tack passed very close to Carraig Mhor. This was fine if it was visible as, depending on the precise direction of the wind, one could pass either to windward or to leeward of the rock. The problem arose when the rock was just covered at, or near to high water. The obvious course of action would be to pass well to leeward, but when tacking hard to windward sailors hate to lose any ground, much as mountaineers hate to lose any height when climbing. The result was usually a few nerve-racking minutes while looking desperately for any evidence of the almost-submerged rock before finally chickening out and paying off to leeward.

The rig was a dipping lug, which was quite easily handled by two people. The rudder was always unshipped when not sailing and the mast was usually lowered when fishing, unless it was for a very short time. When the boat was back at the moorings at the end of the day's work the mast, sail and oars were securely lashed to the thwarts, and this reminds me of a game that Danny and I used to play.

When I was about 17 and Danny was 15 we took the boat out regularly on our own although I think it was probably another year before our father gave up and passed it all over to us. We would sometimes go out in the late afternoon or evening, and as we had to pass the Macleans' house we would make sure that we spoke to Kenny Maclean, and that he was aware that we were going to sail to the South to fish for haddock as this would bring us in to view of Mellon Udrigle. We would then saunter away casually until we were out of sight, at which point we would run the half mile to the moorings as fast as we could with heavy sea boots on.

We had got the business of bringing the boat in, boarding her, unlashing the gear, and shipping the mast and rudder and getting under way down to a fine art. We would be preening ourselves when coming into view of the houses at Mellon within a very few minutes of having left there. Reflecting on this, years later, we realized that nobody took the slightest notice of our Olympian achievements. Still, it was good fun and we got some satisfaction from it all.

I remember an other occasion where our adventurous spirit lead to some parental opprobrium and if the weather had not been kind to us, could have led to danger of foundering. We had set three or four herring nets one evening in August with the hope of catching some mackerel. We had then gone to a dance and, as was the custom in those days the dance did not finish until about 4 a.m. So by the time we had cycled home, the sun was up and we decided to change and go straight out to sea as any catch would be at risk from diving birds.

In the event we had a good catch of mackerel and a few dozen herring. We went back to the moorings, and while Danny ran home with the herring I baited a long line of 100 hooks with quarters of mackerel. As it was still only about 6 a.m. Danny had not wished to wake our parents so he had just put the herring in the barn. When our mother woke up and found our beds had not been slept in she had rather a worrying time until some time later our father opened the barn and found the herring. They realized then what we must have done, but still gave us a good dressing down when we finally got home.

We were unaware of the worry we had caused and sailed off to our chosen spot to set the long line. A long line has its hooks spaced at intervals of twelve feet, so that it measures about a quarter of a mile. We decided to set it just off the reef that runs South from Carraig Mhor where we thought we might catch some conger eel, which are very good lobster bait. We chose to leave the line set until about 4 p.m. but I cannot recall whether we went home for some sleep at this point or whether we carried on with fishing the lobster pots.

I do remember clearly that at about 4 p.m. we started hauling in the long line and that was the greatest haul of any kind of fish that we had ever had in this boat. There must have been a conger eel on every third hook on average with some of them being nearly six feet in length. Hauling from a depth of from 50 to 60 feet, we would have at times maybe three of these monsters off the bottom at any one time. These were all alive and fighting strongly, so getting them aboard was a mammoth task. We were unable to unhook them, so we ended up with a terrible tangle of eels and line. Conger eels will live out of water for hours and are capable of giving a very nasty bite. In fact the large ones could easily sever a finger. We were wearing thigh boots, which was fortunate as we had a writhing living mass of conger eels up to our knees by the time we had finished hauling in the line.

Not only were we being crowded out of our own boat but also the weight meant that we were reduced to only a few inches of freeboard. As I mentioned earlier we were lucky in having a perfectly calm sea, so we were able to row back slowly and steadily to the moorings. It took us a long time to untangle and unhook all the eels and get them landed. We then had to chop them all up and salt them down, filling many barrels, which ensured that we had enough bait for the rest of the season. A very long but also a very satisfactory day.

I mentioned earlier that East winds caused us a lot of problems at the moorings. If the wind arrived while we were at sea, and if we were anywhere West of Opinan, we would head for the port of Opinan. A Mr Banks had built this port, which was not much more than a good boat landing, very many years ago. Was this the Mr Banks of "Endeavour" fame? I remember being told by Kenny Maclean that Mr Banks used to bring his yacht in to this port and that he had also paid for the building of the road that went from Mellon Udrigle to the Opinan port. This is the road that is known to us as the old peat road.

The Opinan port was only suitable within a two to three hour window either side of high water. Because our boat had a lot of stone ballast, which we did not want to remove and replace on a daily basis, we could not pull her up the beach. We used to moor her by using a heavy stone for a stern anchor and a long rope from the bow tied to a point above high water mark. The heavy stone at the stern would hold the boat in position when she floated, but being smooth, would not resist a strong pull on the bow rope by us if we returned the next day while she was afloat. While the strong East wind lasted, we would operate from Opinan and time our comings and goings according to the tide

I remember one time in early November having to go out at 7 a.m. Nothing out of the ordinary about this except that on this occasion Danny and I had again been to a dance, and had not got home until the early hours. We would probably have slept late if we had not been constrained by the tide, but had to set off with only a couple of hours sleep. One of the problems at Opinan was that although we always found the boat afloat, there were some shallows on the way out of the estuary. These necessitated us getting out and pushing from time to time until we got in to deeper water. On one of these occasions Danny got his sea boots full of water. As soon as we had cleared the estuary we stepped the mast and set sail. At this point Danny removed his boots and thick sea boot stockings, wrung them out and hung them in the rigging. While I sailed the boat to the West and around Greenstone Point he lay down on the cold and wet stone ballast and went fast asleep in spite of the cold and having wintry showers of hail.

Protective clothing as we know it now was quite unknown then. We wore sea boots, which came right up our thighs and oilskin coats when it rained. We never took any food or drink with us on the boat. I think this must have been because of the difficulty we often experienced in boarding. Plastic bottles had not been invented then and I don't believe metal thermos flasks were available either. If we were thirsty we just used to land at places where we knew that streams or springs existed. The large bowl of brose which we had for breakfast had to sustain us for however long the day was. We never wore watches either, and after getting back to the mooring and while walking home we would have a competition to see who guessed the time most accurately. I always lost as I invariably guessed the time as being much later than it actually was, owing to the acute hunger that I felt.

I have not made any mention of the market for our catch. The only time that we ever sold anything other than lobsters, was during the war when the local ship-chandler would always buy any fish that was surplus to our requirements. All our lobsters at that time were sent by rail to the Billingsgate fish market in London. They had to be packed in wooden boxes with sawdust to ensure that they arrived at the market still alive.

Getting enough boxes for this purpose was an ongoing problem. The local shops received most of their goods in wooden boxes, so that was one source. We used to scour the shore for miles, picking up any pieces of wood that we could find and make our own boxes. The theory behind the packing of lobsters with sawdust was that, as they were lifted straight out of the sea, all the moisture would drip in to the sawdust that was liberally laid between each layer of lobsters. The lobsters would then absorb the moisture back again. It seemed to work very well, as we never had many dead lobsters arriving at market.

We usually sent them off on Monday or Tuesday. It meant a very early start as we had to get them ashore, packed and labelled, and taken to Laide Post Office for 8 a.m. to catch the mail bus to Achnasheen. There they were put on the train, changing at Inverness and arriving in London early the next morning to be on the Billingsgate market by 6 a.m. Getting them to Laide on bicycles with large carriers was the hardest part. Sometimes you might even have a box strapped on your back.

I can still remember the names of some of the different fish salesmen that we sent the lobsters to. There was Baxter, Barber and Jocelyn. At the beginning of the season we would send a box to each of them and make a judgement as to which we thought was the most honest. There was very little difference in the price paid but some might give short weight, while others would claim more dead-on-arrival lobsters. I seem to remember that Jocelyn was generally our most favoured one. They would send a telegram the same day to let us know the price they were sold at, and a cheque would follow soon after.

Our father once had a friend travelling by train to London the same day that he was sending off some lobsters. As he was travelling on the same bus and train as the lobsters he undertook to watch their progress. He reported back that everything had been handled with great efficiency throughout the journey. He went farther than just the journey, taking a taxi to Billingsgate to watch their arrival there. He then watched the boxes being opened and as far as I can remember his observations tallied pretty well with the salesman's report.

Chapter 7

The Second World War and the Russian Convoys

One thing, which had a profound effect on my youth, but that I have only mentioned briefly before now, was World War II. You might think that living in such a remote area the war would have had very little effect on our lives. Ordinarily, that might very well be true, but this was no ordinary area in wartime, as I will try to explain.

The Admiralty always knew Loch Ewe well, as Royal Navy ships, large and small, often called there in peacetime. It was an obvious choice when they were looking for a place where a large number of ships could congregate and be relatively easily defended. It has deep water, and is ringed by hills, so aircraft have to approach it from a high altitude. With anti-aircraft guns placed on all the hills surrounding the loch and a boom-defence net stretched across the mouth of the loch to keep submarines out, it was very well fortified.

Because of the havoc that German U-boats were creating among merchant ships carrying supplies across the oceans, it was decided quite early in the war that ships should cross the oceans only in large convoys. This made it easier to provide naval escorts for them. The setting up of Loch Ewe as a convoy assembly port required a lot of back-up infrastructure. This consisted mainly of a large naval shore base in Aultbea, and a large army camp at Poolewe. There were other military units here and there around the place, and it was two of those smaller units that gave us, as children, our first and closest encounter with the military war machine.

There was an army unit at Laide Post Office who set up a barrier across the road leading from Sand. Armed soldiers manned this barrier for 24 hours a day. The countryside around Loch Ewe had been declared an area of restricted movement. All civilians, including young children, had been issued with identification papers. These had to be carried around at all times, to be produced on request to military personnel. It was not always soldiers, as sailors manned the barrier leading on to the pier road at Aultbea.

Of course, coming from Mellon Udrigle, we did not have to pass through the barrier at Laide on our way to Aultbea. I suppose it was considered that as this road led to nowhere it would be unlikely to have any spies or other undesirables coming along. This ignored the fact that people could land from the sea at any point on the peninsula and make their way to Aultbea without challenge.

I can still remember the challenge when you approached the barrier on the Sand road. The soldier on duty would raise his rifle and call out "Who goes there, friend or foe" to which you were supposed to answer "friend". He would then say "advance friend and be recognized". At this point you would show him your identification papers. It was not very long before all the locals were well known to all the soldiers, and in true British style, the formalities were soon dispensed with.

I remember very clearly the setting up of this army post, and getting to know lots of the soldiers who served there. However, I do not remember whether they remained there for the duration of the war. I cannot think of any good reason why they would not have stayed, except that the authorities may have felt that there was more useful ways of utilizing this manpower. They certainly stayed long enough for at least one of the soldiers to marry a local woman.

The second military unit that I made reference to, was an RAF unit that was set up in Opinan. The actual camp was built where Kenalick and Jean's house now stands. They were there as an observer unit to spot enemy planes heading for Loch Ewe. The observation post was on the hill immediately behind the house that belongs to Andrew Marr's parents. I cannot understand the thinking behind the positioning of this observation post, as this particular hill cannot be more than 150 feet high. There are plenty of places nearby that would make better observation posts. Maybe the fact that it was accessible by road had some bearing on it

As far as I can remember, the unit consisted of a sergeant, a driver, three telegraphists, three observers, three aircraftsmen and possibly a cook. This enabled them to keep a continuous watch, with the observer in his shelter on top of the hill, the telegraphist sitting by his wireless and the aircraftsman passing messages between the two. They must have worked a three-watch system, but I don't know whether it would be 4 hours on and 8 hours off, or 8 on and 16 off.

You may wonder how I, as a young boy, knew so much about the workings of a military unit in time of war, with all its accompanying secrecy. It is because of the much-heralded Highland hospitality. If any of those men were still alive today and could read this, they would certainly agree.

This unit arrived in the summer of 1940 and very soon after that the men off duty would stroll along to Mellon Udrigle to get away from the boredom of the camp. They used to come along in groups of three. That would have been one watch. There would have been one other watch on duty, and one sleeping, I presume. The very first ones to make contact with the locals happened to be passing our house as our mother was coming in with the evening's milk. She asked them if they would like a glass of milk and they were very happy to accept.

That was the start. The word soon got back to the camp, and the next night a different three arrived about the same time. They were invited in by the Macleans, and on the third night the next three arrived and were adopted by the Macleod family. I don't know if the neighbours had discussed this before hand in order to share out the hospitality, but I think they must have. The same ones kept going to each of the three houses for as long as the camp remained there. I don't remember whether they stayed for the duration of the war, but I don't think they did. The personnel would change from time to time of course. It was much too easy a billet to allow the same people to enjoy it for too long. I can still remember that one of the men from our adopted watch was called Edgar, and that he came from Birmingham. You must realize that we had led a very sheltered life before now, and that having strangers in our midst was very exciting for us children.

It was at this time that we saw our first-ever movie. It was probably not very long after the arrival of the RAF unit that ENZA paid a visit to them. I cannot remember now what the acronym stands for. I think the E was for entertainment. In any case that is what they did, entertain. They were made up of actors, actresses, musicians, singers, comedians etc. I think that the ones who visited Opinan were just a small unit who went around showing films.

I don't know whether they had been to the camp at Opinan, or whose idea it was that the film should be shown in the schoolhouse for the benefit of the village, but that is what happened. Neither can I recall whether any of the RAF personnel shared that showing with us. I do recall that it was a very poor projector and a very small screen, and I was totally underwhelmed by the whole thing.

There was one tragic event affecting this RAF unit during the summer of 1941. I think it was that summer, or it may have been later than that. By this time the men off duty did not always come to our houses. Instead they would go by their own truck to Poolewe. The large army camp there had a canteen where they could go and drink beer with service people of their own age. On this particular evening there must have been about six of them and on the way back they came off the road on one of the bad bends above Aultbea. I think that at least two of them were killed and all the others were injured to some extent. I suppose the War Office would have declared them as having been killed on active service but it was well known locally that it was a clear case of drink-driving accident.

There was another observation post in our locality, which was manned by civilians. It was set up on Meal nam Meallan, the hill that lies between Mellon Udrigle and Udrigle. This was quite a sensible place to have an observation post, as it is the second highest hill on the whole peninsula. It was manned by two men from Mellon Udrigle, one from Opinan, and one from Laide. These were men who were well past the call-up age. In fact one of them was our own neighbour Kenny Maclean who must have been about 70 years old at this time. I think our father must have been away from home working when the recruitment took place for this job as I think he would have liked to be involved. He did at a later time become the relief observer, providing cover for sickness absence etc.

They used to work six-hour shifts and at some point they must have done a double shift so as to rotate the shift pattern. They had a direct telephone link to the Naval Base at Aultbea and had to report all ships that they could see passing up or down the Minch. I think they would have just reported them as ships, but on one occasion when our father was on duty he reported two minesweepers heading South. The operator on the receiving end asked in a rather indignant tone how he knew that they were minesweepers. Our father replied that, having served on minesweepers throughout the whole of the Great War he felt well qualified to recognize them.

Knowing how rough the climb to the top of this hill is from the Mellon Udrigle side can you imagine what it must have been like for a man of 70 years at midnight on a dark and stormy winter's night?

This would have been with the use of only the dimmest of torches, as everyone was subject to black-out regulations. We often climbed the hill to pay a visit to the observation post, particularly when Kenny Maclean was on duty. It was a cosy little hut with a small stove where they could do a little bit of cooking. Maybe just heat things up and make tea.

I mentioned black-out regulations before. These had come into force as soon as war had broken out and we were subject to the regulations to the same extent as people living in towns would be. I don't know about the enforcement, as we did not have any wardens going around, as they would be in town. I think people were trusted to do what they had been told. I seem to remember that we were supplied with the black cloth with which to make the blackouts for the windows. As we had no electricity at this time and only one Tilley lamp, the rest of the illumination being provided by oil lamps or candles, the chances of being spotted from 10,000 feet by German planes must have been quite small.

Our bicycle lamps had to have special shades over them so that they only pointed down at the road immediately in front of you. This was so nearly useless that we went about without any lights most of the time, particularly as it was always difficult to get batteries. At this time the road from Mellon Udrigle to Aultbea was not surfaced. It was just a gravel road with pot-holes and often with loose stones on top. I have had a few falls off my bicycle when going fast down hill in the dark and hitting one of these pot-holes or maybe a loose stone.

We experienced two heavy air raids on successive nights when there were very large convoys in Loch Ewe. The raids started at about 1.30 a.m. and lasted for about an hour and a half. Our mother came to our room and woke us up so that we could see the display. Danny elected to stay in bed and went straight back to sleep. I got up and sat at the window wrapped in an eiderdown and watched the whole thing. In retrospect we realized that it was rather foolish to sit by the window but I remember being quite excited by it all. The sky was lit up with all the tracer shells from the anti-aircraft guns, which ringed the Loch, and from all the guns on the 60 or so ships that made up the assembled convoy.

In spite of the large number of planes overhead for that time, constantly dropping bombs, no vessels were hit, and there were no other casualties as far as we were aware. I believe that this was due mainly to the strategy of having the high hills, which ring the loch, bristling with guns, so that the planes could not dive low enough for accurate bombing without exposing themselves to a withering cross fire.

These were the only major raids that took place, but there were a few isolated visits by enemy planes throughout the war. I clearly remember on one occasion when Danny, our father and I had just come ashore from our boat and were walking up the rise above the mooring when we spotted a plane coming across the sea very low from the East. It was just skimming the waves and heading straight for us. It was fairly clear that even as it would have to pull up to clear the rise it would be very close to us. Our father pulled us down on the ground, as he must have thought it was an enemy plane, but as it passed over us we saw the RAF roundels on the wings and felt rather foolish, although it only missed us by a few feet.

The only casualty that I was aware of occurred during a daylight raid by a single plane that dropped a bomb close enough to a vessel to cause her to roll rather violently. One man fell as a result and broke his leg. The vessel was the Devon City. She was one of the vessels that were stationed permanently in Loch Ewe. I don't remember what her function was. She may have been an ammunition vessel from which the vessels calling in convoys and their escorts would have their ammunition stocks replenished.

I mentioned the call-up age earlier. This referred to conscription for national service, and I will try and explain how it worked. By the second year of the war everyone between the ages of 18 and 40 who was not in an exempted occupation was in one of the three services or the Merchant Navy. All the people who were in the Territorial Army or the Royal Navy Reserve were called up as soon as hostilities commenced. The conscripts therefore had to be brought in gradually as they could not be handled logistically or trained all at the same time.

Living as we did in a very close-knit community we were very well aware of what was going on as these were our friends, neighbours and family who were being taken away from us. As far as I can remember, the first people to be called up after the territorials were the 19-year-olds, and they then progressed up to the 30-year-olds before moving back to the 18-year-olds. They then progressed onwards until they reached the 40-year-olds. This probably took until about 1941. I have not checked any of this and I may be out of line with the dates and ages, but I believe I am fairly close to the truth. One thing I am sure of is that if you were called up at the age of, say, 39 in 1941, there was no way you were getting out when you attained the age of 40. You were in for the duration of hostilities.

Three of the Macleans from next door to us were in this early call-up category, between the ages of 18 and 27, as was our own brother Donald. Donald joined the Merchant Navy and I can only remember him getting home about three or four times throughout the duration of the war. Danny and I, being quite young, were not affected very much by all that was happening, but it must have been a very worrying time for our parents. I do remember several occasions when a long time had elapsed between letters from Donald how we all worried about his safety. At this time merchant ships were being sunk by U-boats on a very regular basis. In the first year of the war figures were released by the War Office, through the BBC, of merchant shipping tonnage lost during each month. The tonnage was so high that the practice was soon abandoned as it was felt to be bad for morale.

We knew a lot of people who were killed in action or lost at sea without trace. There was one merchant ship, the Port Hobart, which was sunk by a surface raider very early in the war. This ship had five local men on it, two of whom were only 17 years old. The sinking of the ship had been reported to their families but with no idea as to whether there had been any survivors. Nothing more was heard for about six months, so you can imagine the joy when word finally came that they were all prisoners of war in Germany. Others that we knew were not so lucky and were never heard of again.

The few men from Mellon Udrigle who were of service age all returned except for one. The Macleods' youngest son was killed in action in North Africa. He was less well known to us as he worked in a bank in London before the war. He was the only one of the Macleods to be called up as the rest were all over 40. His widow came to live at the Macleods' house for a couple of years after he was killed.

I keep talking about men, but it must not be forgotten that women were also called up into the services a little later. There were many more women in reserved occupations, as they had taken on so much of the work that had been done by men before the war. Our own sister Anna told me many years later that she desperately wanted to join the WRNS, but was prevented from doing so on account of working in a reserved occupation. She worked for one of the local general merchants who had the contract for supplying the ships that called at Loch Ewe. It would have been impossible to have totally supplied all the ships that called, but there was a constant need to make up various shortages.

It was as a result of working at this ship chandler's that Anna was able to do something that nobody else in the family was able to do. Donald came in to Loch Ewe in convoys on their way to Murmansk in Northern Russia on more than one occasion. It must have been very frustrating for him, as there was no way that he would be allowed ashore. On one of these occasions Anna found out that the ship he was serving on was one of the ships in a particular convoy. She had some friends in the Merchant Shipping Office, and as they had to board the ship in the course of their duties they smuggled Anna on board, so that she was able to spend half an hour with Donald.

There was great excitement when we next saw her and she told us all about it.

As the war lasted for six years, a lot of my growing up was done during this time. In fact I started my sea-going career in the last year of the war. I will come to that later. Looking back over all those years it is difficult to say how much our lives were influenced by the times we lived in. I think that as children we were less influenced than you might suppose. We suffered food rationing like everyone else, but we never went hungry. While there are fish in the sea and deer in the forest, it is said that a Highlander will never go hungry. I explained in earlier chapters how little we depended on shop-bought commodities.

Sugar is the one commodity that springs to mind as having caused a problem. Rationing started immediately after the outbreak of war as far as I can remember. In any case the whole family was still at home and our mother called us all together and gave us the option of continuing to have sugar in our tea and no more baking, or doing without, and having some home baking. Donald, Anna and I volunteered to forsake sugar in tea. Our mother had stopped taking sugar during rationing in the first Great War. That left our father and Danny, who as the oldest and the youngest members of the family were reluctantly excused.

We kept ourselves informed about the progress or otherwise of the war and any other news by the radio and newspapers, although I think that we were aware even then that the papers carried a lot of propaganda. The main evening news in those days was at 9 p.m. and most people tried to be indoors to listen to it. I can still visualize old Alexander Macleod pulling out his fob watch when Big Ben sounded the time signal and muttering about their lamentable time keeping if it did not agree with the time on his watch.

The people who were either too young or too old to be called up for national service could not do just as they pleased. The government had powers to direct people to work in places where their labour was needed. Our father worked away from home for a whole winter on the construction of Dalcross Airport, which is now the civil airport for Inverness. I think that was probably the first winter of the war. During the next winter he was skipper of a fuelling barge in Loch Ewe, something he must have found much more congenial. In the spring and summer he worked at the salmon fishing at Laide. It is strange that this would have been considered a reserved occupation, as salmon was very much a luxury food in those days.

I think that concludes my wartime memories. It is truly amazing that a world war of six years duration can be condensed into a single chapter, a mere footnote in the history of my life.

Chapter 8

The Salmon Fishing Station

I have made several references to salmon fishing at Laide in previous chapters. I will now tell you about it by describing the season during which I worked there.

When I was 16 years old my father asked me if I would like to work with him at the salmon fishing at Laide. I don't believe there was the slightest doubt in his or my mind as to what the answer would be, but it was nice to have been asked.

In those far-off days the fishing season ran from the end of February until the middle of August. The season started with just one boat operating, and working five nets. This would have entailed having five men working the early part of the season, increasing to nine when the second boat came in to operation and by then working at least eight or nine nets. Each boat would have a crew of four and there would be one man ashore all the time mending nets. This was in the days before monofilament nets.

In 1944 we started with five men in the last week of February, and I was very proud to be one of those. My father was the general foreman, and also the skipper of the first boat. The boats were all locally built at Port Henderson near Gairloch. They were about 24 feet long and heavily built in larch on oak ribs. They were powered by oars when there was no wind, otherwise by a heavy brown canvas lugsail. There was also a smaller boat, which was kept on an outlying mooring and used mainly for ferrying the crew out to the big boats that were anchored farther out.

The first job would have been to rig the outlying mooring and get the small boat launched. After that it would be the turn of the first of the big boats. It took a fair amount of manhandling to move them from winter quarters in to the sea. Once the big boat was safely afloat we would start breaking out the anchors and warps for the first of the nets. These salmon bag nets were rather complicated so I will try to briefly explain how one net would appear when ready for fishing.

The final trap, in which the salmon swim freely, is a net enclosure having four sides, a top and a bottom and is a cube of about 12-foot sides. It is not an absolute cube, as the side nearest to the shore is in the form of an inverted 'V' with an opening from top to bottom held open by wire stretchers every foot or so. From the corners of this final trap, or bag as it is

My father in a salmon fishing boat at Laide jetty.
I presume the lady had bought the salmon

usually described, long net wings run off at a 45-degree angle. These terminate in a pole from which a warp is led to the shore where it is secured to the rock by pitons. A rope is led from the opening in the 'V' directly to the shore to where it is connected. This rope is replaced by a leader net during the time that fishing is permitted. The bag is kept rigid by having a pole attached to the bottom at one end, which is led up through a ring in the top of the bag where it is lashed. To hold the whole thing in place a warp is attached to its outer end and is then run straight out to sea for about 200 metres with a heavy anchor on the end of it.

When returning to the river where they had been hatched from their long sojourn at sea, salmon swim along parallel to the shore, and when they are confronted by the leader net they turn and swim either in towards the shore or out to sea. If they choose to swim towards the shore, they soon realize that there is no way through that way, so they then head out to sea. They may make many turns as they encounter the afore mentioned wings, but they are inevitably led finally into the bag. They swim about in this space quite freely but because of the 'V' do not find their way out again.

When the fishing boat arrives at the net, it is easy to see if there are any fish swimming about. If there are, the lashing on the pole holding the bag rigid is released so that the bag becomes loose. The bend in the leader corks indicates the direction of the current and, as the salmon will always swim against the current when trapped, the boat is placed on the down-current side and the crew grab the net, making sure they have the bottom of the bag. They then haul the boat over the net as the salmon swim away from them until there is no further to go. At this point the end of the bag, with all the salmon in it, is swung on board. There is a laced-up section in both walls of the bag so, no matter which side it is fished from, the opening is there. The lace is then undone and all the salmon fall out to be quickly despatched with a sharp tap on the head with a short club.

I mentioned earlier that this was in the days before monofilament nets. In fact, man-made fibres were indeed somewhere in the future at this time. This largely explains why it took a crew of four to man these boats. It was in reality because of the weight of the nets, which were made of heavy cotton. When wet it took four men to lift them. They also got easily covered in slime and had to be changed more frequently. They also tore more easily and were constantly being examined and repaired.

I found all this very exciting and not least the talk amongst the men. I will try and draw a word picture of each of them. My father you have met from time to time throughout these pages, so it is sufficient to say that I loved and respected him in equal measure. He was wise and very experienced, a great motivator and a great leader of men.

The oldest man in the team was Duncan Mackenzie, known to everyone as the Dean. I think he was 65 years old at this time but a fitter or stronger 65-year-old I have never come across. He had been a fisherman all his life and was a superb handler of sailing boats. He became the skipper of the second boat in the later part of the season.

The next oldest would have been John Macaulay. He also was a great sailor. He carried on into old age single-handedly sailing all round Gruinard Bay in his lobster boat. I mentioned earlier how much I enjoyed the chat among the men. I was thinking largely about John Macaulay who had some wonderful stories to tell about his earlier life at sea.

He had been at one time the Mate on a vessel serving the remote light-houses on the coast of Alaska and the Aleutian Islands. The stories he had to tell about these times gripped my imagination. Some of them I still remember and they might be worth repeating. Just one family to each one, with no reliefs, manned these lighthouses and they had no radios. On one occasion the husband half of the crew of one of these lighthouses broke his leg. They did possess a small rowing boat into which the wife placed the husband and rowed 150 miles across the treacherous waters of the North Pacific to the nearest habitation. I don't remember if we were told what happened to the light while they were gone, but it is quite possible that they had children who would have been quite capable of tending the light. They were a resourceful band of people.

Another story involved two families on widely-separated lighthouses, one of which had a son and the other a daughter. They must have got relieved occasionally although I don't think it would have been on the regular basis that we would be familiar with. In any case the story goes that these two families met up somewhere and the two young people who had never seen each other before got married and went off to man another lighthouse.

There was another elderly man living in Laide at that time whose nickname was Grockan. He had spent some time in western Canada and I believe he may have been to the Klondike gold fields. John Macaulay actually traced him to a little hut somewhere in the wilderness where he was panning for gold. He may have found some because he never worked after coming back to Laide, and although not wealthy he seemed to have enough to get by on. He spent all his time while I remember him digging drains on his croft even though the land seemed perfectly dry. It was almost as if he was still looking for that elusive pot of gold.

Anyway I am wandering off track a little, so let us get back to the pen pictures. John Macaulay, having spent a lot of his life away at sea got married quite late in life and had two daughters. His house was just above the salmon fishing station, so he always went home for his lunch while the rest of us had our ours in the bothy, so I don't know when he would have told us these stories. There was never much time spent lazing about, although when we were at sea and sailing between nets there would have been some respite. Many years after this I took Alasdair when he was about fifteen years old to see John as I must have been telling him some of these stories, and he expressed an interest in meeting him. I think the resultant meeting underlines the mistake that can be made sometimes in re-visiting somewhere you were very happy in when you were young. John by this time was one of the oldest people living in the district, and unfortunately was almost completely deaf. Although mentally alert, it was almost impossible to have a proper conversation with him.

The final member of the early team was Ronald. I am not sure about his surname, but I think it may have been Macdonald. He came from some-where to the south of Gairloch, maybe Torridon or Diabaig. He did not have the greatest grasp of the English language and was reputed to have told someone in Gairloch, when asked where he came from, that he came from the backside of the mountain. As he was pointing in the general direction of Beinne Eighe I think my assumption of where he came from may have been correct. Ronald was very good company and had a good sense of humour.

He lived for the season in the bothy that we shared with him for our lunch breaks. He had a small stove with no oven and I think his only attempt at cooking was with a frying pan. On one occasion, this led to one of his practical jokes . He knew that the Dean was very fussy about hygiene, so when he brought out his frying pan one day to cook up some-thing for lunch he made sure that everyone saw the footprints of a mouse in the congealed fat. The Dean was spluttering with indignation at the thought of anyone cooking without cleaning out the pan, but Ronald calmly remarked that the footprints would soon disappear when the fat got hot. He told the rest of us later that he had made the mouse footprints with a fork just to wind the Dean up. It seems highly likely that there would have been mice around, nevertheless.

Ronald had been a fisherman all his life and in those days he crewed on a boat from Gairloch every winter, line fishing for cod. He was very good at repairing nets, as a result of which he became the permanent shore man and could be relied upon to keep all the nets in good order.

All the salmon caught was stored initially in an icehouse and then sent off by mail bus and rail about twice a week, maybe more frequently during the summer when more fish were being caught. The icehouse was a quite substantial stone building set right in to the cliff with no windows and only one small door. It was partitioned off, and the ice was stored in the inner compartment, which was so well shaded and cold that the ice stayed frozen right through the summer.

In later years the ice was bought, but at the time I was involved every-thing was very much DIY. Each winter my father waited anxiously for a period of very hard frost. I don't think he was ever disappointed, as I seem to remember that we generally got a hard frost, usually in January. Beast loch was the source used. My father would wait until the ice on the loch was at least two inches thick and he would then set the process in motion by hiring as many people as were needed, which usually meant just about all the fit men and boys in the area. All those with horses and carts were required to bring them as well, and there would be at least one lorry on the job.

He kept a lot of equipment at the fishing station, which he would have brought to the loch. This would include long-handled wooden mallets, wide but light metal forks, large net scoops, etc. A flat-bottomed boat was kept permanently at the loch. The ice at the edge would be smashed up with the wooden mallets until there was enough space to launch the boat. The broken ice was loaded into the carts and the lorry and transported to the icehouse. When the boat was launched two or three of us would get in it and smash our way out. The broken floes would be pushed back to the shore where others would break them into smaller pieces before loading them. I remember that Murdo Urquhart and I were first into the boat, and how much we enjoyed leaning over the bow and smashing the ice with our wooden mallets. There must be something in the human psyche that derives pleasure from smashing things up; witness the pleasure that most people get from throwing bottles into the bottle-bank

As the icehouse was built into the cliff face the approach from the road was level with the top of the gable end which had a heavy wooden door set in it. One man would be stationed here to open the door each time a load arrived and to close it after them, as it was felt necessary to keep the place in darkness. I don't know how much ice would be collected but I would guess it would be in the region of 40 or 50 tons. In spite of the location I think there would be some loss through melting by the end of the summer.

I have mentioned that all the salmon caught was sent by mail bus and rail. I think it was always sent to Edinburgh. I wonder why some of it did not get sent to the London market. It did not always go by bus and rail. When I was very young I remember that a fishing vessel called the Barbara-Anne used to call once a week. I believe that she would have collected salmon from stations all round the coast, but I am not sure where she would have delivered them to. Her time of arrival must have varied from week to week, but I clearly remember my father having to get up at 4. a.m. on some weeks as the week's catch would have to be loaded on to one of the boats and they would sail out to meet the Barbara-Anne well out in the bay. She would also be collecting from the Scoraig station at the same time. After starting to consign the salmon by rail the Laide boat had to meet the Scoraig station boat as well as the boat from the Mellon Udrigle station every day. These two latter stations closed after 1939 although I believe the Scoraig station opened again for a few years after the war.

Back to summer 1944 again. The second boat started early in May and it became necessary to recruit more men. This was not very easy as all the men of working age were either away at war or were in some reserved occupation that they could not leave. The problem was resolved by deciding to reduce the boat crews to three per boat. This meant that with one man on shore mending nets, it was necessary to bring in only two more people. One of those was an elderly man called John Matheson, known to everyone as Matson. The other one was Charlie Mackenzie, who was the Dean's grandson.

My father was skipper of one boat with John Macaulay and Matson as his crew. The Dean was skipper of the other boat with Charlie and I as his crew. This was quite a change as we went from having four able-bodied men per boat to one boat with two able-bodied men and one elderly man, and the other boat with a 65-year-old man and two boys. I was 16 years old and Charlie was 15. We were very fit and strong for our age and the Dean was just about the fittest 65-year-old that I have ever known.

Charlie and I got on very well and we had some great fun together. The working day was from 7 a.m. to 5 p.m. with a two hour break at noon from Monday to Friday and 7 a.m. to 7 p.m. on Saturday with a three or four hour break between 11 a.m. and 3 p.m. As I mentioned earlier the salmon would only go into the nets when the leaders were set and we were limited as to what hours we could legally fish. This was to allow a period when salmon could have an uninterrupted run into the rivers. The permitted hours in 1944 were from 7 a.m. Monday until 6 p.m. Saturday, hence the working hours. We obviously could not get all the leaders in and out at the exact specified times but we were required to be as near as possible to these times, while always erring on the side of legality.

I don't remember exactly what we were paid, but I think my wage was around £3 for a 48-hour week. The older men probably got £4, with my father getting a little bit more. Because of the shortage of prime wild salmon during the war the price was very high. I am almost certain that the landing price at that time was £1 per pound. When you think that we were landing as much as 1,000 pounds per week on average, the profits for the owner were pretty good.

It was very heavy work, particularly when there was no wind and we had to row these heavy boats. Wet nets had to be carried on stretchers from the jetty to the drying green. These stretchers were made for four men, but as we had crews of only three, the strongest man had to take one end on his own. In our case this was the Dean, and I can still visualize him walking along the track from the jetty with his end of the stretcher where there should have been two men while Charlie and I had the other end.

At the end of the season all the nets, warps and anchors had to be taken ashore. The nets were washed and dried, as were all the anchors and warps. A large metal pot was filled with tar, which was then heated over an open fire. All the warps were coiled and then dipped in the hot tar and after drying they were stored in the shed. The anchors were also tarred, but were then left outside. One of the last jobs was getting the three boats in. They were turned upside down and tarred before being lashed down securely for the winter.

Chapter 9

Big Wash Days, The Sabbath, Anthrax and Other Stories

The preceding eight chapters have told the story of my life up to the age of 16+, fairly comprehensively. Reading through them now, it occurs to me that there may be a few more incidents scattered randomly through my early life that could conceivably be of some interest.

I referred in an earlier chapter to big wash days. At that time there were no laundries in the area, in fact there still are not, as far as I am aware. There were no washing machines. Indeed the only equipment was a large wooden tub and a washboard.

Because of the problem of heating enough water to do a decent-sized wash it was easier to concentrate the job into one big wash day. A fire would be lit in an open stone fireplace outside, over which a very large iron pot would be set. This would be filled from the wooden cask that had collected the rainwater from the house. Two wooden tubs would be set up on trestles, one for washing, and one for rinsing. The only aid that our mother had was a ribbed washboard. She did not even have a mangle, so everything had to be wrung out by hand. The neighbours in question would have been Mary Macleod, Flora Maclean and our mother. My memory of these days was of lovely warm sunny weather. We, the children, would create a dam in the burn so that the water would be deep enough to draw pails of water from. That would probably have been our job as well. The biggest iron pot that was available would be set on the fire, which was fuelled by peat.

As the water heated it was transferred to the wooden tubs and the women would tuck up their long dresses, remove their shoes and get in to the tubs to stamp up and down on the blankets. We used to find this highly amusing but would be careful not to show this too much as I think we were a little bit frightened of Mary Macleod. We used to tease her at different times and she used to chase us and shout at us. I am quite certain now that she had meant us no harm.

We would have used this same dammed area of the burn during warm weather to bathe in. By that I mean have our baths in. We would go down with towels and soap, strip off and have a good bath. After a long hot summer's day the water would almost be at bath temperature.

Talking about damming the burn reminds me of another use that we put this to. We would dam the burn and then, when all the water ran out from the down side of the dam, we would turn over stones and find young eels. We would select only those that were about six to eight inches in length. We would take these to our father who would skin them and thread a fairly large hook through them with the shank coming out through the mouth and the operational end of the hook protruding from the belly. These would be attached to traces, which were also hand made, and then on to lines and used for trolling for lythe.

When I was growing up in the 1930s the Church played a quite signifi-cant part in our lives. Not in any oppressive way but as something that was always there in the background. In fact it could be argued that the Free Church was less fundamental in its teaching then than it is nowadays, yet the congregations now are a lot smaller than they were then. When I was young just about everyone went to church. Up till about the age of ten we went to church for the whole day. After that we just used to go to the evening service on our bicycles.

Going to church in the morning for the whole day was something of a social event for us. For a start, it was the only day on which we got dressed up in what really was our "Sunday best". Morning service was from noon until 1.30 p.m., and evening service was from 5 p.m. until 6.30 p.m. This left a long gap in the afternoon, which was filled by going to the houses of different relatives or friends for lunch. This was the part that we loved. Most often we would go to our Grandmother's house as a whole family. By that I mean our father and mother with Danny and me. Donald and Anna being older must have gone their own ways, as I don't remember them being with us on any occasion.

Our father and mother would often split up as our mother had lots of friends from her young days that she liked to visit. We would go with our father on almost all occasions, the exception being when we went to our Uncle Duncan's house in Mellon Charles. We had an uncle living at the old farm end of Isle Ewe and distant cousins living at the other end of the island where their descendants are still living. A visit to either of those was a great adventure, as we had to go across by boat.

When our Uncle Kenneth who was our father's older brother lived there, there were at least four families living at that end of the island.

One of the other families living there was our Great Aunt Lena who shared a small cottage with her husband. I don't think they had any children. As all, or most, of these people would have been at church they must have used two or three boats. All that I can remember is that we were in our uncle's boat and that there seemed to be a lot of people in it. I cannot ever remember sailing across, though these would have been sailing boats. Maybe it was considered good for the soul to have to row on Sunday.

We always went to our uncle's house for lunch and after that was eaten Danny and I would go out exploring with our cousin Donald, who was a few years older than us. Prior to the Great War of 1914–1918, the whole island had been a single farm and the four houses that were there had been the farm workers' cottages. In 1919 the farm was broken up into crofts. One or two of them were still occupied by the same farm workers, who had each taken a croft. The others had come along later.

This made it an interesting place to us as a lot of evidence of the big farm was still there in the 1930s. I still remember how awestruck we were at being shown the water wheel that had powered the corn mill. I believe that the water wheel can still be seen there, although I doubt if it is still in working order. I also remember the very old graveyard there, where the graves were marked by ordinary stones stood on end.

All the families at that part of the island vacated their houses and moved to the mainland in 1939. I think they must have been forced to move by the Admiralty, as Loch Ewe was such an important area during the war. There is not a trace of these houses now as seen from the mainland. If these people were forcibly evicted, why was Willie Grant allowed to carry on living at the other end of the island?

On checking through my genealogy book I find that Willie Grant was a first cousin of our father's. I believe that I was unaware of this at the time, and thought that the relationship was farther removed than that. At that time it was the only house at that end of the island and he lived there with his wife and three sons. I can remember only two of the sons, who were probably the younger two and were then in their teens. There are now four houses at that end of the island all occupied by Grants.

All the sons went off to the army and the navy as soon as war started, leaving their father and mother alone as the only people living on the island. They seemed to have carried on living as if nothing had changed. Willie could often be seen sailing his boat out among all the vessels at anchor waiting for their convoys to be formed to get to his favourite fishing grounds. He must have been in his mid-60s then. He was well known among the fishermen who manned the fishing vessels that were working for the Admiralty in Loch Ewe, and to most of the officers in charge of the naval base. They must have felt that with three sons away with the armed forces he did not pose any security risk.

I am moving ahead of the story. We are still back in the mid-1930s, and we are still having our adventurous Sunday lunches. Willie Grant's was the other favourite place to go. I think he was a man a little bit ahead of his time. He had a walled-in orchard where he grew all kinds of fruit, which was a rarity for that part of the world at that time. He had also built a quite substantial smoking shed where he used to smoke a lot of the fish that he caught.

He and our uncle owned a fairly large fishing boat, which they worked in partnership as lobster fishermen. Our uncle had the nickname "Grunt" which I believe was bestowed upon him by Willie as he was wont to answer any queries by Willie when they were fishing with a grunt, or at the very best with the shortest of monosyllables.

When we went to our Grandmother's house for lunch it was about one and a half miles and we used to walk in a large group where the adults would be sharing all the local gossip. A lot of the men from these parts went away to sea and when they were home on leave there was nothing I liked better than listening to their tales of far-off places. Stories of their visits to places like Montevideo and Rio de Janeiro fired my imagination and must have played some part in my desire to follow in their footsteps, which was fulfilled, although I never got to the aforementioned two places.

This seems to have been a catalogue of social events, but to enjoy them we had to "endure" a morning and evening service.

The observance of Sunday was fairly strictly adhered to. Food was cooked, but all the preparations had to be done on Saturday. Children were not allowed to play. The only book that could be read was the Bible. No drinking of alcohol, no singing or whistling, no listening to radio. The list goes on.

The people followed the Old Testament with its emphasis on a judging, vengeful God, rather than the New Testament with the greater emphasis on grace and the road to redemption. Surely the heart of the gospel is more about liberty than punishment.

In spite of the impression given by the elders of the church of being stern and unforgiving, they were amongst the most generous and truly good people that I have ever known. The ability of these communities to look after their old, their sick, and their troubled, is something that you never hear about. People looking in from outside tend, inevitably, to focus on the restrictions that Calvinism imposes on Sunday.

Thinking about looking after the sick, I well remember the numerous times our mother sent me off on my bicycle with fresh fish that we had just caught to the home of someone who was ill. We were always catching fish, and there always seemed to be someone somewhere who was ill, and there must have been a strong belief that steamed fish was the right food for invalids. I personally cannot think of anything less appetizing.

Did all this make us better people? I certainly feel that we had a good moral grounding with strong emphasis on honesty, integrity and upright-ness, but I also think that it would be the height of arrogance to suggest that these same attributes could not be achieved by other means.

I mentioned earlier that we went to church for the whole day only up to about the age of ten. Our parents still went away for the whole day but as we did not have to go we had to cook our own mid-day meal. I can only remember one meal that we ever cooked, and as it was one of our favour-ites we must have cooked it each time. It was a large pan-full of fried pota-toes taken with a large jug of milk. The potatoes would have been boiled on the Saturday, but we must have been trusted to use the frying pan.

On the days that we were left on our own, we probably did not adhere strictly to the rules about not playing, but we were very discreet about it and ensured that we were well out of sight when we were playing. There was a fairly large flat ledge of rock on the shore some distance beyond the schoolhouse that was our aircraft carrier. At least it seemed large then, but I have looked at it since then and it does not seem very large. It was all chiefs and no indians, as one of us would be an admiral and one a captain. The rest of the crew existed only in our imaginations.

The salmon fishing station a short distance along the shore afforded a great play area. The poles that were used to spread the nets on for drying and mending, especially the horizontal ones that were used to spread the leaders on were, as far as we were concerned, as good as any gymnasium. We spent many happy hours performing all sorts of acrobatics here.

The station was occupied from Monday to Saturday during the summer season but was deserted for the rest of the year. The boat at the Mellon Udrigle station was manned by four men, as they all were. Two of these men were local, the skipper being John Maciver, Alice and Jessie's father, and the other being Willie Urquhart, my friend Murdo's father. The other two men were brothers, Roddy and Willie McLennan. Roddy lived in Mellon Charles and Willie in Isle Ewe. As work started at 7 a.m. on Monday and did not finish until 6 p.m. on Saturday they were provided with a bothy to live in. Conditions were rather primitive as I remember, with hard wooden bunks, and a small pot-bellied stove to cook on.

Willie had a bicycle to cycle to Aultbea but then had to get a boat across to the island, so he would not arrive home until quite late. Roddy did not cycle so had to walk all the way to Mellon Charles, which probably made him even later getting home. Because of the early start on Monday morning they left home on the Sunday evening, so what with going to church twice on the Sunday they did not get to spend much time with their families during the summer.

Although religion played a significant part in the lives of most people there was a tendency towards the supernatural with quite a number of people. These tendencies were not necessarily mutually exclusive as was shown by some of the stories. There was an old man living in Opinan who was known to us as the Dehohan who was credited with the second sight. He had many stories but I only remember the one where he claimed to have seen a woman standing by the burn that flowed past his house. She clearly wanted to cross the burn, but when he put his hand out to help her across she just disappeared.

Another story concerned a very religious lady who lived in Mellon Charles and was a cousin of our neighbour Kenny Maclean. On the night that she died a number of people reported seeing an angel hovering over the house at the moment of her death. I would normally have put Kenny Maclean in the sceptical category, as the following story will illustrate. As a young man, he was walking home one dark wintry night. When coming round the bend in the road above Beast Loch, a place that was reputed to be haunted, he saw something white waving from side to side and about four feet above the road coming towards him. I think a lot of people might have fled at this sight, but he just walked right up to the apparition only to discover that it was a cow with a white blaze on its forehead. I think this took some courage, and talking about courage in the face of the "supernatural" there is another story concerning Danny.

For you to appreciate this story I will have to tell you about the traditions concerning deaths at that time. There were no funeral parlours, so the dead stayed in their own home until burial, which admittedly was usually within a couple of days. It was the tradition for two men from the village to sit up all night while the family slept. Different men would take their turn for subsequent nights.

At this time a middle-aged man called Roddy Asher lived in what was then the last house in Opinan, the house now occupied by Andrew Marr's parents. One Saturday evening he was expecting a visit from two of his nephews who lived in Inverness. He had prepared a meal for them and was so excited about their visit that he dropped dead from a heart attack as they walked in the door.

This was in 1947, and I happened to be home on leave at the time. One of the nephews came along to the telephone box to call for the doctor and came down to our house to tell us what had happened. I went back to the house with him, and spent the night there. The next night Danny and someone else took their turn at the "wake". At some point during the night Danny felt the need to go outside for a breath of fresh air and saw an apparition at the cliff edge, some distance from the house and waving its arms. I think a lot of 17-year-olds would have gone back in, preferring the company of the dead to the unknown. Not so Danny, who walked right up to the "apparition" only to discover that it was a scarecrow that Roddy had erected on the day that he had died. Thus was another incident prevented from passing into supernatural folklore!

There may have been no mystery surrounding Roddy's death but there was some mystery about his life. He had spent some years in Canada during the early part of the 20th century and when he came home he modernized his house and never worked again except for about four years during the war. Although he had a few cows and sheep, and lived fairly frugally, he never seemed to be short of money. Although he was friendly with everyone, he was a very private man and nobody ever heard him talk about his time in Canada.

Lewis Mackenzie, an old friend of ours, was convinced that Roddy had either found gold while out there, or that he had robbed a bank. He was further convinced that there was money hidden somewhere on Roddy's croft. Whatever it was, Roddy took his secret to the grave with him. There is one other little story that has a quasi-religious aspect. Soon after I left school, the school at Mellon Udrigle closed, never to open again as a school. At that time Danny was the only pupil so he had to go to Laide School. As this was over three miles distant he had to be provided with transport. While our father suggested that a good modern bicycle would be very suitable, the Education Authority said it had to be a car. The contract for taking him to school was given to Miss Munro, who also happened to be the teacher at Laide School.

One summer day on the way to school, and when passing Beast Loch, Danny saw a horse that he recognized as belonging to the Macivers stuck in a bog. He got Miss Munro to turn the car around and they went back to tell the Macivers. When Danny got to their house and dashed in shouting that their horse was stuck in a bog he found them all on their knees at family worship.

Family worship took place in every home, morning and evening, with a reading from the Bible, and a prayer. At Danny's interruption the prayer came to an abrupt halt as they all jumped up and called for Danny to go to the fishing station at Laide to get his father to come along with some men with poles and blocks and tackle so that they could rig up some sheer-legs. Danny did this, but I am sure that Miss Munro would have insisted on going on to school after that.

I think that I mentioned in an earlier chapter that we probably suffered less from the effects of rationing during the war than people who lived in urban areas. This was largely due to our own efforts in growing food and rearing animals. It was also due to our hunting/gathering instincts. I have already spoken about fishing and catching rabbits. There was another source of food of which we availed ourselves once a year, seagulls' eggs.

There is a loch about half a mile West of Greenstone Point called Loch of the Birds, which has an island in its centre. This island is the nesting place for hundreds of seagulls at the breeding season, or at least it was when I was a boy. Danny and I used to walk across the hills to this loch around the middle of April with a couple of pillow cases with which to carry home our spoils. There was a causeway out to the island but it was about a foot below the surface of the water and as a result was very slippery. This was fine for going out empty handed, as we did not worry about falling in.

There must have been hundreds of birds nesting on this island, as you had to walk very carefully to avoid stepping on a nest. We looked for nests that had only one egg in, as this would indicate the beginning of the lay. If there were not enough of those we went to nests with two eggs but only took one. We usually got sufficient eggs to fill our two pillowcases in this way. Gulls never lay more than three eggs in the nest, but they will always replace the ones that we took, so we did not feel any guilt about what we were doing.

We packed the eggs in moss and hay, so we probably ended up with about four dozen eggs in each pillowcase. We did not risk slipping on the causeway on the way back so we stripped off and half waded half swam through the deeper water next to the causeway. Rather surprisingly, after the long walk home, I don't recall many broken eggs.

The eggs were a lovely dark green colour with black spots and were excellent to eat. We never had them boiled, as we could never be sure that they were not addled, but I can still remember the monster omelettes our mother used to make for us.

I mentioned in an earlier chapter how we used to count the days until our holidays. Well, I have been reminded by Danny of the day we broke up for one particular holiday and of the traumatic event that took place that day. Danny and I had cobbled together a kind of buggy from old pram wheels and bits of wood. We used to drag this thing along to any reasonably smooth hill that we could find, then both of us would sit on it and hurtle down to the bottom. On this particular day we were having fun as usual when Danny fell off the back and banged his head.

We took no great notice of this at first but after a while I must have noticed something odd about Danny's behaviour – that is, more odd than usual. It became clear after a little while that he was suffering from total amnesia. My cure for this was to sit him on a stool in the byre and question him vigorously for two hours. I can still remember my amazement that he could not remember that we had broken up for school holidays that day. He did not even know what school was. It was complete and total amnesia brought on by concussion, and talking to medical friends in later years, I found out that the treatment could not have been more wrong. We did not tell our parents until we were able to give a clean bill of health. This took two hours, which might have been due to the appalling treatment. No further action was taken, such as calling a doctor and it certainly did not seem to do Danny any harm.

Talking about hurtling down hills reminds me of another fun vehicle that we made use of. This was a real motor bike that had belonged to Archie Macrae, Mary and Sadie's father. He used to come to Mellon on a motor bike when I was very young, but the bike had eventually expired and was left at the back of the Macleans' hen house. This was more or less on the spot where Alice Maclean's house now stands. I was probably only about nine or ten years old when Murdo Urquhart, Danny and I used to get on the bike at the top of what was a reasonably high starting point and go hurtling down the green. The foot brake still worked so we would come to a skidding halt just before we reached the shore. We would then struggle to push it all the way up to the top again for our next run.

We did not always come through our escapades unscathed. Two accidents that I can remember both took place while playing on the sand dunes below Alice and Jessie's field. The first one concerned Danny. I don't know what game we were playing, but it entailed Danny crouching under a bank while Murdo and I jumped down off the bank. In the course of this game the bank underneath which Danny was crouching collapsed, burying him completely. We must have been aware of this fairly quickly as we started digging for him. Danny's version differs slightly from my memory of the event. He says that he fought his way out on his own to see Murdo and I digging frantically in a different place. I seem to remember that we were digging in the correct place, but that maybe he did force himself out. It could quite easily have ended tragically, as being buried under a large mound of sand is worse than drowning. You cannot breathe, and you don't even know which way is up. I don't think we told our parents about it, at least not for a long time afterwards.

The second accident happened to me. Once again I don't remember what the game was but it entailed me being mounted on Murdo's shoulders and don't forget he was less than one year older than I was. I think that I was probably about nine years old at the time. In the course of this game I fell off Murdo's shoulders and landed rather heavily on my right arm. I think that we were aware fairly quickly that there was something wrong because I could not straighten my arm. Murdo, who was never short of a cure for everything, had me walking around with a heavy stone in my hand in the belief that this would straighten out my arm. He was not that far out as it transpired.

This accident was not something that we could have kept hidden from our parents as I was in some pain by the time we got home, and the deformity was obvious. I think it was probably on the next day that the doctor was sent for. We had a lady doctor at that time, a Dr Nicholson. Her remedy for my ailment was to get my father to find a heavy weight and tie it to my wrist and hang my arm over the back of a chair. This was much the same as Murdo's treatment and it was just as ineffective. I suffered a lot of pain, largely from having my arm over the back of a hard chair. After several days of this torture my father took pity on me and did away with the heavy weight and started to manipulate my elbow. After only five minutes there was a distinct crack, my arm straightened, and all my troubles were over. We never had much faith in Dr Nicholson after that and not very long after that she left the district and Dr Hunter arrived.

This chapter seems to have been very largely about play but even when we were quite young we had tasks that we had to perform as I have described in earlier chapters. I also listed some of the jobs that were available to people at that time. One of the ways in which money could be earned and which I did not mention was picking winkles. This was something that we got involved with at quite a young age helping our father, and something that Danny and I did on our own as teenagers.

I don't remember that our father did a lot of winkle picking, but I do remember doing it with him and being surprised that we did not seem to feel the cold even although it was always during winter. I can remember better doing it with Danny. There were no vans collecting such as there are now and the only market was the Billingsgate in London. We used to send them to the same salesmen as the ones we sent the lobsters to. They used to send us the empty bags. Heavy hessian bags, not the net bags that are used nowadays.

We put each day's collection in old hessian sacks and covered them with stones until we felt that we had enough to send off. We would then empty them all out on a clean, flat area of grass and pick over them, discarding everything except the best winkles. These would then fill the salesmen's bags, which weighed one hundredweight (50kg). We would then load them on to the horse and cart and take them up to Laide in the evening where they would be loaded on to the Mail-bus for the start of their journey to London.

We did most of our collecting at Opinan, but we had noticed at some time when we were at the shore at the Loch of the Birds, probably when collecting seagulls' eggs, that winkles were very plentiful there. We set off one day with some bags and two creels and having arrived at this distant shore we found the winkles to be very plentiful and of excellent quality. We collected two large bags, which we then loaded into the creels and on to our backs. I think we realized at this point that our strength barely matched our enthusiasm, but were determined not to discard any of the beautiful winkles. That was an agonizing walk across the hills with us having to stop and rest every hundred yards or so. It took us the whole of the rest of the day and we swore never to attempt this again.

When describing how we went about our lobster fishing in an earlier chapter, I think I mentioned only one incident that was somewhat risky. There was one other time when our father and I had a very close encounter with drowning.

I was about 15 years old at the time, and was having my first season as a full time lobster fisherman. It was quite late in the season, late October or early November and we were fishing creels from Opinan West to Greenstone Point. It was a calm, heavily overcast day, and my father had a premonition about the weather. He suspected that we were going to get strong northerly winds, so when we picked up a ground net that we had set for lythe he decided that we would not reset it. We also kept all the creels as we hauled them. This created something of a problem as the net was rather bulky and had brought a lot of water in with it. I think that I had explained in an earlier chapter that we had about a ton of stone ballast in the boat, some of which we would have got rid of, if we had pre-planned the lifting of all the gear. The other problem was that in our haste to get all the creels lifted we had covered the bailing well, so that not only did we have the whole fleet of creels, plus the heavy net, but all the water that we had shipped.

I might add that my father had an uncanny knack for predicting the weather, which I never attained, even although in later years I studied for, and passed rigorous examinations in meteorology. On this particular day even I was aware before we had finished that we were in trouble. We hauled the last creel at Greenstone Point and the wind by then was from the Northwest although still only a light breeze. There was a heavy ground swell building up, which indicated a gale out at sea. The wind was fair for us to run back to Opinan so we raised a shortened sail but the danger of being pooped due to the heavy swell and our overloaded condition was such that my father removed the short tiller and used a long boat hook so that he was able to stand amidships. To help raise the stern a bit more he had me almost hanging over the bows.

We got back safely to Opinan, and saved all our gear. By that evening the storm had arrived and was of such ferocity that we would have lost everything. The wooden bottomed creels with stone sinkers that were used then always got smashed up whenever there was a heavy ground swell.

I remember an occasion, probably in that same year, when my father and I had set a 300-hook small line for plaice. We had an excellent haul and after keeping enough to eat and give away to friends and neighbours we used the rest to bait all our creels. We then set them all the way to Greenstone Point and never saw them again. A terrific storm had blown up the same evening that we had set the pots and lasted for a whole week. When we were finally able to get out we did not find a single creel. We did retrieve a fair amount of wreckage on the shore, which was used to start building up our fleet again. I think we were most annoyed about the loss of the unusually good quality of fish that had been used for bait. I never ceased to be amazed at the equanimity with which our father took these severe setbacks to his business. The loss of all the fishing gear could wipe out the profit for a whole season as well as the immediate loss of income.

Something that should have been recorded in the chapter on wartime experiences was the incidence of anthrax that caused a lot of anguish at Mellon Udrigle. In the late summer of 1942 a group of scientists with the help of the navy put a flock of sheep on Gruinard Island and exploded a "dirty" bomb containing anthrax germs among them. This was all very secretly done and indeed not admitted until many years later. We would probably never have known about it, had not one of the dead sheep fallen into the sea, presumably in its death throes.

Gruinard Island lies about a quarter of a mile off the coast at Gruinard and about two miles from Mellon Udrigle. As ill luck would have it, the wind was from the East and the carcass of the sheep was washed up on the shore at Mellon. From there we deduced that a dog had eaten some of the contaminated meat and was later sick on the moor. We were never exactly sure about how the anthrax was spread, but we were quite certain that a sheep from the island did wash up on our beach. Was the cause due to this contaminated sheep or were the germs airborne from the island?

At first it was just the odd sheep that died, which did not cause too much concern. When cows started to die and then the Macleans' horse died, we knew that there was something seriously wrong. I don't remember how we had informed the authorities, but before long several Ministry vets descended on the village, and in a few days they inoculated every living animal in the place.

Only the Macleods, the Macleans and ourselves lost any animals. A total of five cows, two horses and a good number of sheep. I remember very well the day our horse died. My father and I were gathering hay on what was known as Hanna's croft. I was using the horse and cart to take the hay to where my father was making a stack. The horse began to stagger, and my father seeing this shouted to me to get him unyoked as quickly as I could. I did this, and on my father's prompting led him towards a soft area of ground where it would be easier to dig a grave. By the time I got him to the chosen spot I was quite literally holding him up, and so expired the faithful Jimmy. We may have chosen the softest part of the field, but on digging the grave we found that it was not quite deep enough. We dumped poor Jimmy in on his back and my father sent me home for a saw, and we sawed his four legs off and buried them beside him. At that time we did not know that it was anthrax or the tremendous risks that we were taking. We were instructed later to bury all animals very deep and fence off the burial ground for fifty years. I think we complied as well as we could but fences fall into disrepair and dogs tend to dig up bones. Anyway it is well past the fifty-year mark now and there has never been a re-occurrence.

The loss of our horse meant that a replacement had to be found. I don't remember how my father went about this, but in the fullness of time he heard of a horse for sale in Letters, a little village on the West side of Loch Broom. As I explained in an earlier chapter, very few people had telephones then, but the jungle drums were very efficient. Maybe there was some correspondence by letter, or did my father just go along with a few pounds in his pocket and do a deal.

However it happened, he set off on his bicycle early one Saturday morning. He rode his bicycle to some point beyond Dundonnell and then walked over the hill to Letters. I don't ever remember seeing him look at a map other than a school atlas, so I don't know how he knew what line to take over the hill, or how he found the croft that had the horse for sale, but he completed the transaction to everyone's satisfaction. He then walked back over the hill with the horse to where he had left his bicycle and started to walk back home leading the horse and wheeling the bicycle. At some time after dark I decided to set off on my bicycle to meet him. I got as far as the top of the hill at Second Coast before I met him. He was very pleased to see me and got on his bicycle and left me to walk the horse home, which I was delighted to do.

The horse was called Alan and had at one time been a milk-cart horse in Ullapool. This caused a little problem when he was used for carting. He would not pass a house until he was given a biscuit. He really dug his hooves in and no matter how much you tugged and yelled at him he would not move until he had his biscuit. It must have been a bad habit that was formed in his milk-cart days. Fortunately our house was the only one close to the road so I just used to fill my pockets with broken oatcakes at the start of the day and we got on very well.

One forms a very close relationship with a working horse, and he had such a sweet temper except when I used to try and ride him bareback. During bad weather in winter he was always kept in his stable throughout the day except when I would take him down to the burn to drink water. I always mounted him bareback after he had drunk and galloped back to the stable. Well, that was the intention, but I never made it. He got back alright, but invariably left me flat on my back in a nettle bed or in the mud. He obviously did not like being ridden, and while galloping along apparently enjoying himself he would buck suddenly and send me flying. In spite of this we remained very good friends.

Chapter 10

Going to Sea

From a very early age my ambition had been to become a sailor, and the opportunity presented itself in September 1944 when I was sixteen and a half years old. I had of course learnt the craft of seamanship as a fisherman under the tutelage of my father, so I was quite well prepared for my first sea-going job.

That first sea-going job was on a vessel so small, it was not really much bigger than the fishing boats I was used to. It had a place in the scheme of things that was rather obscure, and was crewed mostly by men of no sea-going experience, so I hardly think it counts in the annals of my life at sea. However, as it was the first it must warrant a paragraph or two.

I talked in Chapter 7 about the Naval Base at Aultbea. It was the assembly point for convoys of merchant ships, many of which were bound for Russia. Royal Navy ships, which acted as escorts, were always in and out of Loch Ewe and these, as well as the merchant ships, needed servicing. Quite early in the life of the base the Admiralty requisitioned about twenty trawlers, herring fishing drifters and some smaller fishing vessels. These were manned largely by the men who had been on them when they were fishing.

It was on one of these smaller fishing boats called the Nyanza that I started my sea-going career.

The crew consisted of a skipper who, as far as I know, had never been to sea, a mate who had definitely never been to sea before, and an engineer who had been an engineer on deep-sea vessels and I suppose was over-qualified for the job. The mate, although inexperienced, was a quick learner and seemed reasonably proficient at his job. The engineer who was called Billy Gow was my real mentor and guide in my duties aboard, which included being the cook as well as a deck hand. Billy was married to a lady from Laide who only died in 2002 at the great age of 104. She was known to everyone in the area and at the Isle View nursing home as Annie.

The Nyanza was more like a yacht than a fishing boat, and came with a complete set of sails. These were stowed in the forepeak and never used while I was on board. She had been brought round from Ullapool by another crew and I do recall seeing her on the way round under sail. The fish hold had been converted into sleeping quarters, and there was a small engine room that was also used as a washroom and toilet. She was flush decked and had a large tiller instead of a wheel.

I have no clear recollection of any work that we did, although we must have done some, as I do remember steering the boat round the back of Isle Ewe. I was there for only one month. One incident that I do recall was being in the company of another Ullapool vessel. I think it must have been alongside the Aultbea pier. The other vessel was called the Senorita and one of the crew called Geordy joined us for supper. He played piano accordion and I think it quite likely that this was why we invited him. We were having cold meat for supper and Geordy started to choke on a piece of meat. He was on the point of collapse when I noticed what was happening and gave him a good thump on the back. A large piece of gristle shot out and he breathed easily. Somewhat to my embarrassment he never tired for weeks afterwards of telling anyone who would listen to him about how I saved his life.

After a month on the Nyanza I was called before the officer who was responsible for allocating civilian crews to different vessels and told to pack my bags and join the Neves. I think it is quite possible that the Nyanza had broken down, or was taken out of service for some reason. Whatever the reason I was quite pleased to be moving to a larger vessel. The Neves was a Lowestoft steam drifter with a crew of seven or eight

I joined at the same time as another local boy called Lal. He was a cousin of the Wisemans who live in Mellon Charles now. We were told that one of us had to be the cook and that we could sort it out among ourselves. Neither of us wanted to be the cook as we were rather keen on being deckhands. We finally agreed that the only solution was to alternate the job. One week as cook and one week as deckhand. The skipper agreed that this seemed a sensible solution and we continued like that for the whole of the time that we were on the vessel, which must have been about nine or ten months.

When acting as cook one also had to do all the catering, which meant buying at the local shops. This was quite a responsibility for callow youths such as we were. I don't think we provided a very varied diet. We had an advantage over the civilian population in that we had Merchant Navy ration books, which were much more generous, especially as regards meat. I seem to remember that we had meat on the menu every day. It would be fried steak one day and a stew the next, always accompanied by boiled potatoes. That is about all that I can remember about the cooking, except for the puddings. One day it would be semolina and the next it would be a steamed pudding. It was a sort of spotted dick and I can still remember quite clearly making this in a large tin with a vent on the top. It would be served with custard. All the rest of the crew except for us two boys came from the same fishing town on the Moray Firth called Cullen. They were all herring fishermen, and as anyone who knew the East Coast fishermen in those days could tell you, they were extremely frugal. This must have impinged upon our catering, although I cannot remember ever being hungry.

The crew consisted of skipper, mate, chief engineer, 2nd engineer, two deckhands and a cook. The skipper had a cabin on the deck in front of the wheelhouse. The Admiralty had added this, as they considered it to be improper for the skipper to share quarters with the rest of the crew. The rest of the crew members were all together in the after cabin, where, in civilian times, the skipper would also have been found. The after cabin was below decks, in the stern of the vessel, and was 'U' shaped. The bunks went right round the stern, and were no more than wooden shelves that were half enclosed by sliding doors. When I think about it now it must have been rather claustrophobic, although at the time I just thought it was very cosy.

There was a table down the centre of the cabin with a narrow bench all the way round following the contour of the bunks. Breakfast was very easy if it was not my week to be the cook. I just rolled out of the bunk on to the bench and that was my place at the table. The rest of the crew always slept fully clothed. This was not for the usual reason where seamen like to be prepared for an instant abandon ship when subject to enemy action. No, this was because of their training as herring fishermen, where the time available for sleeping was so short that they would not waste the minutes required for undressing and dressing again.

Forward of the after cabin was the combined engine room and stoke-hold. I soon made friends with the 2nd engineer who mostly tended the boiler, and this was the warmest place on the vessel. Because we did not do a great deal of steaming, and when we did do, they were only short trips, the stokehold was a clean, tidy and relatively peaceful place to work. This was in direct contrast to what it would have been like when engaged in the peacetime occupation of herring fishing where long trips to the fishing grounds and back to market would be done at full speed. In these conditions the stokehold would be an inferno with the engineer on duty stripped to the waist shovelling coal into the furnace as fast as he could, and drawing out ashes which would be all over the floor. I saw these conditions later when we delivered the vessel back to Lowestoft.

Because of the amount of time we spent at anchor or tied up at the pier there was plenty of time to keep the engine-room tidy even though a head of steam had to be kept up at all times. The chequered plates in the engine-room and stokehold were regularly rubbed down with emery paper so that they shone. Likewise, all the bright metal on the engine shone. The engine was a triple expansion compound engine. I learnt quite a lot about steam engines and about how to raise steam in a Scotch boiler. Although I didn't appreciate it at the time this was to stand me in good stead many years later when taking my Masters.

The engine-room was not the only warm place on the vessel. There was a position just aft of the funnel, which was an open grating over the stoke-hold. This had a narrow seat across it which was just wide enough for two people to sit upon. I seem to remember that it was called the fiddley. This spot was in great demand on cold days, but was usually taken by the older members of the crew.

I learned quite a lot of seamanship during my time on the Neves, such as rope handling and anchor handling. As a matter of fact I learned how to *cat* an anchor, a skill I was never called upon to use again, as every ship I served on subsequently housed their anchors up the hawse-pipe. I never got a chance to steer the vessel, which was a pity, as a later incident will show. I suppose the trips were so short that the skipper seemed to do all the steering.

Our work consisted mainly of taking various officials out to the ocean-going vessels anchored in Loch Ewe at the south side of the island. We would also take some stores to some of the vessels in the convoy. I spoke earlier about the food rationing that everyone had to endure in wartime. The other shortage, which caused almost as much anguish, was the shortage of cigarettes and tobacco. Now it so happened that this shortage did not apply to Merchant seamen of whatever nationality, although there always seemed to be more to spare on American ships. I think you can guess where this is leading. As the youngest, and probably the most active member of the crew, I was sent scampering up the rope ladder with some money to try and buy cigarettes from anyone who was happy to have English money. I was successful most of the time, and it was usually a full carton of 200 cigarettes. Lucky Strike is the brand that I remember best.

Writing about the shortage of cigarettes reminds me of a story that Kenalick Maclean told us at this time. He was coming home on leave from the RAF where he was serving and had some time to kill in Inverness while waiting for his train. He was down to his last cigarette and was going from shop to shop, but with no success. He eventually spotted a man whom he took to be a local man walking purposely towards a shop where he had already been refused. He convinced himself that the man was going to buy cigarettes and followed him into the shop. As he suspected, the man was surreptitiously handed a pack of cigarettes from under the counter. Kenalick then stepped forward briskly and asked for another of the same. They could hardly refuse him, even though they had told him a few minutes earlier that they had none. In times of shortage most people find that they can be quite cunning.

The nine or ten months that I spent on the Neves seemed to have passed very quickly. It was a long time ago, and I have difficulty in remembering many details. I was young and impressionable, and I just got on with enjoying life. I do recall a very severe snowfall that lasted for some time. My sister Anna, who at that time worked in George Maciver's shop, or maybe it was the NAAFI by then, was worried that our parents were cut off by the snow and would be getting short of supplies. She made up a shopping bag of essentials and I walked to Mellon Udrigle through the snow in sea boots. I think I used to get a night off about once a week when I would cycle home. We all used to go to dances every other week or so in the long since demolished drill hall, which used to stand somewhere near where the Aultbea Butchers now stand.

The most exciting thing that happened to us on the Neves was when we were ordered to rendezvous with another vessel outside the boom-defence to take a German prisoner from them and land him at the naval base. He was an airman whose plane had been shot down. At the time, with so much wartime secrecy we did not know the story behind this.

I have since then heard a version of this story, which I have no reason to believe to be untrue except that, in its ending, it differs somewhat from my recollection of my small part in it.

The story, as it is told by others who were involved, is that the German plane crashed into the sea in Little Loch Broom and that the pilot, who was the only survivor, walked into a house in Scoraig where there lived a 14-year-old girl with her mother. They fed him and cared for him until they got a message out in some way to the authorities, and a vessel with the Aultbea policeman on board picked him up and brought him to Aultbea. It is at this point that my recollection of the affair differs. Why did the vessel that brought him from Scoraig not land him, instead of transferring him to our vessel, the Neves? I have no recollection of a policeman being involved either. What I do remember quite clearly was that he still had his holstered revolver strapped round his waist, but I cannot remember any escort. That does seem very odd, but there cannot be very many people left alive now with first-hand knowledge of the event.

The next exciting event was the day the war ended. That must have been a day of great relief to most people, but to some, whose loved ones would not be returning, it must have been tinged with sadness. At a little over seventeen years of age I gave little thought to the awful waste of it all and just got caught up in the excitement of the moment. All the ships in Loch Ewe, and that was a considerable number, blew their steam whistles continuously for hours it seemed. As many people as possible went ashore and I am sure there were many toasts drunk that night. I think we held a dance in the old drill hall, and I don't think many people got to bed that night.

Very soon after the end of the war the Admiralty started sending the vessels that they had commandeered back to their owners. I am almost certain that by the end of May we had received our orders to proceed to Oban, there to await further orders. We spent three weeks there before the orders came to proceed in our own time to Lowestoft, which was the home port of the Neves.

I am not sure if the orders included the "in your own time" as I was not privy to the actual orders, but that is certainly what we did. I don't think we ever steamed for more than six hours in any day, and very often it would be less. This was a perfect example of the "more days, more dollars" syndrome. These men were all fishermen and were probably not looking forward to going back to that hard life after the relatively easy life that they had enjoyed for a few years. There was a general euphoria through all echelons of society so our skipper must have made the decision to stretch the voyage out to its limits by just making very short trips. We also contrived to stay for two nights in most of our stops. We went by way of the Caledonian Canal, which was very interesting. There were no lock keepers, so we had to do our own opening and closing of gates and sluices.

The Caledonian Canal brought us to Inverness where I seem to remember that we spent a weekend. That seems rather strange to me now as the next port of call was Cullen in Banffshire where most of the crew came from and I would have thought that they would have been anxious to get to their own homes as quickly as possible. I don't remember how long we stayed in Cullen for, but I guess it must have been one of our longer stops. It took two more stops to get as far as Aberdeen, and it was while we were there that news came of the end of the war in the Far East with the surrender of Japan after the dropping of the atomic bombs on Hiroshima and Nagasaki.

There was great jubilation in Aberdeen that night with dancing in the streets and everyone just going wild with joy.

The stops that I can remember after that were Methil on the Forth, South Shields, Scarborough, Grimsby, and then finally our arrival in Lowestoft. It took another two or three weeks for us to be paid off, which must have happened late on a Friday as Lal and I could only get as far as Inverness on the Saturday owing to the slow tortuous train journey involved. We stayed for the weekend in my uncle's house in Inverness.

This was the same Uncle Kenneth that I mentioned before as having lived on Isle Ewe. Two things that spring to mind when I think about him are his reputation as a very strong man, and our fascination with a finger that was missing on one of his hands at the first joint. I think he lost the finger in an accident at a sawmill. The best example that I can think of to illustrate his strength was as follows. He had loaned his plough to his cousin Willie who lived about one mile away. When he went to get it back Willie asked him to hold on until he yoked the horse to pull it back. Uncle Kenneth said "don't bother, I can easily carry it", saying which he just swung it on to his shoulder and stepped briskly back to his own croft. Years later when Uncle Kenneth left the island our father bought quite a few of his implements, including the said plough which was the heaviest single plough that I had ever seen. When Danny and I were about 13 and 15 years old respectively we were considered very strong for our ages but I can well remember how the two of us struggled to get this same plough lifted on to the cart when we wished to move it from one area to another.

The Grants generally were reputed to have great physical strength, or at least as far as the earlier generations were concerned. I can trace myself back five generations to Kenneth Grant who died in 1818. The name Alexander occurs throughout my family tree, so it seems quite possible that the Great Slaggan Bard, who was called Alexander Grant, was a brother of Kenneth Grant. Alexander was born about 1742 and died in 1820. Kenneth died in 1818. I mention the Slaggan Bard because of his well-documented reputation as a very strong man of gigantic size. In fact the epithet great was more because of his size than his greatness as a poet. Dixon in his book on Gairloch states that the Slaggan Bard could take a handful of winkles in one hand and crush them into small pieces. Moving forward in time, my great grandfather Kenneth, who was a grandson of the original Kenneth, was also a man of great strength. He used to go as crew on sailing herring drifters out of Buckie every summer, and when his son John was 14 years old he took him with him for the season. They walked all the way from Opinan to Buckie with a kitbag each. When they got to Inverness, the young John was so tired that his father first of all took the two kitbags, but later on took John on his back as well and completed the journey to Buckie with John and the two kitbags on his back. I knew the said John Grant, who was my father's uncle and still lived in the original family home in Opinan. Not exactly the original home, but a later one built on the same foundations. He died aged 85 when I was about eight years old.

When I got home from Lowestoft I had a season at lobster fishing. Conscription was still operable then, and would be for a few more years, so my thoughts were now turning to what I wanted to do with my life. I suppose I must have been somewhat overtaken by events because the next thing that happened was being called forward to be medically examined and tested for the armed forces. The Royal Navy and the Air Force had more stringent tests than the army did and I was pleased to have passed the tests for the navy.

Before my call-up papers could arrive I decided that I would prefer the Merchant Navy to the Royal Navy and to this end I joined a fishing vessel, working out of Greenock, on the River Clyde. I was enabled to do this through the good offices of our cousin Roddy Grant (Rover). He was the Mate of one of the other vessels working there. I have no clear memory of what we did there, but I do remember that we went out of the harbour every morning, so I think we must have been taking supplies out to vessels anchored at what was known as "The tail of the bank".

I think that must have lasted for no more than two months. The vessel I was on was then moved to Lochgoilhead on Loch Goil, which is a branch of Loch Long. Our work there was very interesting as we were working with scientists who were experimenting with listening devices while creating 10 foot waves artificially.

Our function was the placing of rafts in pre-determined places in the loch. The positioning had to be very exact, and was determined by using rangefinders. The rafts would be towed to the approximate position and four anchors would be dropped with roughly 90 degrees between them. The exact position would then be found by adjustment of the lines leading to the anchors. To start with the scientists were very much involved but they soon realized that I was quite adept in the use of the rangefinders and could be relied upon to get all the rafts set in the correct positions.

There were two Royal Navy vessels involved in these experiments. They were two MTVs and one of them was the fastest ship in the navy at that time. By travelling at maximum speed in the narrow confines of the loch they hoped that they would raise a ten-foot wave. I don't think that was ever achieved but I believe the experiment was a success nevertheless.

There were two jetties in Lochgoilhead one of which – the town jetty – had to be kept clear at noon each day for the MacBrayne's ferry that called daily from Gourock. The run from Gourock took two hours each way. After we had been there for some time I was due to go home on leave. This entailed getting the ferry to Gourock, then a train to Glasgow in order to get the night train to Inverness. This was followed by the morning train to Kyle of Lochalsh, getting off at Achnasheen and from there on the slow mail bus, getting home about 6.00 p.m. This was a journey time of 30 hours to do what you could do now in about four hours by car.

I did not mention that the captain of this particular ferry was a very irascible man who would fly into a rage if he found the town jetty in use by us or one of the MTVs. On the day that I was supposed to be going on leave one of the MTVs was lying at the jetty, and when they did not get off quickly enough the ferry turned round and sailed off back to Gourock without ever landing. I was rather upset about this, as it would mean a whole day of my leave lost. However, the Lieutenant in command of one of the MTVs told me not to worry, as they would run me across to Gourock. Just imagine, if this were to happen today there would be questions asked in parliament. We set off about an hour later at high speed and caught up with the ferry before she was half way across to Gourock. That was not the end of the story as they decided to teach the captain of the ferry a lesson by passing so close to him at high speed that they made his vessel roll violently. I suppose it seems a little bit juvenile now, but I thought it was great fun at the time and was very happy to get home for a short leave

This was a very happy time, during the summer of 1946 when I was just a lad of 18 years. Halcyon days indeed. We were more or less adopted by the village of Lochgoilhead. I was a member of the village football team and we used to travel around Argyllshire playing against different villages. There was only one other person of my age on the vessel. That was Walter the cook. The rest of the crew were a little older and were all married. There were a few young girls of our own age in the village who we used to meet up with. It was all very innocent. There was not a lot to do except go for walks around the beautiful countryside. Strangely, I don't remember any competition from the Royal Navy boys.

After about two months of this idyllic posting we were told to proceed to Lamlash on the Isle of Arran. On the morning that we left there were towels and sheets being waved from the windows of most of the houses lining Lochgoil as we used up all our compressed air blowing the ship's siren in farewell.

When we arrived at Lamlash we found out that our work was to act as liberty vessel to a fairly large fleet of landing craft that were anchored in this sheltered bay and still fully manned. I don't remember other liberty vessels there but there must have been at least one other. We were kept very much on the move from morning till at least 10 p.m. There must have been another vessel and we probably were on duty only every other day. We did not like it as much here as the people did not seem to be very friendly. I think the Royal Navy got in ahead of us this time.

The crew numbers on the MFV were the same as they had been on the Neves: captain, mate, two engineers, two deckhands and a cook. There was no sharing of cooking duties here and I was one of the deckhands. As far as I can remember there were no reliefs when someone went on leave. We all just shared out the duties. At one time the chief engineer was on leave, and the 2nd engineer, whose home was in Glasgow, wanted to go home for a weekend. I think there may have been some domestic problem that he had to go and sort out. This was my chance to make a lasting impression on the whole enterprise.

With the natural curiosity of the young I had shown a great interest in the engines, and wanted to know how everything worked. The engineers, particularly the 2nd engineer was quite keen to show me the ropes. He probably had an eye to having someone who could take over from him when he wanted some time off. In any case I got trained in starting, stopping, and operating the engines. This was in the days before bridge control was thought of and all engine manoeuvres had to be performed in the engine room to instructions transmitted from the bridge by telegraph.

The bridge telegraph showed Dead Slow, Slow, Half Speed, Full Speed and Finished with Engines, both ahead and astern, the ahead being on the forward quadrant of the telegraph and the astern on the rear quadrant. The telegraph was polished brass and mounted on a hardwood base that stood about three feet tall. It would be positioned in the middle of the wheelhouse, but on large vessels it would be replicated on each wing of the bridge. There was a corresponding telegraph in the engine room close to the engine control position. When an order was passed from the bridge to the engine room by moving the handle to the desired position a bell rang in the engine room and a pointer moved to the same point. The engineer had to move a handle on his telegraph to the same position that in turn rang a bell on the bridge before executing the desired order.

When the 2nd engineer went home for the weekend I was very happy to take charge of the engine room. Apart from having to perform all the engine movements as required by the bridge the main responsibility was in ensuring that the compressed air vessels were fully charged at all times as they were used every time the engine was started. There was also regular lubrication to be attended to. The fun part as far as I was concerned was in trying to be very prompt in executing the engine movements as required by the bridge. At the end of the first day the skipper told me that he found his ship handling was much improved with me in the engine room, as he seemed to get greater power when going astern. What neither he nor I had realized was that I was moving the throttle lever into the emergency position each time I went astern. There had been red paint to indicate the emergency section but it had got worn off and I had not been told to avoid this.

The end result of this neglect was that on the second day there was a loud bang from the stern and a great deal of vibration. Upon investigation we found that one of the blades had sheared off the propeller. We were laid up after this with no work to do. I decided that I was not cut out to be an engineer and started making enquiries about going deep sea on big ships, which should be the subject of a new chapter.

Chapter 11
My First Deep Sea Voyage

After making my decision to leave the MFV, and Admiralty employment, I found out that I would have to sign on with the Shipping Federation, known colloquially, and hereafter as the Pool. I don't remember now how I found out what I had to do in order to join the Merchant Navy proper, but I do remember taking the ferry across to Ardrossan and a train to Greenock, which was the nearest port at which the pool operated. I cannot think why I did not go to Glasgow to start with, as it became my home port eventually.

The recruitment process must have been very quick, as I don't remember spending any time in Greenock before joining the M.V. Luxor bound for the Persian Gulf on the 6th of September 1946.

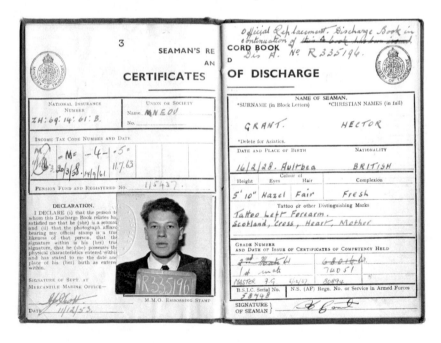

Discharge book, front pages

The exact dates of joining and leaving vessels are known from now on as one of the first things that I was issued with on joining the pool was a discharge book, or to give it its full title a Continuous Certificate of Discharge. My first book had space for 24 entries and my second had space for 60 entries. I still have these books and the first is filled up and the second is filled up to number 39.

I have seen discharge books dating back to the 19th century and the format has not changed to this day. There are eight columns and six lines per page, and one line covers a whole voyage. The first column is the name of the vessel with its official number and tonnage. The next two columns contain the date and place of engagement and discharge. The next is rank or rating followed by description of voyage. This is either home trade or foreign. The next two columns are the important ones as they are a copy of the report of character. The first is for ability and the second for general conduct. Anything less than very good in both is considered bad. In fact there are only two stamps that can be used to fill these spaces. The one that everyone wants is the VG for very good. The other is DR, which means decline to report. A DR in either column was usually considered the end of

Discharge book certificates

a career. These were stamped in the books at the end of the voyage and you would stand a very poor chance of being signed on by any other ship if you got a DR. The final column was for the signature of the Master and an official from the Shipping Federation.

The dates in the discharge book referred to time on articles, which might not be the whole time spent on the vessel. Articles were usually opened on the day before departure, and were closed again on arrival back in the UK. The closing of articles did not necessarily mean the end of your employment. If it had been a relatively short voyage and you wished to sail on the same vessel again you just carried on as before on the same rate of pay until such time as articles were opened again at the start of a new voyage. The only difference was that this time did not appear in your discharge book. This became critical for me at a later stage, in getting sea time in before taking examinations.

The articles were a legal document, which spelt out in detail the responsibilities of the crew as well as their rights. I cannot remember the rights as taking up a lot of space in the document, but it did spell out the minimum amount of different staple items of diet each person was entitled to, known universally among seamen as the Board of Trade diet or the pound and pint diet. A copy of the most important parts of the articles had to be displayed in a glass-covered frame in a conspicuous position near the crew's quarters. The main part, which all crew members had to sign, stayed in the Masters safe with a copy in the shipping office. Or was that the other way round?

A brief description of the watch system with general duties entailed and the manning of vessels in the 1940s and which pertained until the 1970s would be useful here. Automation had not arrived yet and crews were much larger than they are nowadays.

The manning scale for an ordinary 10,000 ton tramp steamer would be: master, chief officer, 2nd officer, 3rd officer, radio officer, chief engineer, 2nd engineer, 3rd engineer, 4th engineer, bosun, carpenter, 8 ABs, 3 ordinary seamen, donkeyman, 3 greasers, 6 firemen, chief steward, 4 assistant stewards, chief cook, 2nd cook and a galley boy. That adds up to 40 people. This would be the minimum if I remember correctly, as there would be many more engineers on a twin screw vessel and it applied only to European-crewed vessels. In companies that employed Asian crews the numbers were much higher. On twin-screw cargo liners on which I sailed some time later with Indian crews, the total numbers were in excess of 80.

Generally speaking articles were opened on the day before sailing and all of the crew signed on. The bosun would have the task of placing the deck crew into their watches even though watches would not be set until immediately after sailing. There was always so much work to do before sailing in getting the ship ready for sea that all the crew were required on deck. There would be five or six hatches to be secured, and in those days that meant heavy beams and single hatchboards. There would be anything between 10 and 32 derricks to be lowered and secured, and many other tasks too numerous to mention. It is worth noting that when overtime was paid for working more than eight hours in a day, this did not apply to the day of sailing or the day of arrival. On those days one had to work for more than ten hours before becoming eligible for overtime. This was a good example of the parsimony of shipowners generally.

Once the ship was at sea, watches were set. The bosun, carpenter and one AB, usually the most senior one, were on day work while the rest were in watches two ABs and one ordinary seaman or OS per watch. The watches were 8–12, 12–4, and 4–8. Once you were picked for a watch, you remained in that watch for the whole of the voyage, however long it was. I cannot remember if we drew lots for the watch or it was just an arbitrary placing by the bosun. Some people had different preferences for watches but generally speaking the 8–12 was most favoured as it offered a more natural sleeping time. As one had to perform all kinds of deck work between the hours of 7 a.m. and 5 p.m. when not on bridge duty the 4–8 was favoured by the work-shy. The OS, although the junior member of the watch, performed exactly the same duties as the ABs.

Let us assume that we are in the 8–12 watch and go through one day at sea. Someone from the 4–8 watch would call the three of you at 7.30 a.m. and the OS would run along to the galley and bring the breakfast for the three to the mess room. The quality of food varied enormously between very good and atrocious depending on the company. There would be porridge with bread and tea. On Thursdays and Sundays there would be bacon and egg but I don't remember what would follow the porridge on other days. I remember one ship that had a thin and runny fish curry quite frequently for breakfast. I did not like curry before then, but I was forced through hunger to eat this disgusting mess. I started with rice with a little bit of curry and gradually increased the amount over time. I have loved good curry ever since, even though my introduction to it had been by way of a rather poor imitation of the real thing.

As soon as breakfast was eaten and the dishes washed, one of us would make his way to the bridge to take over as helmsman at exactly 8 a.m. The other two would present themselves to the bosun for orders. The duties were many and various: overhauling running gear, splicing wires and ropes, replacing running and standing gear, washing down paintwork and painting – all the maintenance work that goes into keeping a ship in good order. One of the two working on deck would relieve the helmsman at 10 a.m. for his two-hour stint at the wheel. The one who was relieved would have a quick smoke before joining those working on deck, who would be his watchmate and the day-work AB.

At noon we would be relieved by the 12–4 watch and go to the mess room for our lunch. This, like breakfast, varied in quality from ship to ship, but being young and healthy we devoured it, if not with relish, at least with equanimity. For the rest of the day we were free to do as we wished. Maybe a little nap in the afternoon, some reading and probably some hobby work. Most ships were reasonably well supplied with books and most sailors were avid readers. The expression "money for old rope" must have originated among sailors, as old rope was the raw material for so much of the things we used to make. Not that I ever sold anything but I made quite a few mats by teasing out the yarns from old rope, plaiting it, and forming it into fancy shapes, and stitching it together with sail-twine. We had to wash, repair and press our own clothes as well as keeping our cabins clean and tidy.

Our next watch is due at 8 p.m. and the duties here are a little different. The one who had not done a stint at the wheel in the morning watch would be first on as helmsman from 8 until 10, followed by the one who had done the first stint in the morning. Before doing his 10–12 stint, he would have been on lookout from 8 until 9. The 8–10 helmsman would be on lookout from 11 until 12, and the 9 –11 period would be covered by the "farmer", the name by which the person who did not go to the helm was universally known. The rotating system was designed to give everyone an equal share of duties over a period of time. You moved up one place in each consecutive watch: farmer, 1st helm, 2nd helm. When not on lookout or at the wheel, you were considered to be on stand-by and had to listen out for a whistle blast from the officer of the watch who might require you to do some errand for him. This might be reading the log, which was streamed from the stern, or he might want the sea temperature taken if you were in iceberg waters. The lookout was always posted during the hours of darkness. During bad weather this would be on the windward wing of the bridge. The officer of the watch liked to have the lee side to himself. In reasonable weather, provided there were no seas being shipped over the forecastle head, the lookout would be posted there. The attention of the officer of the watch was drawn to any lights that you spotted by ringing the bell: one peal for the starboard bow, two for the port bow and three for dead ahead. Owing to the much greater elevation of the bridge, the light should be visible from there much sooner if a proper lookout was being kept but you never made that assumption.

The bell, which was struck to indicate time, was on the bridge, close to the wheel so that the helmsman could strike it. When the lookout was on the forecastle head, he had to reply by striking the forecastle head bell. Eight bells coincided with the watch-changing times: noon, 4 p.m., 8 p.m., midnight, 4 a.m. and 8 a.m. One bell was at half an hour later and so it continued with an additional stroke for every additional half-hour until 3.30, 7.30, and 11.30, when 7 bells would be struck. One bell was also struck at 3.45, 7.45, and 11.45. This bell was the signal for the new watch to get dressed and ready for their watch. I think that sets the general scene, so I will now attempt from memory to describe some specific voyages.

The first voyage is probably the most memorable, as everything is new to you. The one thing that was not new on this voyage was the ship itself. I don't know when it was built, but it was very close to the end of its working life when I joined it. Around that time most ships would have twin cabins for all of the crew, but not on the Luxor. All the crew lived together in the forecastle: deck crew on the port side and engine room crew on the starboard side. There was a fore and aft bulkhead down the middle separating them. Bunks lined both sides and there was a long table down the middle. She was heavily infested with rats, which I find strange, as she was an oil tanker, which limits the spaces for rats as well as making the finding of food more difficult. I don't think we left much in the way of scraps from our meagre diet. The rats used to run along the beams above the bunks all night. I think that my fear and revulsion at rats dates from this time. As soon as we got to warmer climates, most of us just took a mattress and a sheet out on deck and slept under the stars.

Our first port of call was Port Said at the northern end of the Suez Canal. This was also my first introduction to foreign lands and very exciting I found it. We arrived in the early afternoon and lay at anchor very close to the town until the next morning. I don't think they had the convoy system as well organized then as it was later, or maybe we were just waiting for orders. As soon as we were anchored we were surrounded by a flotilla of small boats selling everything from melons to crocodile handbags. These were known as bumboats. There was one particular man who was known to us as George Roby. I kept seeing him regularly over the years as we passed through the canal. His sales technique consisted of listening carefully to the accents of most of the crew and then mimicking it. He could do Scots, Geordy, Scouse or Cockney like a native of these places. I remember mostly buying fresh fruit as this was never in very good supply on the ship. We did go ashore at night but I don't remember much about that. I do remember being pestered a lot by young boys trying to sell you anything, including their sisters. On the way back I think that one of our group must have hit one of these boys, because we were suddenly attacked by a large group of men and only just made it back to the taxi-boat that was taking us back to our ship.

I learned a lesson that night. That lesson was that if you want to avoid trouble, don't go around in a gang. There is always going to be someone in that gang who wants to start trouble and you get dragged into it whether you want to or not. In the course of a lifetime you are going to get involved in enough scrapes of your own making without seeking to get involved in those of others. I hesitate to cast aspersions on my shipmates, but to say that they were a hard-bitten lot might be understating the case. They were all from the town of Greenock and some of them may have come with a questionable reputation. Most people would have considered the Luxor a bad job, and in later years when I learned how the system worked, I realized that the Shipping Masters in the Pool tended to send the bad boys to the bad ships. It was my misfortune, although I had no reputation, good, or bad at this time, to have been available when the Luxor was being manned.

While we lay at anchor in Port Said, we all took the opportunity to swim in the harbour. I find it surprising now that we were allowed to do this. As we were without cargo the deck was quite high above the water and most of us jumped in feet first while holding our noses. We must have been at least 25 feet above the water as I can still remember how deep we went and with all the flotsam in the harbour it was not without some risk

We must have got our orders fairly quickly if we did not have them already, as we left Port Said the next day bound for Abadan in the Persian Gulf in what is now Iran. Before leaving Port Said, we received a large and powerful searchlight with an operator. This light was mounted on the bows for use when transiting the Suez Canal at night. The canal is too narrow to allow ships to pass so a convoy system was devised whereby all southbound vessels left Port Said at roughly the same time as northbound vessels left the port of Suez at the south end of the canal. About halfway along its length the canal passed through the Bitter Lakes where the convoy that arrived first would anchor until the other convoy passed through.

I seem to remember that we steamed through the canal at something close to normal speed so this required accurate steering. At this point I should explain that steering a large ship is quite different from steering anything else, including small vessels. For a start, nothing happens when you turn the wheel, as there is quite a delay before the ship answers to the helm. Putting the wheel back to 'midships is not enough either as you have to put on opposite helm to stop the swing. It is all a matter of anticipation as you are usually taking off the helm and indeed reversing it sometimes before the ship has started to swing. It is an art that only comes with experience. When steering a compass course the lubber line, painted on the forward rim of the binnacle, indicates the ship's head and first-time learners find it difficult to understand which way the ship is swinging. It seems that it is the compass that is swinging, when in fact it is the ship that is swinging round the compass. Turning the wheel the wrong way when the ship goes off course is known as chasing the lubber line, which learners tend to do.

I think that I must have been on the 8–12 watch on the way out and had not quite mastered the art of steering in the ten or twelve days to Port Said, and was never pulled up by the 3rd mate whose watch that would have been. When steaming through the canal I had the first helmsman duty at 8 p.m., and soon after taking the helm the chief officer arrived on the bridge to find the ship shearing about rather erratically. He berated the 3rd officer for having a novice at the wheel in such restricted conditions, and had me relieved immediately. As far as I can recall that was the first and only time that I was found to be less than very competent in any of my duties, and indeed as far as steering was concerned I became a first class helmsman. Maybe my pride had been hurt.

After clearing the canal we proceeded on our way to Abadan. This must have taken at least ten days and during this time we spent all our working hours down in the tanks cleaning them in readiness for the next cargo. This must rank as one of the worst jobs I ever had to do at sea. There was a thick black oily sludge that we had to try and move to the suction point using squeegees. It was then pumped over the side. Care for the environment was still something in the distant future then. All this horrible dirty work took place in temperatures of 40°C. The rate of pay for an AB at this time was £24 per month, and for an OS it was £16. There was a special payment of 3 pence (equivalent to just over 1p today) for each session worked down the tanks. Alternatively you could accept a glass of rum as you emerged from the tank and forfeit the money. Needless to say we all chose the rum, as it was such a paltry sum of money, and you had to wait until the end of the voyage to get it anyway.

We eventually arrived at the loading terminal in Abadan. In common with most tanker-loading ports we were miles from any town, or any habitation for that matter. There was a club of sorts, which was run by the Missions to Seamen, or was it The Flying Angel? Both these religious organizations which were totally non-denominational, provided a very useful function to seamen of all nations. They served snacks and beer and would have rooms where table tennis, darts, snooker etc. could be played. They could be found in most ports of the world, although I don't remember them being on the Indian subcontinent. They were well patronized by the local girls who used to organize dances. Football and cricket matches could be organized between different ships through the auspices of the mission. In the major British and European ports they provided very good living accommodation at very reasonable prices.

I am not sure now whether the club at Abadan was a mission or whether it was a club provided by the oil company, which I think was the Anglo-Iranian Company. It was very small but it did have a small swimming pool, which was very welcome. It showed a film every evening in what was quite a small room, but I think we enjoyed it nevertheless. We did not have real money, only vouchers which could only be spent in the club. There was some bartering going on with people who came aboard with watches and other jewellery. We bartered for these with spare second-hand clothes. I got my first-ever watch there. I seem to remember that it was a Roma, which was quite a good watch, and so it proved.

I think we spent about two days in Abadan before leaving with a full cargo of oil for Hamburg. I don't remember much about the trip home except for arriving in Hamburg in very cold weather during the month of November.

At the time I seem to remember being told that we were the first tanker to enter the port since the end of the war. I find it hard to believe that they could have existed for the eighteen months since the end of the war without any oil imports, although they had existed throughout the war without any oil imports by sea.

The work of reconstructing the country had not really started at this time. I can still see the scene of utter devastation in the port and city. From being the third largest seaport in the world there was hardly a usable berth left in the whole port. I can still visualize the cranes lying at drunken angles all around the docks. It was the same when we went in to the city. There were more flattened bombsites than there were standing buildings. I made many trips back to Hamburg over the next ten to fifteen years and saw it rise again to its former glory.

At this time the country was still governed by an allied commission. As far as I can remember we were issued with vouchers which could only be spent in premises belonging to the allies. This did not stop resourceful sailors finding ways of visiting local establishments. Cigarettes were the universally recognized currency of the times and these were cheap and plentiful on board ship. You could have a great night out on the proceeds of one pack of cigarettes.

Talking about the allied commission that ran the port, and indeed the whole country reminds me of something that I only found the answer to many years later. The national flag at the time of my first visit was the letter C in the international code of signals. The current national flag replaced this a few years later. In 1962 I was chief officer on the Caledonian Coast and one day while chatting to the captain, a certain Frederick Mara, we got talking about Hamburg. I learned that he had been seconded from Coast Lines to the harbour commission in Hamburg to help in getting the port back to some semblance of order. At his very first meeting the question of a temporary national flag came up. He suggested the letter C as it stood for commission, and this was accepted and acted upon. What he had not told anyone was that the letter C was the house flag of Coast Lines and he was extremely loyal to the company, having served with them from cadet to captain.

On completion of the discharge of our cargo we made our way to South Shields where we paid off on the 16th of November 1946. My abiding memory of our arrival in the UK after a foreign voyage was of the intrusive manner in which the Customs officers treated us. They were much more vigilant than they are nowadays, although coming from war-torn Germany there was not much that we could have been smuggling. I suppose that because of the shortages at home there was scope for trade in cigarettes. I seem to remember that some people had bartered for some goods. Small musical instruments including mouth organs were available on the black market. I had not indulged in this practice, so I don't know if the Customs people were interested or not.

After paying off we all made our own way home, although with only two days leave for every full month served on articles I realized that I would have used up most of my leave in travelling so I just made my way back to Glasgow. I had realized by this time that it would make more sense to have Glasgow as my home port. I think that I was able to keep the four days leave that I had earned to be added to subsequent leave, but maybe not. Rights were not so easily enforced in those days and justice was pretty thin on the ground. In any event I took up abode in the Sailors Home and reported to the Pool for my next ship. The Sailors Home provided good clean accommodation with food as good as could be expected at that time with all its severe food shortages, and all at a very reasonable price. So ended my first foreign voyage, the first of many over the next almost twenty years.

Chapter 12

Sailing Around the World

I see from my discharge book that I signed on my next ship exactly seven days after signing off the last one, and as this week would have included travelling time and a weekend it shows how quickly jobs were found in those days. This ship was the Baron Ruthven and I signed on in Glasgow on the 23rd of November 1946. In retrospect this was another bad signing although happily it was a very short trip and also I think I can honestly say it was the last "bad" ship that I sailed on.

As the name might indicate, this was the Baron Line. All the ships were named after some baron or other, and the company was owned by H. Hogarth. The company flag had the letters HH on it and the company was inevitably known as Hungry Hogarths. The epitaph was not unjustly earned as I remember the food being fairly appalling. There was no refrigerator or freezer on the ship, so when fresh food ran out after a few days we relied on canned food and salt meat. It was the only ship on which I served that carried barrels of salt meat. This really was harking back to the days of sailing ships. I don't remember much about the food that was served up, but when you are young and healthy you will eat almost anything.

This voyage took us in ballast to Huelva in Spain to load a cargo of manganese ore from the Rio Tinto mines. This was of course in the time of General Franco, and the absolute poverty of the region was sad to see. A memory of this time has stayed with me all of my life. As the youngest member of the crew, I was appointed as the 'peggy' while in port. This was the name given to the person who acted as mess boy. You were not excused any of your deck work, but in your own time had to carry the food from the galley and wash up the dishes after the meal, and clean the mess-room. Just after I had cleared up after lunch one day and had dumped all the leftovers in the slop bucket a young boy of about ten years of age came aboard and started digging with his hands into the slop bucket. There was a layer of cold watery custard overlaying congealed gravy and cold potatoes and not much else of nutritional value given the low standard of fare provided. I was shocked at this sight and told the boy that he could stay aboard and help me in future in return for being given all the leftovers before they were dumped in the bucket.

I have been back to Huelva twice since that time, the most recent visit being in 2005 when on holiday in the region. I found that it had changed beyond all recognition in that time, which I was very happy about.

We loaded our cargo in two or three days and sailed back to Glasgow where we were discharged on the 15th of December 1946.

I spent an even shorter time between jobs this time as I see that I signed on the British Wisdom on the 19th of December 1946.

The British Wisdom was a 12,000-ton tanker belonging to the British Tanker Company or BTC, as it was then known. This was the company that is now known as BP. The ship, as distinct from all my previous ships, was almost new, this being only her second voyage. This was the standard tanker of this time and there was nothing larger than this at sea then. This did not hold for long as within a few years the standard became 30,000 tons, then 60,000, and within quite a short time scale we had 250,000 ton tankers. The rapid increase in size was commercially driven by the closure of the Suez Canal as the economies of scale made the long trip round the Cape of Good Hope more profitable.

I am jumping ahead a little here, so let us get back to 1946 and the beginning of what turned out to be quite a long voyage. As I said earlier this was only the second voyage for this ship, and to us she was the last word in modernity. Experiences in later years showed that this was not the case. Everything was nice and new and clean, but really quite basic. Seamen were berthed two to a cabin in the stern. There was a common washroom without any showers. It was just a fairly large room with a hot and cold tap and a drain in the floor. We were each provided with a bucket and the method that everyone used was to fill the bucket with warm water, strip off, and wash down completely, and then tip the bucket over your head. It was just as effective as having a shower.

I saw the British Wisdom under another name carrying a cargo of vegetable oil in Bromborough Dock where I was the manager, about 25 years after I had sailed on her. I could hardly believe that I had thought of her as a nice modern ship then. She was at this time rather decrepit, I suppose not surprisingly, as she really was at the end of her working life.

Although I was being quite truthful when I said that my previous ship was the last bad ship that I sailed on, the present one left a lot to be desired in the culinary department. Breakfast was always a bit iffy. It frequently consisted of thin porridge with watered-down condensed milk followed by an even thinner and watery curry with boiled rice. Being forced through necessity to eat this concoction, which bore only a passing resemblance to the real thing, I might have been expected to be put off curry for life. This was not the case, however, as in later years I served on ships with

Asian crews where the cooks were either Indian or Bangladeshi and the curries were superb.

I am sure that by now the reader must have noticed the apparent obsession with food. I make no apologies for this. Firstly we were all young, healthy, and working hard with lots of good fresh sea air, so we were hungry most of the time. Secondly there was a distinct lack of social life aboard ship, so meal times became the highlight of the day. Don't forget that transistor radios, cassette players, video recorders *et al.* had still to be invented. Old-fashioned valve radios were big and cumbersome, but a few people made an effort to carry one aboard. Even then one was usually limited to the BBC overseas programme. I do remember that on this ship someone must have brought a gramophone aboard because I can remember Frank Sinatra being played rather a lot. I think it was at this time that I fell in love with the voice of Ella Fitzgerald. Great arguments ensued about the relative merits of Frank Sinatra and Bing Crosby. I was a Bing man in those days. Probably because it was the minority view, which I was always inclined to take.

Our first stop on this voyage, after passing through the Suez Canal, was Abadan in Iran. This happened to have been my first port abroad on my first voyage. We made four intermediate trips from the Persian Gulf before loading for home. The first was to Adelaide and Port Lincoln in Australia followed by a trip to Durban in South Africa. We then loaded in Bahrain for a short trip to Port Sudan in the Red Sea and back to Abadan to load another cargo of aviation fuel for Durban again.

I enjoyed the trip to Australia but had to wait until I was in my sixties before visiting the country again, and then I had to pay my own way. I don't remember a lot about Adelaide but in spite of it being just a sleepy little town I remember Port Lincoln quite well. That part of South Australia was at that time short of young men and it was not unusual for seamen to jump ship and lie low for a few months before integrating into the population. The other ordinary seaman and I got friendly with a local man. I think he owned an ice cream parlour. My friend had trained as a butcher before going to sea and the ice cream man who must have had connections in the meat industry was very keen to recruit him. In fact he proposed to take both of us to a cabin that he owned about 150 miles inland where his teenage daughters would look after us until the hue and cry about our disappearance died down. I think we were tempted, but as he never produced the daughters we did not trust him. I don't think I was ever very serious about it, but my friend was.

I have happy memories of Durban as well. Of course I visited it very many times after that and never got tired of it, but the first time is always the most exciting. Not that I can remember much about it. One clear memory is of walking along Point Road and seeing all the handsome Zulus with their rickshaws. Of course we had to do the tourist thing and have a ride in a rickshaw and I can still remember how amazed I was at the speed at which they could run and the sheer athleticism of their powerful bodies.

The next trip was from Abadan to Port Sudan and that is memorable only for the fact that there was no respite from the excessive heat of the Persian Gulf and the Red Sea. I think that it was on this trip on the way back to Bahrein Island in the Persian Gulf that my two watch mates succumbed to heat exhaustion. It was on the afternoon watch, and when the first one collapsed at the wheel the next one took his place. He did not last much longer and I had to take over then even though I was the farmer in that watch. I lasted until the end of the watch with no ill effects. I will always remember how ill they looked, with their eyes sunk right in to their heads. They had just allowed themselves to get dehydrated and the wheel-house was completely airless. This was in the days before air conditioning was available on ships.

We loaded in Bahrein for Europe. I say Europe with some reservations as I know the voyage ended in Falmouth but I am almost certain that we discharged our cargo of oil in Antwerp first. My discharge book shows only the port at which we were signed off and that was Falmouth on the 16th of August 1947.

I made my way home from Falmouth via Glasgow for the first time in over a year. I must have accrued about three weeks of leave in this time but in fact I stayed home for more than four months. I am not sure now how I managed this as I note that in the following year I was home for almost three months. I know that in one of those years my father had a long spell in hospital and I was able to claim compassionate leave to look after the croft. I suspect that this was in 1948, so the 1949 long spell remains a mystery. The Shipping Federation must have forgotten about me.

I, however, as this was one of the seasons where Danny and I were hard at work at the lobster fishing as described in an earlier chapter, did not waste the time. It is worth mentioning that I was probably earning twice as much as I would have been at sea as an ordinary seaman.

The Pool finally caught up with me, or maybe I decided that I had been home long enough, as I see that I joined my next ship in Glasgow on the 8th of January 1948

This was the Beaconsfield and easily the best ship I had sailed on up to that point. I don't remember the name of the company, but all their ships were named after districts around London. I think they only had about six ships in total. They were a very paternalistic company. They had framed paintings of members of their family in every cabin. It was made clear to us that this was so that we did not need to put pinups on the walls, something that we were forbidden to do.

The food was excellent on this ship, as was the accommodation. The general configuration of this ship was fairly standard for that period. A raised forecastle head, then No 1 and No 2 hatches, then the bridge structure. This had the accommodation for the captain and the deck officers as well as the dining saloon. I think the galley was at deck level in this block. Then came No 3 hatch followed by a one-storey structure, which was over the engine room. This structure had engineers cabins and crew mess-rooms and, in davits above it, four lifeboats: two to port and two to starboard. The after deck, which had No 4 and No 5 hatches, was a flush deck with the crew's quarters being in the very stern below deck level. We sailed the next morning for St Johns New Brunswick on the eastern seaboard of Canada. It may not have been the best time of year to be making my first transAtlantic crossing in a 10,000-ton vessel but I was happy to have a change from tropical climes. We were engaged in carrying lease-lend goods to war-torn Europe.

As the St Lawrence River was frozen over in winter, we used St Johns in New Brunswick, but in summer we went up the St Lawrence River to Montreal, generally calling at Quebec and sometimes Three Rivers. The discharge ports in Europe were Antwerp, Rotterdam and Hamburg. On our first trip to St Johns I became ill while there and ended up in hospital for ten days with a mastoid infection. I quite enjoyed my time in hospital as I was not really very ill and the nurses made a great fuss of me – the "poor young sailor thousands of miles from home" syndrome – and I guess I played up to it for all it was worth.

I don't think I will ever forget the day that I came out of hospital. It was snowing hard and blowing a blizzard. We were due to sail that evening and as was always the case there was a tremendous amount of work to be done. All five hatches had to be closed and secured and all the derricks had to be lowered and made secure as you are straight out into the Bay of Fundy which is a very treacherous stretch of water. When everything was secured we cast off and sent all the mooring lines below. At this point the captain called us all to the bridge and had us all pass the 1st officer, who stood inside the wheelhouse door with a large glass and some bottles of rum. Each person was given a large tot and I don't think I ever appreciated a drink so much. Sea-going watches were then set and those of us who were off watch were able to get to bed after what had been a very hard day, especially for someone like me who had just got out of a hospital bed.

That voyage across the Atlantic Ocean bound for Antwerp was quite memorable for the severe storm that we encountered. In eighteen years of going to sea I have experienced a few bad storms but that one must have been in the top three or four. I think that we were probably about half way across and had been battling along with a northerly gale on our port beam for a day or two when it suddenly got very much worse. I was on watch as the helmsman around 3 p.m. in the afternoon watch when a monstrous wave swept across our decks. When we looked out after the wave had passed we found that the companion ladders leading from the deck to the first level of the bridge had been swept away, the two starboard lifeboats had been swept across the boat deck and smashed up. Even more amazingly the steel roof of the 'midships accommodation had been torn off and curled up like a sardine tin lid over half its length.

There are two courses of action that you can take when weather conditions are so bad that you cannot maintain your course. The first is to "heave to". In other words steer straight into the wind and reduce the speed so that you just hold your own. The second is to turn and run before the wind. We chose the latter, which is by far the most comfortable but has the disadvantage of sending you a long way off your course. When I say we chose the latter, neither I nor any other member of the crew had any part in the decision making. The captain alone had to decide. We ran South for about two days before the gale had abated sufficiently to resume our course

When we arrived in Antwerp we had some temporary repairs done, then called at Rotterdam and on to Hamburg where most of the cargo was destined for. I am rather vague about what happened next. I think we went from Hamburg to Tilbury where we had all our repairs done. We changed quite a lot of the crew here although at least two of the original crew from Newcastle signed on again. One of those was a particular friend of mine. By the time we got across the Atlantic this time the St Lawrence River was open and we called first at Quebec for one day and then up river to Montreal.

This friend of mine whose name I cannot even remember had been on the ship for the trip before I had joined and had made friends with a family who lived in Verdun, an outlying district of Montreal. I was introduced to this family who had a daughter of about my age with whom I became very friendly. Everything was very proper and I don't remember ever meeting her except in the company of the whole family. On my next, and last, voyage to Montreal they packed a large box of goodies for me to take with me, as I knew I would be going home on leave when we got back to the UK. We were still in the throes of severe food rationing at this time so this box had been filled with all the things that could not be bought at home.

The only thing that I remember was a large bottle of maple syrup, which I don't think we had ever seen before.

I am jumping ahead here, as we are still only on the second voyage. The scenery on the St Lawrence, which is approached by the Gulf of St Lawrence, a long meandering gulf that eventually becomes a wide river, entranced me. By the time you have travelled upstream to Quebec the river has narrowed to less than a mile. It remains as narrow as this all the way to Montreal except for one place where it passes through a lake. The valley through which it flows is steep-sided and heavily wooded. I was reminded of it many years later, when travelling along the Mosel in Germany, the only difference being that the valley sides on the Mosel were covered in grape vines and not pine trees.

I loved the time spent in Montreal, which was probably about nine days. Most of my spare time was spent at the home of the Potts family or going out on the town with them. They did seem to do everything as a family group. On my next, and last, trip when I was the only one left of the original crew I spent a weekend with the family at a lakeside camp somewhere up-country from Montreal where we swam and picnicked

I think it was at the beginning of the second trip that the chief officer realized that I was being wasted as a watch keeper and got the bosun to place me on day work. This may be seen as rather a strange decision, as the day worker was usually the most senior seaman on board. I was the most junior rating on the ship but he had seen enough to realize that in spite of that I was clearly the most talented seaman on the ship.

This was not an idle boast on my behalf and I need make no apologies for it. I had learnt my seamanship as a boy in fishing boats and could splice ropes and wire and was competent in all the fancy knots and ropework, which was the pride of all the old sailors. There was by now, however, a new breed of sailor coming to sea who did not all have this pride in their profession, and this is what the Chief officer had spotted. Bearing in mind that I received only half the pay that the mainly incompetent ABs did, it was a wonder that I did not feel any resentment. I can assure you that I did not, and was perfectly happy to get on with my work. Maybe I was a bit naïve but I took a lot of satisfaction from being the best at my job.

As I mentioned earlier, on my third and last voyage on the Beaconsfield I was the only one left of the original crew. I must have kept in touch with the friend whose name I have forgotten and who lived in Gateshead, as I spent a day or two with him and his family after paying off from the Beaconsfield in South Shields on the 8th of August 1948. I was much saddened some time in the following year to receive a letter from his sister telling me that he had died suddenly of a brain haemorrhage. She must have got my address from the Shipping Federation.

I overstayed my leave again this year just as I had done in 1947 and spent the time very profitably again, lobster fishing with Danny. It was only for three months this time rather than the five months of the previous year as I note that I joined the SS The Earl on the 5th of November 1948. This was a coaster, which I joined in Troon, having been sent there from Glasgow. I had asked to be given a coasting vessel so that I could leave at a time of my choosing rather than at the end of what could be a long foreign voyage. The reason for this was that my sister Anna was getting married in late January or early February 1949.

I still did not have enough sea-time in to be promoted to AB, but I had sufficient time in to allow me to take an examination for the rank of EDH (efficient deckhand). This was equivalent to AB on the pay scale and I passed without any problem. I shared the forecastle accommodation with the other AB who was Polish. There were only the two of us, captain, chief officer, chief engineer, 2nd engineer and a cook: seven in total. Our first trip was to Hamburg with a cargo of potatoes. After discharging this we loaded a cargo of scrap iron, a lot of which was still to be found in Hamburg.

I shared a surname with the chief officer and I don't know whether it was for this reason or not, but he had taken a dislike to me and always gave me the worst jobs. One of these jobs was renewing the ratlines on the foremast shrouds. On a nice warm day this would have been a very pleasant task, but the end of November in Hamburg is anything but warm. The shrouds are the three wire stays to each side of the mast. The outer ones are about six feet apart at deck level and converge at the top of the mast. The ratlines, which are made of tarred hemp, form a ladder for climbing the mast so they have to be frequently renewed. This is done by splicing an eye in to one end of the rope, lashing that to one of the outer shrouds, half hitching it to the middle shroud, then cutting the rope at exactly the correct length, splicing an eye in to that end and lashing it to the other shroud.

The correct and traditional way to do the job is to place the coil of rope on the deck, taking one end up with you and doing all the work aloft. As it was such a bitterly cold day I worked out that if I cut several lengths of rope of ever-decreasing lengths I could at least splice the eye in to one end of these lengths in the shelter of the forecastle. The system worked perfectly well and I was wasting no more than three or four inches from each length. After about an hour the chief officer came along to see the progress, and although he could not fault my work he made me revert to the traditional way of doing it. This was rather counter-productive as my fingers were numb with the cold and it was taking me twice as long to splice the eyes in the rope. This day was memorable for another reason, which would also give it an exact date. It was the day on which Prince Charles was born.

I did not particularly enjoy my time on this ship. At that time I did not think that going to sea in coasters was the life for me. This is interesting in view of what happened later. I don't remember the tonnage of The Earl but it must have been around 600 tons, so never spent much time in port, and at sea we worked four hours on and four hours off. Life was quite a hard slog and there was not much friendship except with the other AB. I remember spending a whole day wandering the streets of London with him. It was a Sunday and the streets were completely deserted, which would be a rare phenomenon today. I have no recollection of how long he had been out of Poland but he knew all the places in London that one should visit much better than I did.

I am surprised to see from my discharge book that I paid off on New Year's Day, 1st January 1949. Maybe the fact that I was discharged ill with blood poisoning and sent to hospital clouded my memory. This was in Grimsby and I spent ten days in hospital before being discharged and making my way home in good time for Anna's marriage to Bill Manson.

I want to end this chapter here and devote a whole chapter to my next ship where I spent the happiest two years of my sea-going life – and would you believe, it was a coasting vessel.

Chapter 13

A Family Wedding and
A Happy Ship

Before joining my next ship we had the happy occasion of Anna's marriage to Bill Manson. Because Bill's family were scattered all over Scotland and England, they had decided to have the wedding in Inverness so as to make it easier for everyone to get to it. The family and all the friends from the West hired a coach for the day. This would have been Alfred's bus. Donald was still going to sea at this time and he was unable to make it to the wedding. I had missed his wedding for the same reason the previous year. Danny had by this time joined the Royal Navy to do his National service, but was able to get a 48-hour pass to come to the wedding. All the way from Plymouth I think. I had managed to wangle time off, as I explained in the last chapter.

The marriage ceremony was conducted by the Revd Mackinnon of Aultbea in the Caledonian Hotel, and the reception just carried on from there; very convenient. My most enduring memory of the proceedings was at some time in the evening sitting at a table having a drink with my father and Danny. It was memorable because it was the first time it had ever happened, and if my memory serves me right it was the last time. My father was not a pub-going man, although he had no strong objections to drinking. In fact he quite enjoyed a very occasional drink. He was, however, without any help from drink, excellent company and great fun to be with. It was the first time that any of us had met any of Bill's family. I remember particularly his younger sister Marie with whom I kept in touch for a while. I remember going to visit her some time later that year. She was sister-in-charge, or matron, of the Cheshire VC home somewhere in Hampshire. This was the Home Hospital that Group Captain Cheshire VC had set up after the war to care for airmen who had been badly burnt and wounded on flying duties

The evening finally came to an end and those of us going west got on to Alfred's bus. I remember that Danny got on it as well but only went as far as Strathpeffer. Our cousin Ian Macrae who had been to the wedding with his wife Etta put him up for the night as he had to catch an early morning train back to Plymouth. Ian and Etta must have been living in Strathpeffer at that time. I can remember Isabel and Murdo Macleod being on the bus, probably going to Loch Luichart, and Murdo singing Gaelic songs all the way.

I don't know how long I was at home for after that, but it probably was not for very long as I think that I felt by this time that I had used up any remaining goodwill that the authorities had regarding extended leave. I therefore made my way back to Glasgow and reported to the Pool.

I wanted to go back to deep-sea ships again after my less-than-happy time on the last ship, The Earl. Maybe it was as a form of punishment, or maybe they thought I liked coasting vessels, but my next ship was the Cranborne, a small coasting vessel which I joined in Glasgow on either the 8th or 18th of February 1949. The date stamp is rather blurred.

This ship was even smaller than The Earl being capable of carrying no more than 360 tons when fully laden. The crew numbers were the same, a total of seven, which was standard for this size of vessel at that time. I shared a cabin with the other AB whom I thought of as an old man. He was probably in his forties. I felt quite aggrieved when I found out the terms of pay that applied on this ship, which were not in accordance with Board of Trade standards. There was no overtime payment, however long the hours you worked. There was a fixed sum paid weekly, which I think was finan-cially equivalent to six hours work, which I thought was a joke as we must have worked close to 80 hours a week. We also got paid a sum of money for each cargo that was carried which I think was also equal to six hours pay, and as we probably carried on average two cargoes a week, it did not work out so badly.

The mate was also an older man. In fact he must have been in his fifties, as he used to tell us stories about his time fighting in Mesopotamia during the Great War of 1914–18. We are still fighting there today, although we call it Iraq now. I had not been on board for many weeks when the older AB left and the mate left to become captain of one of the other ships belonging to the company, the Purbeck. The company was based in Poole in Dorset and they named their ships after areas or towns in Dorset. They only had three ships but I am not sure that I remember the name of the third one. I think it may have been the Cranmere.

The new AB and the new mate were about my own age and we got on so well together that almost overnight we changed from being just another hard-working ship, to being a very happy ship. We still worked just as hard, but life was no longer a chore.

One can look back over one's life and recognize different points at which one's life changed, or at least one's attitude to life. This was one such time. I had gradually come round to the point of view that job satisfaction was far more important than financial reward. Taking pride in your ability to do your job well and working happily within a good team was reward enough.

When at sea we worked four hours on and four hours off. The senior AB was in the captain's watch, and I had become the senior AB very soon after joining. The captain was a rather lazy man who liked his bed very much and in a very short time he had come to the conclusion that I could be trusted to be left on watch on my own at night.

I should explain here for the benefit of those who know about ships and the usual layout of navigational aid, etc. The short answer is that there were hardly any. In the wheelhouse there was a magnetic compass, which was marked off in quarter points by which we steered and that was all. There was no standard compass on the monkey island – or flying bridge, as I believe it is more commonly called now – for taking bearings or for checking the compass for deviation by taking azimuths or amplitudes of heavenly bodies. Neither was there a chartroom, the chart in use being open on the saloon table, which admittedly was only one deck down. The chart that seemed to cover most of the voyages that we made was known as the three-channel chart which was canvas backed and covered the sea area from the Mull of Galloway to the Thames; in other words the Georges Channel, the Bristol Channel and the English Channel.

The afore-mentioned chart had the courses between most of the ports in these areas permanently pencilled in, but we hardly ever had to refer to the chart as we navigated very much as sea pilots do, relying very much on local knowledge and absolute familiarity with the coast within the area defined above. We did sail to many places outside this area, in which case other charts would be brought out. The only log entry would be a note on a slate of the time that a particular lighthouse, light vessel or point of land was abeam. This would be copied in to the rough log that was kept on the saloon table with the chart. We did not even have to consult the chart for the course to the next waypoint in most cases, as we were so familiar with the coast.

In my time on the Cranborne we must have visited every port, large and small, from Glasgow on the west coast to Hull on the East coast including the whole east coast of Ireland and a great many on the west coast plus every French channel port and many of the ports as far east as Hamburg. We were prepared to go anywhere within Home Trade limits, and indeed did from time to time, but we seemed to spend the great majority of the time in the Irish Sea and in the English Channel as far round as London Docks. It made for a very interesting life, as we never knew in advance where our next voyage would take us.

At this point I should describe the accommodation and the general layout of the vessel. There were two hatches, one forward of the bridge and one aft. The bridge superstructure consisted of the saloon at deck level with the captain's cabin opening off to starboard and the mate's cabin to port. On top of this stood the wheelhouse, which was reached by outside companionways to each wing of the bridge. I have already described the minimalist wheelhouse. Each hatch was served by one derrick and one motor winch. The trick when working cargo with a single swinging derrick was to keep a slight list on the vessel: a list towards the quay if discharging cargo and away from the quay when loading. This allowed gravity to swing the loaded derrick, while it was quite easy to pull the empty derrick back.

While the captain and the mate had their accommodation amidships the rest of the crew were housed in raised accommodation on the after deck. On the starboard side there were two single cabins for the chief engineer and the second engineer and on the port side there was a cabin for the two ABs and one for the cook. Across the stern there was the galley and the mess room.

Everyone ate in the mess room, which had a serving hatch from the galley. It was also the social centre of the vessel where we all met to play cards etc when in port and if not going ashore. The chief engineer was the captain's older brother and had an older brother's influence on the running of the vessel. Meal times were, breakfast at 0800, lunch at 1200 and tea at 1600. This was unusually early, and it meant that work for the day finished earlier than normal but was at the instigation of the chief engineer who was an avid moviegoer. He liked to go to the earliest house so as to leave him with plenty of time to go to the pub, which was his other great hobby.

Home Trade vessels are different from deep-sea vessels in many respects, one of which is that the company is not responsible for feeding the crew. The cook, who is paid a fixed sum by each member of the crew, normally takes on this function and I don't believe that many of them make any profit out of their shipmates. I don't remember that the sum to be paid was ever discussed with a view to increasing it in line with infla-tion, or even whose decision it would have been. I think it would have been done in a democratic way, but as wages had not increased in the two years that I was on the ship, neither did the rate that we paid for our food. I remember quite clearly that the sum we paid was £1 per week. It is an interesting reflection on the times that this figure could be kept unchanged for two years, at least between 1949 and 1951, as indeed was the basic pay for an AB at £6 per week. I think the cook did very well to feed us all for a total of £6 as it was always understood that he fed out of his profits.

I think the food was plentiful and wholesome, but not very varied. I think we had porridge and tea for breakfast. Lunch was the main meal of the day and I cannot remember more than two dishes, which were served up on alternate days. The first was called soup, but was in reality a thin beef stew served up with boiled potatoes. The second one was a local Appledore dish known as "Schooner on the rocks". I can still visualize the cook making it. He layered the bottom of a large roasting tin with peeled potatoes, put a half pound lump of lard on it, some boiling water and on top of this he placed a joint of lamb and the whole thing went in the oven for a couple of hours.

It does not sound such an extraordinary dish, but I think it was memorable to me in that it appeared in exactly the same way every other day for two years. I must admit that I never got tired of it, although occasionally its greasiness became a little difficult to stomach if you were being tossed about in a gale somewhere off the southwest coast of Ireland.

I don't remember as much about the menu for tea. Fish figured quite frequently as I recall, and cold meats at times. This was during food rationing of course, but we were lucky in the Merchant Navy in having special ration books which enabled us to get far more food than the civilian population. Due to having tea at such an early time we were always hungry in the evening and always went to the local greasy spoon café or for a fish supper in whatever port we were in. At sea we made do with bread and jam. There was a big metal pot of coffee always sitting on the galley stove when we were at sea so that you could help yourself during the night watches.

I mentioned earlier about being on watch all on my own, and it was a long and weary time, particularly from midnight until 0400. Fortunately, the chief engineer who was always in the captain's watch used to appear from time to time with a mug of coffee to keep me awake. He would also take the wheel for a spell if I needed to go to the toilet, or down to the saloon to check the chart.

I should explain here that all the crew except for the other AB and I came from Appledore in North Devon. They had all served in sailing ships in the 1930s. These were schooners and ketches, which were owned by merchants in Appledore, Bideford and Barnstaple. One or two of the ketches out of Barnstaple were still plying their trade during the time that I was on the Cranborne. There were also coasting schooners working out of Eire at this time. One in particular that I remember well was the De Wadden out of Arklow.

This early training in sailing ships made superb seamen and navigators out of the Appledore men. I have mentioned how little we possessed in the way of navigational aids, and it is fairly certain that these sailing ships would have possessed even less. This made it necessary for them to rely more on their own senses and instincts. There was an apocryphal tale about the schooner captain from Appledore who navigated his way along the north Cornish, Devon and Somerset coast at night by the difference in sound of the various flocks of sheep grazing on the cliff tops. He would listen attentively for some minutes and then pronounce that these were the sheep belonging to a particular farmer and that this enabled him to establish his position.

That may or may not have been true but I personally experienced instances of the uncanny ability of these sailors to tell where they were by instinct alone. We were in Exmouth at one time, having just discharged a cargo of bricks when we received orders to proceed at our best speed to Jersey for a cargo of the first new potatoes of the year. This must have been in April 1949. We were told that there would be ships arriving from all ports in the UK, and the first to arrive would be the first to be loaded. It must have been a little like the phenomenon of later years when the race was on to get the first of the new season's Beaujolais across the channel.

Soon after leaving Exmouth we ran into dense fog but kept going at full speed. This was not very fast of course as we could only do 8 knots flat out. I have spoken before about how poorly we were provided with navigational aids. This would not have been true of most of the other ships making their way to Jersey. The majority of them would have had Radio Telephone, while many of them would have had Gyro compasses, and a great many would have had a Decca navigator. I merely point this out to illustrate what I said before about the quality of seamanship to be found in these men of Appledore, in view of what happened next on this trip.

I was on watch on my own but called the captain to the bridge when I guessed that we were within half an hour or so off our destination, having not seen or heard anything since leaving Exmouth. The captain just stood with his head out of the wheelhouse window apparently listening and after a while he seemed to become alert and stopped the engines. He asked me if I could hear anything and I said that it sounded like gentle surf breaking on a beach. When the way was of the vessel he told me to go forward and drop the anchor and pay out three cables. I complied with this order and on my way back to the bridge I found that the captain had already gone to his bed. He just shouted to me as I passed his cabin to give him a call when, and if, the fog lifted.

The fog did eventually lift some time before 0800. I was amazed to find that we were anchored about a quarter of a mile from the harbour of St Helier and all we had to do was weigh anchor and move in to our berth. This was either a great big slice of luck or a piece of sublime seamanship. At that time I was inclined to think the latter, although having heard some years later that the captain actually lost the Cranborne on the rocks close to the South Stack on Anglesey in dense fog, some questions were raised in my mind.

They had only started to harvest the potatoes in Jersey and there was only about 40 tons available for us, and we were told to proceed to Cardiff with this part cargo. We did however steal a march on all the other ships, which had only started to arrive as we were sailing. What is more, there would be no potatoes for them for some time. I can remember the price that our cargo was being sold for in the shops the next day as one shilling per pound, which is equivalent to 5p today. I think that, as this was 1949, it was more expensive for the first of the Jersey Royals than they would be today. Being such an expensive commodity they were packed in what I believe to have been 14-pound paper bags, and one of these mysteriously found its way to the galley, so we enjoyed the delights of Jersey Royals for the next week.

One of the places that we used to go to fairly often was Hayle, which was the port for St Ives. We went there with cargoes of coal for the power station. It was one of those berths where we dried out at low water, and we always took the opportunity to scrub the ship's bottom and clear it of marine growth. If we were there for more than one tide we would turn the ship round, so as to get both sides clean. The bay of St Ives has a large expanse of sand, which dries out at low water, and besides cleaning the ship's bottom we went out on the sands and dug up about two bucketfuls of cockles. These would be cooked and thoroughly cleaned of sand after which they would be set on the mess room table in a large basin with vinegar for everyone to help themselves whenever they felt like a snack.

On one of the other occasions that we were in the port of Hayle I went to see Danny in Falmouth. At this time Danny was in the Royal Navy doing his National Service. He was serving on an Air Sea Rescue craft, which was one of two that were permanently stationed in Falmouth harbour. One of them would be fully manned and ready to set out to sea at a moments notice. I don't know how we arranged the meeting, as this was many years before the advent of mobile phones and texting. When in harbour this craft would be tied up to a buoy, and not alongside, but I have no recollection of getting aboard. I have a very clear memory of being there. When I asked Danny about this he said that we would most probably have met in a pub, but I don't think this was the case.

I mentioned before that we visited every known port within Home Trade limits. It goes farther than that as we visited many ports that were so insignificant that they were unknown to most people. This was largely because of our size and shallow draft. We went quite frequently to a quarry in Cornwall to load crushed stone, which we always took to London for road making and for concrete, as the major rebuilding of the city was taking place after the devastation of the war. I don't know now where that quarry was. It was no more than a break in the cliff and we just had to pick up a mooring wire that was attached to an offshore rock. That became our stern line and we just threw a bow line to someone on the cliff. The stone was held in a large hopper and enough to fill one hold was released in minutes. We then moved so that the other hold was under the hopper and the action was repeated. We were loaded and on our way in less than one hour.

We did keep on returning to the same ports regularly and some of those were our favourite places, but some we did not like at all. We loaded coal from Garston on the River Mersey very many times. This would most frequently be for Ireland, either North or South. If it were for the North it would most likely be to Belfast. We would then load potatoes back to Preston, or sometimes to Bristol. These might be loaded in Belfast, or more often in some of the smaller ports along the County Down coast such as Dundrum and Kilkeel. These potatoes were not for human consumption, and were sprayed with a dye to avoid them being passed into the food chain. The Potato Marketing Board imported them and there were suspicions that some disreputable traders were getting hold of them, washing off the dye and selling them to the public. I don't think there was anything wrong with them. I think it was an early example of what tends to happen when Governments interfere with market forces. One is reminded now of butter mountains and wine lakes etc.

One of the oddest trips that I can remember was when we loaded lumps of pitch at Dagenham for one of the French Channel ports. I think it was Dieppe. After loading and making our way down the Thames a severe gale blew up. We anchored off Margate in company with many other vessels, large and small. This was in August and the sun shone the whole time. After about four days the wind abated and we got under way. We arrived in Dieppe on a Saturday morning to find two large grab cranes ready to start unloading us. We were told that the unloading would be completed by noon and that we were to sail for Ostend. The first grab came down into the hold and closed. When it was swung out and opened over a railway wagon nothing came out. At this point we realized that the hot sun while lying at anchor for four days had melted the pitch, and it was now one solid hard mass, the temperature by now having dropped quite a lot.

The discharge in the end took a whole week, as they had to bring pneumatic drills on board and painstakingly drill the whole cargo out. I don't remember if we went from there to Ostend that time although I do remember taking a cargo of Italian pears and apples from Ostend to London on one trip. As was usual whenever we had anything edible in the cargo, some of it found its way into our mess room. This fruit must have been treated with a particularly noxious spray, and as we ate it unwashed and un-peeled we ended up with upset stomachs and a heavy rash all over our bodies. I don't know if that taught us a lesson or not. It was rather irrelevant really as the opportunity to get anything worthwhile out of our usual cargoes was very rare. You cannot eat coal, bricks, timber, china clay etc, and that is what we carried most of the time.

China clay at this time was a major export cargo from Cornwall. The big ships used to load in Fowey, but we always loaded in Par, a few miles to the west of Fowey, near St Austell. I seem to remember that motor racing used to take place on Par sands before the war. There was not much to do in Par, but the village of St Blazey was nearby and was one of our favourite watering holes. China clay is used in the manufacture of a multitude of different things and is exported all over the world. We always took it to Paisley, where we understood that it was used in the manufacture of Plaster of Paris. For this reason the holds always had to be spotlessly clean and dry as they were subject to a very rigorous inspection before loading could commence. Failure to pass inspection usually meant one more day in port and it is not beyond the realm of possibility that we may have engineered this.

I don't think it would be possible to spend two years on a small ship all around the wild seas of the British Isles without having some close encounters with disaster. I think there were quite a few hairy moments, but the one that I remember very clearly took place off the Pembroke coast. We were probably coming from some Irish port and heading for one of the South Wales ports. We were in the vicinity of the Bishops and Clerks, a group of dangerous rocks off St David's head, when the Chief Engineer came up on deck and reported a bad leak in the engine room and that the pumps were unable to keep pace with the inflow of water.

The weather at the time was fairly atrocious with a strong westerly wind and driving rain and much reduced visibility. In the circumstances, there was only one course of action, bearing in mind that we had no radio, run for the nearest shelter. This was Milford Haven, and did we need a haven! As soon as we were far enough in to the shelter of the land we dropped anchor. I then saw for the first and only time in my life the classic textbook repair executed. This is something that every seaman reads in books on seamanship and is taught in college but very few get the chance to put into practice. A rivet popping out usually causes the hole in the ship, and indeed this was the case with us. Any thing much bigger would be difficult to deal with. First you find a cork, tie a long piece of string to it, and push it out through the hole. When the cork finally surfaces you reach for it with a boat hook and pull it up on to the deck with the string attached. You then remove the cork and tie on a bolt, which has a large washer, and a tallow soaked grommet fitted. The string is tied to the bolt by having had a hole drilled through its end. You then throw the bolt over the side and haul it in by the string. Finally you thread another grommet, washer and nut on to the bolt and tighten down. I think that as a further precaution we built a cement box over the repair. We always carried some sand and cement on board for doing running repairs.

Recounting that story reminded me of how much I owed throughout the rest of my seagoing life to the training I had on the Cranborne. She was an ill-equipped vessel, even by the standards of those days, but we competed successfully with the very considerable British merchant fleet of that time. I spent the rest of my time at sea after leaving the Cranborne as an officer and I always had complete confidence in my own ability to deal with whatever life and circumstances threw at me. Most deep-sea sailors are happy only when all land is well below the horizon, but I was at my best when surrounded by hazards, in the form of rocks and sand banks, so that I could exercise the skills that I had learned on the Cranborne. The incident with the repair in Milford Haven was just one of many such incidents, although this was probably as close as we had come to a real disaster.

Although there were times of hardship and danger, my over-riding memory of the two years spent on the Cranborne was of a very happy time. We went back to the same places so often that we got to know lots of people, and we generally managed to have a very good time. We also had the excitement of visits to strange and out of the way places. One such place was on the far northwest coast of Ireland. I had only been on the ship for about two months at this time, so I was not taken into the confidence of the captain and was just told which was the next point to steer for. I would not have seen the chart and for this reason I am not very sure of where we did go to. I know that it was beyond Lough Foyle, as I had been up as far as Londonderry and Moville in Lough Foyle on previous occasions. I am almost sure that it was Letterkenny in Lough Swilly as I do remember that it was a long way up from the open sea.

The captain must have been told how far up the loch he had to go before getting a pilot because we anchored mid-morning in a beautiful part of the loch. There were no signs of habitation, but we could hear the constant braying of donkeys. We lay there all day and all night, and sometime the next morning an old man was rowed out from the shore and he said that he would pilot us up to our berth. Looking at the map now I wonder if this really was Letterkenny, which seems a reasonable sized town. My memory of the place that we got to was of a small village with one pub. I also remember that we were told that we were the first ship to have docked there for a year. The berth was just barely long enough for us to lie alongside. We were to load a full cargo of 360 tons of potatoes so you can imagine our consternation when the first consignment arrived on a donkey cart, all six bags of it.

This was in April 1949, so things may have improved a bit since then. I know that it was April because when we were on our way up the loch I had spotted a lovely little island that was full of nesting seagulls. It was about three miles below our berth but memories of boyhood escapades with seagulls' eggs stirred me into making the trip down the loch in the ship's boat with my friend Roy, the other AB. If I remember correctly we did not take any eggs. I think there were young chicks running around so we concluded that it was too late in the season and that most of the eggs were at the point of lay. It was a very nice way to spend the afternoon nevertheless.

It took us almost a week to get loaded and on the last evening in port Roy and I had gone to the pub. We got chatting to a couple of the local lads who told us that they had a car and were going to a dance in some other town and invited us along. Not knowing what this was going to lead to, we happily agreed. I think we may even have bought a case of Guinness.

The town where this dance was being held at must have been about 50 miles away as it took us about two hours to get there. The dance was in full swing when we got there and we soon joined in and were having a good time. At some point in the evening we noticed that our newfound Irish friends were spending all their time with a particular pair of girls, and it seemed to us as if they knew them, and had in fact met there by arrangement. Soon after this our suspicions were confirmed when these two lads told us that they were going to spend the night with their friends and that we would have to make our own way back. We asked them when the next bus would be going our way; only to be told that the bus only went one day a week, and it had already been that day. This caused some consternation, as we knew that there were only a few more donkey carts of potatoes to be loaded the next morning and that we would be sailing away. We knew that we could not afford a taxi because of the distance involved even if we could find one. At this far distant time I cannot recall just how we did it, but somehow, with a mixture of charm and threats, we persuaded them that it would be far more honourable to bring us back to our ship than to spend the night with these lovely girls.

I can still remember that awful sinking feeling when our dilemma unfolded. The stuff of bad dreams; like getting back to a car park, only to find the gates locked for the night, or as in one of my regular recurring dreams where I find myself arriving at an airport with little time to spare and realizing that I did not have my passport.

We got back on board sometime in the early hours of the morning and loading was duly completed and we sailed away. I do wish I could remember where that place was.

Appledore today has a large, modern and important shipbuilding yard, but in the 1940s it had one small dry-dock. Our captain must have had a lot of influence with our owners because he arranged for us to have our annual dry-docking done at Appledore on each of the two Christmases that I was on the ship. This was very convenient as all the crew except for the two ABs were natives of Appledore. We happened to like the place very much as well, and thought of it as our second home.

Looking through my discharge book I see that I took two holidays during the two years that I spent on the Cranborne, and surely by coincidence I find that they were at the same time of the year within one day. At some time fairly early in 1950 when he finished his National Service, Danny joined us as the second AB and he was still there after I finally left. We had some great times together for almost a whole year that we spent together on that ship. Specific instances are more difficult to bring to mind, but there was one incident that I remember quite well. Danny might not thank me for recalling this, but it did really happen. We were in one of the smaller French ports, which was still big enough to have a casino. We had gone there to enjoy a few beers, and were not in the least bit interested in the gambling. We had not started off with a lot of money and we were soon down to our last few cents. We pooled the little that was left, and as there was only enough for one beer between us, Danny picked up this loose change and went off. He was soon back with two beers and a pocket full of money. I don't remember what he had put the money on. Was it the roulette wheel? It might have been a one-armed bandit. Whatever it was he had made enough money to last us for the rest of the evening.

It is difficult to remember things in sequence, so some of the stories will relate to the first year that I was on the ship when Roy was the other AB, and others to the second year, when it was Danny. I remember on one voyage from Hamburg to Hull, realizing for the first time that the captain, while quite brilliant at local navigation, was technically ignorant. We had dropped our pilot after clearing the River Elbe at a point that happened to be on the same line of latitude as Spurn Point, which we were heading for. I had not seen the chart, but was told by the captain that he had been saved the trouble of drawing a pencil line on the chart and that I was to steer due West. For the benefit of landlubbers I would explain that the lines of latitude on a chart are set out as true east and west. Magnetic variation is the difference between true and magnetic north, and at that time it was about 12 degrees west. As our compass was a magnetic one we should have been steering west by north to make true west. I did not say anything but as the captain had done his customary vanishing trick I slipped down and asked the mate to check the chart and confirm the proper course to me. He did this and confirmed that I was right. We agreed that it would be too embarrassing to tell the captain, but as he seldom visited the bridge he would probably never notice.

It must have been around this time that I started to get ambitions about improving my career, but had decided that it should be done formally with the proper certificates. I should explain that at that time it was not necessary to have any certificates in Home Trade vessels except where passengers were carried. In fact the certificates were called Certificate for Master of Home Trade Passenger Vessel, or Mate as the case may be. There were only the two certificates or tickets, as they were always known. The rules differed for deep-sea vessels where there were three tickets – Master, Mate and 2nd Mate – and at least one of each had to be on board, regardless of whether passengers were carried or not. The 3rd mate did not have to be certificated.

The height of my ambition then, was to get a Home Trade Mate's ticket, and see where it went from there. To this end I bought a lot of books, including the ubiquitous *Nicholls's Concise Guide*. A lot of my spare time was now spent studying, but as I had nobody to tell me what was required of me, I found out when I eventually went to college that I had studied to a level that was far above what was required. That is a subject for a later chapter.

Besides studying hard the work of the ship still went on as before, and I don't think I curtailed my shore going to any great extent. According to my discharge book I came back to the ship on the 14th of October 1950 from my second holiday and rejoined as mate. I think this must have been planned before I went on leave. Eric Hallet, who was the mate, must have been due some leave, and I think he went to one of the other ships to do some relieving. In any case I see that I was the mate for six weeks.

I remember that during this period we made a lot of trips to Dungarvan with coal from Garston. There must have been a contract to move a certain tonnage over a short period because we came back light each time so that we were getting two cargoes a week delivered.

We got to know Dungarvan well and liked it very much. There was a pub on the quayside whose landlady was known to us as Mother Carey. She had two or three daughters, which I think enticed us as much as the Guinness. I remember on one occasion the captain having to send the cook to get us back on board as the discharge was complete and the ship was due to sail in half an hour. We got back on board and set to immediately, getting all the beams shipped, all hatches on and covers, and everything lashed down and secured, and ready for sea with about two minutes to spare. We believed then, and I still believe, that this showed a very high degree of efficiency. We were constantly testing ourselves and trying to improve on the way we did things, and took a lot of pride in our ship.

When I was Mate, Danny became the senior AB and did the captain's watch. On the trip back to Garston after we had blotted our copy books by staying late in the pub the captain took to his bed as soon as we sailed and did not appear on the bridge for the whole 30-hour trip. Near the end of the voyage I came on watch when we were approaching the Liverpool bar lightship to find Danny still by himself on the bridge. Our tonnage was such that we did not need to take a pilot as long as we had no cargo on board. We had been up and down the River Mersey that many times that I was quite happy to navigate the river on my own and see how long it would be before the captain appeared. I think he may have appeared before we got to Garston because of what happened next. At this time Garston was a very busy coal port. There could be as many as ten ships arriving to load on each tide. This was well in excess of the number of loading gantries; so as to be fair to everyone ships were loaded in the order of their arrival. There was a system known as stemming, where the mate of each ship had to sign a book in the Lockmaster's office. This established the order for loading, so there was always a rush to see who got there first. The term stemming came from the practice of pushing up on the mud until the stem of the vessel was up against the dock wall, when the mate could jump ashore and get his name in the book.

The desire to be first to load, or not as the case might be, depended on the time of the tide, and whether being early meant you could get all battened down and ready for sea, but still have a night ashore. That was the case on this particular trip, on our way in from Dungarvan. We could push up on the mud to a distance of only about ten or twelve feet from the dock wall and, as there was another vessel that looked like beating us, I took a long wooden ladder up into the bows and dropped it on to the dock wall. I clambered along the ladder and went to the office where they could not believe that I was in a position to stem the vessel, but they had to accept my signature. Such were the tricks that we got up to, just to get a night ashore, or to get loaded quickly and away so as to get to the next port, maybe to have a weekend.

I mentioned earlier that we always spent Christmas in dry-dock at Appledore. In the second year that I was there we must have come out of dry-dock between Christmas and New Year as I remember that we spent New Year in Bideford which is only two or three miles from Appledore. We were there with the ship so I think we must have moved up there from dry-dock. We did occasionally take a cargo to Bideford. The quay is in the middle of the town, as Bideford stands on the River Torridge. Most of the town stands on the west bank of the river and the part on the east side is known as East the Water. The river is fairly wide here, so the bridge connecting the two parts of the town is quite long. It was a tradition in Bideford to race across the bridge in the time it took the town hall clock to strike midnight on New Year's Eve. You can imagine what a shambles this was, as every participant would have been imbibing the local nectar in the many nearby pubs right up to the start of the race. It was much more fun than falling out of the pubs at closing time and starting to fight in the streets.

I had finally accrued sufficient sea time to qualify for my Home Trade Mate's certificate and made arrangements to attend the navigation school at the Royal Technical College Glasgow. I left the Cranborne in Swansea on the 14th of February 1951, after what I always look back on as the happiest two years of my time at sea. I got a great send off from all the crew who came to the station to see me off. Danny would have been among those as he stayed on for quite a long time after I left. In fact he later joined one of their other ships as Mate. I am not sure if I went home on leave before joining college or after my exams. I think this is a good place to end this chapter, as my life had just reached another important turning point.

Chapter 14

College Days

When I look at the date on which I left the Cranborne, which was the 14th of February, and the date on which I joined my next ship, which was the 27th of May 1951, I feel sure that I must have taken some extensive leave before going to college as I know that I did not have to do the full course, and the college would have been closed for the Easter break. All the indications are that I must have joined after the Easter break.

The standard course ran for ten weeks, with two weeks over for revision, and exams taking place after that. I had only been on the course for about three or four days when the tutor asked to have a word with me in private. I went in to his office with some trepidation, only to be told that I was far too good to be on his course. He had already spoken to the college principal and it was agreed that I could switch over to the 2nd Mate Foreign Going course. When I had my sea-time checked by the Ministry of Transport I was short of the required time due to my having spent so much of my time at sea in Home Trade vessels where time only counts half towards Foreign Going certificates.

It is to that tutor, whose name I cannot event remember, that I owe so much in that he changed my perception of my own capabilities and inspired me to aim rather higher than I thought possible. When I finally did join the 2nd Mate's course in the following year my first port of call was his lecture room in order to thank him, only to be told that sadly he had died a few weeks earlier, while only in his mid thirties.

I knuckled down to the course that I was on, having got over the disappointment of not being able to go on the 2nd Mate's course, and within three weeks was ready to sit the exams. I passed the written and oral parts, but failed on signals. It is worth pointing out here that the signals part of the examination is the same for all levels of certificate, from the lowest which is the Home Trade Mates, to the highest which is the Foreign Going Masters. This is one of the areas where the Merchant Navy differs from the Royal Navy where all signalling is done by trained signalmen, who presumably do nothing else but that. In the Merchant Navy the officer of the watch, among all his other duties, does all the signalling.

The signalling examination consisted of sending and receiving coded messages and plain text in Morse code by Aldis lamp; sending and receiving messages by semaphore; sending and receiving coded messages by the international code of signals. One also had to know every single flag hoist without reference to the codebook and a lot of the most commonly used two- and three-flag hoists.

As I had started from scratch without any knowledge of signalling, it would have been pretty well impossible for me to reach the pass standard in three weeks. Having got the main part over early I was able to concentrate all my efforts on getting up to speed on signalling. The biggest problem was getting someone to actually send to me by the lamp. We did not use a proper Aldis lamp at the college but just used a pinprick of light in a darkened room. A couple of weeks of intense cramming and I passed the signals part and became the proud owner of a certificate that told the world that I was capable of being the mate of a Home Trade passenger vessel.

When I reported back to the officers' section of the pool I was hoping to get a 3rd mate's job on a deep-sea vessel so as to amass my sea-time more quickly. This did not happen, as I was told to make my way to the port of Barrow-in-Furness and join the River Fisher as mate. I had to make my way down overnight to join the vessel on a Sunday morning. I see from my discharge book that this was on the 27th of May 1951, though that might have been Monday's date when it is more likely to have been the day that I would have signed articles.

I believe that the River Fisher was the very first ship to run a regular container service across the Irish Sea. There may have been some earlier, but I was certainly not aware of them. Fishers of Barrow, who were our owners, had a contract with British Rail, and it was their containers that we carried. These were not standard ISO containers, but were the type carried on railway flat cars in those days, and were only ten feet long. We made three round trips each week. We sailed from Barrow each Monday, Wednesday and Friday, and from Belfast each Tuesday, Thursday and Saturday. We had a nice quiet day every Sunday and a night in bed on Sunday night. Nowadays this service would have been operated with two crews, or at the very least three crews for two ships. Not so back in the early fifties, when you were expected to work until you dropped.

We had a slightly larger crew on this ship than we had on the Cranborne. We had three ABs instead of two, and a petty officer who was actually signed on as a lamp trimmer. It is a title that goes back to the days when ships had oil lamps for navigation lights. The bigger and better found ships still carried lamp trimmers who were in fact assistants to the bosun. The lamp trimmer took a watch with one AB under the watchful eye of the captain, and I took the other watch with two ABs. It was a ten-hour passage each way given good weather, but instead of splitting this into two five-hour watches it was split as two hours, then five hours, and three hours at the end. Because the middle five-hour watch had the tricky part of negotiating the King William bank and rounding the Point of Ayre, I always did the middle watch. This was because the lamp trimmer could not be trusted with that bit of navigation and the captain did not want his sleep disturbed.

The foregoing will have indicated that I did not get much sleep all week, so Sunday really was a day to look forward to. I had to be on deck all day seeing the containers discharged and the new cargo loaded and secured. The first two-hour watch off was hardly long enough to get to sleep before being up again, although I probably slept pretty soundly on the last three-hour watch below. I must have managed to get a few winks at different times or I could hardly have lasted the week.

This was a much better equipped vessel than the previous one. We had a gyrocompass and a Decca Navigator, which was then the very latest thing in navigational aids. Put very simply you had special charts with red and green lines on them. These lines radiated out from slave stations placed around the British Isles and the northern countries of Europe. Signals were received on a console from which the navigating officer could interpret his position by relating to the lines on the chart.

The only really serious crew discipline that I was involved with in all my years at sea happened on this vessel. Two of our ABs were from Belfast and were very bad characters. I cannot at this time recall what their misdemeanours were but they must have been quite serious as I remember very clearly putting them ashore in Belfast just before sailing. I think we must have signed two replacements for them in Barrow the next day. When we returned to Belfast the following day, they were there to meet us, but I just made up their wages to the day that they left and signed them off with a DR (decline to report). I think I explained in an earlier chapter that this would make it rather difficult to get a job at sea with any good company.

I had not been on the River Fisher for very long before I heard in the company office that the Sea Fisher, one of their larger ships, was going to make a trip to South Africa. She was normally employed running coal from Newcastle to the various power stations on the River Thames. There was something special about her as she had been built during the war specifically to carry the mountings for 16-inch guns for warships. Her gross tonnage was about 3,000 tons with two hatches. The number two hatch bulged out about half way along its length, so that the coaming at that point came within eighteen inches of the outside rail. From the known tonnage and from my extensive experience I would guess that the maximum beam of the vessel would be in the region of 45 feet, so that would give a circular hatch opening of 42 feet.

The purpose of the trip to South Africa was to pick up a 16-inch gun mounting from HMS Vanguard. I got to know quite well, and got friendly with, one of the directors of James Fisher whose name I remember as Albert Jones. I was able to persuade him that I would be of more value to the company as 3rd mate of the Sea Fisher than as mate of the River Fisher. I have no real memory of these machinations, but it was not long before I was on a train bound for North Shields, where I joined the Sea Fisher as 3rd mate on the 23rd of June 1951.

Captain Watson must have been close to 60 years old. Mr Macquiston the chief officer was in his early fifties and the 2nd officer whose name I don't remember was in his mid fifties. The only one of my age was the radio officer, who was probably a couple of years younger than me. There was quite a large crew as she was a coal burner, so there would have been four engineers, a donkeyman and six or eight firemen. There would have been at least nine ABs/OSs as well as four catering staff.

After signing on and talking to the other officers I realized that I would have to buy a sextant and had no trouble in finding a shop selling a variety of second-hand navigational instruments. I bought a beautiful old Bell sextant that had been manufactured in 1903. I still regret that in later years, when I thought that I would have no further use for it, I gave it away to an impecunious 4th officer in the Clan Line. It was of the vernier type as opposed to the more modern micrometer type coming into use then and would be quite an antique artefact now.

A couple of days after joining the ship we sailed to Antwerp where we loaded a full cargo of nitrate fertiliser for Durban. After spending nearly three years on motor ships, I found the silence of steam engines very disconcerting. I kept waking up and wondering why we had stopped. I would look out the porthole and realize that we were still steaming away quite merrily. After a few days I got accustomed to the change and it did not bother me any more. It is rather strange that when on noisy motor ships one always wakes up if the engines stop.

It did not take long to load our cargo of about 4,000 tons in Antwerp and we set off on our long voyage to Durban. I probably learned more about astral navigation on that long slow trip down to South Africa than I did in any other comparable time. Mr Macquiston, the chief officer was an excellent tutor, and I spent a lot of my watch below on the bridge with him when he was on watch. I learned to recognize and name the 60 or so principal stars used in navigation, and how to take sightings from them, and work up our position from this. Mr Macquiston had known better things than being mate of an old tramp steamer, and it was only later on the voyage that I got a clue as to the reason for his fall from grace.

He told me lots of stories about his time in the Blue Star Line where he had served on some of their passenger ships. He had been torpedoed during the war and had spent a long time in a lifeboat before being picked up. His father had been the MP for one of the Newcastle wards in the early thirties. One of his stories concerned a visit to the area by King George V. The mayor, accompanied by the local dignitaries including all the MPs for the area, was showing the King around. When they came to a very muddy area the mayor, using the local vernacular, said to the King "mind your feet in the clart your majesty".

The captain was also very helpful to me. I think they could both see that I was very keen to learn, and went out of their way to help. The captain gave me a book on the Marc St Hilaire method of navigation, which I had not studied before then. The 2nd mate had only a 2nd mate's ticket, which probably accounted for him being in what was essentially an East Coast collier. I don't know if he ever tried to progress through college, but if he did he must have failed.

We did not have enough bunker space to carry enough coal to get to Durban, so had to call at Walvis Bay for bunkers and fresh food. I think that we were there for two days before proceeding to Durban. It was on the day that we arrived at Durban that I first became aware of the problem that haunted the mate. At that time brandy used to be carried in the ship's medicine locker and the mate, who had the key for the locker, removed and consumed all the brandy that was there just after we had docked. Albert Jones, the aforementioned director of James Fisher had flown out to Durban on the day that we arrived, and it was he that told me that Mr Macquiston had been a captain in Blue Star ships but had been sacked for alcoholism. James Fisher had taken him on in spite of this, and indeed, apart from the occasional lapse, he was a highly competent officer.

This was not my first time in Durban, but it was the first time I was qualified to visit the Officers Club in that fair city, and a very congenial place I found it to be. When we completed discharging after three or four days we received on board a large amount of material that could best be described as a giant meccano set. It transpired that this was the base on to which the 16-inch gun mounting was to be loaded. This was also the reason that Albert Jones had come to South Africa, as he was the only person on board who had seen this thing erected, or who had been involved at any previous time when the Sea Fisher had carried the big guns.

Before loading the big gun in Durban we went up the coast to Lourenço Marques or Maputo as it is called now. We went there to load a part cargo of manganese ore, which, because of its high density, would not encroach upon the space required for the gun. On the way up the coast, and while waiting to load, the whole crew set to under the supervision of Mr Jones and erected the giant meccano set. When the ore was loaded we sailed back to Durban and loaded the massive gun, which just fitted neatly down through the special hatch.

While in Durban I did a lot of eating out. Food was so cheap and plentiful in South Africa that it was very nice to get away from the humdrum diet that we had to endure on the ship. I can still remember having a massive mixed grill for what was the equivalent of 25p. I can also remember the delights of the Playhouse, which had a cinema where the ceiling depicted the night sky, with all the stars and planets glittering.

We eventually sailed on the homeward voyage, bound first for Rotterdam where we were to discharge the manganese ore. It was in Rotterdam that I first experienced the ritual of lodging protest about the weather. We can all protest about the weather from time to time, but I am talking about an official protest sworn before a Justice of the Peace. An extract of the log is made up where all the worst weather experienced during the voyage is recorded and this is taken to a JP by the captain accompanied by an officer. I am not sure if it is necessary to have a witness as I have never been asked to do it again, but I did on this occasion accompany the captain. I remember quite clearly going to the office of the JP and lodging the letter of protest, and afterwards going to a small café and having coffee and cognac with the captain.

I must tell you about something rather strange that happened during the voyage. We have all heard at some time that the moon can have an influence on one's moods and indeed on one's whole personality, but most of us will treat this with a degree of scepticism. I relate this story, not as proof or disproof, but purely as it happened and let readers decide for themselves. We had a young cabin boy who went about his duties with commendable efficiency. These duties entailed cleaning the officer's cabins and serving at table in the dining saloon, where on this ship only the captain and deck officers sat.

All went well until the first full moon of the voyage when the boy began to act very strangely. This lasted for a few days after which he returned to normal. We were all aware of this and discussed it amongst ourselves, but just passed it off as a one-day wonder. However, at the next full moon he was even stranger. One day at lunch the captain asked him what the soup of the day was, and by way of reply he took a ladle full of soup and poured it over the captain's head. Fortunately for the captain he had compounded his error by bringing unheated soup to the table. At this point it was

The 16-inch guns from HMS Vanguard being
loaded on to the Sea Fisher in Durban

generally agreed that this unfortunate boy would be of less harm to
himself and others if he were to exchange duties with one of the young
OSs. This was arranged and as far as I can remember we had no further
trouble, except that a very close eye was kept on him at full moon.

After discharging the manganese ore in Rotterdam we sailed to
Newcastle where we discharged the big gun from HMS Vanguard. It was
while we were in Newcastle that the mate again demonstrated his love of
the bottle. I had been given the task of going through the voyage accounts
for the captain. At the end of the voyage the captain on tramp ships had to
make up the wages, with all that that entailed, for the whole crew for the
whole voyage, and this had to be ready before the articles were closed,
which usually meant within 24 hours of arrival. He must have had most of
it written up before arrival and my task was to fill in the last few bits and
add up all the figures. No calculators in those days!!

The Mate and 2nd Mate had gone ashore while I was busy at this work, and I think it must have been mid afternoon when the 2nd Mate burst in to my cabin in a very dishevelled and distressed state saying that I had better come quickly as the mate had fallen in the river and was probably drowned. He did not come with me but just went to his cabin and collapsed. Quite clearly a lot of drink had been taken. When I got down the gangway I found the mate sitting on the quayside in an even more dishevelled state than the 2nd mate with his trouser leg torn and his leg covered in blood. There were some dockworkers with him and I heard from them what had happened. They had seen these two men weaving their way back to the ship and saw one of them falling over between the quay and the ship. They saw the other one making his way to the gangway, but they ignored him and ran to the quayside. They found that the mate's fall had been broken by landing across the wire backstay between the ship and the quay. They were able to reach him and pull him up to safety, and all he suffered was a badly cut leg. He was also considerably more sober by this time. There were no repercussions from this incident. I think the mate went to the local hospital for a check-up and when the 2nd mate woke up and was told that the mate was alive and well, he swore off the booze forever. I don't know how well he kept his promise, but I cannot recall any other peccadilloes before I left the ship ten weeks later.

After arriving in Newcastle we closed articles, and opened them again in South Shields and I note that these were Foreign Going articles although I am fairly certain that we did not go outside the Home Trade limits. In fact I can only recall one more round trip before leaving the ship, although the time scale indicates that we should have done more. I do remember that we went to Hamburg where we loaded a full cargo of scrap metal. I also remember the voyage from Hamburg to Ardrossan, mainly because of the severe weather we encountered in the North Sea. I don't think I remember it because of the weather, as one experiences enough storms in 20 years at sea to make only the most violent ones memorable.

No, I remember it because of a happy encounter I had later on. Because of the bad storm in the North Sea we were running very low on food, and as we were due to dock in Ardrossan early on Sunday morning it was felt that we could not wait until Monday. In those days shops did not open on Sunday. We were passing through the Sound of Mull on the Saturday afternoon so it was decided that we would anchor about one mile from the town of Oban. The captain instructed me to hoist an international signal indicating our distressed condition. I don't think anyone could read this signal or decode it. In any case nobody came out to enquire, so the captain then instructed me to launch the motor lifeboat and take two seamen with me and head for the shore to purchase some victuals. Instead of heading for the main ferry terminals, I headed for a small jetty on the east side of the bay. I could see that there were two or three men on the jetty, and as I drew alongside imagine my surprise and delight on finding that one of these men was none other than Duncan Maclean from Mellon Udrigle. These were the Macleans who were our next-door neighbours at Mellon. Duncan had lived and worked in Oban for most of his adult life, but we knew him well, as he came home frequently on holiday. He was a true gentleman and very well liked by everyone. I remember that on his last night at home before going back from his holidays, he would come to our house to say goodbye and he would still be there saying goodbye at midnight. This meeting at Oban, besides being very pleasant for me was also very useful as Duncan had a car with which he took us to the best store in town and got all our purchases back to the boat. I think that at that time he was working on the small ferry that ran out to Lismore.

We were now sufficiently provisioned for the weekend, so it was up anchor and away to Ardrossan where we must have arrived in the early hours of Sunday morning. I think I must have been in touch with Danny before this to try and arrange getting home at the same time over the Hogmanay period. We succeeded in this as I got a few days off while we were discharging in Ardrossan. I think Danny got home before me. I left on the Sunday and got as far as Evanton, where I stayed the night with Anna and Bill.

The storm that had bothered us in the North Sea had returned with a vengeance on the Sunday. I think the date would have been the 29th December 1951. It was one of the worst storms of the century in the West of Scotland. I remember that when I returned from leave seeing a Clyde puffer stranded in a field about 200 yards from the sea. My trip up to Evanton was not without incident. The head wind was so strong that an additional engine had to be used to get the train over the Pass of Drumochter. I took a bus from Inverness to Evanton, but fallen trees about a mile south of Beauly blocked the road and we had to walk in to Beauly and catch another bus for the onward journey. Trees were still crashing down as we walked along, and most of the people ran. I could not run as I was carrying a suitcase and a very heavy box with a dinner service that I had bought in Durban as a belated wedding present for Anna and Bill.

I finally got to Anna and Bill's house. They were then living in Livera Street. I spent the night with them and caught a train to Dingwall in the morning, and from there I caught the Inverness to Kyle of Lochalsh train to Achnasheen. I remember meeting my cousin Annabel on the train. She was also going home for the Hogmanay holiday. I believe that she was working in London at that time.

Annabel and I had some fun on Alfred's bus on the way home. There was an elderly lady called Hannah on the bus. Hannah had lived in Mellon Udrigle until some time in the late 1930s. Our father took over the croft in 1940 – I think. It was henceforth known as Hannah's croft. Hannah was known to be a very inquisitive person and an inveterate gossip. You could be quite sure that any information that she gathered would be well and truly disseminated. She knew who I was but did not know Annabel, so we told her that she was my wife. We did not leave it at that, as we elaborated on the story, adding some really juicy bits of scandal. I don't remember much about it now but I do recall that we kept this up for the whole journey. I think Hannah lived in Gairloch so I don't know if any of this gossip got to the ears of any people who knew us, but as neither of us spent much time in the area, we certainly never heard any more of it.

I got home on the Monday evening to find that Danny was already there, having got home a couple of days before me. We had a short but very enjoyable time together although I am sorry to say that our parents did not see as much of us as they would have liked. I think Danny had to leave on the Thursday to go back to his ship, and I left on the Wednesday. Danny, at this time was mate on the Wimborne, a new ship to the John Carter fleet.

I am unsure what happened after rejoining the Sea Fisher on the 3rd of January as I can see from my discharge book that I signed off on the 13th of January 1952. I did not join my next ship until the 9th of February. What was I doing in the meantime? I remember going to Gothenburg and Halmstaad in Sweden but I cannot remember if it was before or after Christmas. An amusing encounter with the Swedish licensing laws happened when we were in Gothenburg. Soon after our dinner one evening the radio officer and I went ashore to have a drink. We could not find a normal drinking place and ended up in a rather posh restaurant where we ordered a couple of beers. The waiter could not speak English any more than we could speak Swedish but we understood that we could have a drink only if we ordered food. Even though we had just dined, we felt that we could manage a snack, and indicated as much. Some kind of starter course arrived which we consumed with our beer, but when we ordered another round of beer it arrived with a second course. I don't know why we did not give up at this point, but if I remember correctly we ended up having a four-course meal just so that we could have four beers.

I don't believe I went home on leave again, although that is a possibility as I had only had a few days off in all the time that I was on the Sea Fisher, and these were unofficial. I think it is possible that the Sea Fisher was going to go on to Home Trade articles and I must have left her to find a Foreign Going ship, as I was anxious to get my sea time in more quickly.

There is no disputing my discharge book, however, and I can see from it that I joined the SS Jura as 3rd Mate on 9th February 1952. She belonged to the Glen Line and was a small general-purpose tramp steamer, of which there was many built in the United States during the war and were known as Geeps. It was an acronym for general-purpose ship. I cannot remember if the 'e's meant anything. Her gross tonnage was only 1,813 and her cargo capacity would be only about 3,000 tons. We sailed in ballast for Turku in Finland. At that time Turku was known also as Abo. I think it was in the process of having its name changed, possibly under Russian influence. As we were still in the grip of the cold northern winter I remember stocking up with warm clothing and fur-lined boots in the army and navy surplus stores, in anticipation of the even colder weather in Finland. Clothes rationing still persisted in Britain, hence the army and navy stores.

My anticipation of the cold weather was borne out when we arrived off the coast of Finland. When we stopped at the designated position for picking up our pilot the sea ice immediately closed in around us, and to my utter amazement the pilot appeared around a point of land on skis. He skied right up to the ship's side, removed his skis, slung them on his back, and climbed up the pilot ladder. Although the ice was thick enough to allow the passage of a man on skis it did not seriously impede our progress into the harbour at Turku.

We loaded a full cargo of timber including deck cargo to a height of nearly ten feet. The cargo was consigned to many different importers, and we were required to stow these separately. The 2nd mate and I went on to the quay at 7 a.m. every day and counted the planks in each stack of timber, which we knew would be the first to be loaded. When the quantity destined to a particular importer was loaded, we would stop the loading and paint lines across the cargo with cheap water paint, using a different colour for each consignee. I can still remember how cold it was in the early mornings, but the weather throughout our stay was calm, clear and cloudless, so that for the few hours that the sun was up it was very pleasant, if bracing. After all our work in keeping the different parcels of cargo separate, and providing a stowage plan to the receiver's agent we were rather disappointed that when we discharged the cargo in the port of Preston, the separations were totally ignored and the whole cargo was mixed together.

We were lucky to have been able to discharge a full cargo of timber as we had encountered my second severe storm of this winter in the North Sea. When we were half way across, the storm had reached such intensity that we were in danger of losing the deck cargo. The danger here lies in the fact that the cargo might all go from one side, so the vessel would acquire a dangerous list. We hove to and all hands were called out on deck to try and secure the cargo that was shifting dangerously. This was on the fore deck and the captain stayed alone on the bridge with one helmsman and the mate stood with his back to the foremast watching for hand signals from the bridge. When very big waves came along, the captain would signal and the mate would shout to us and we would grab the safety lines that we had rigged up. Somehow we managed to get the cargo secured although I think it took us most of the day.

I have no recollection of making any other trips on the Jura, although six weeks seems rather a long time to do a round trip to Finland. The only indisputable evidence however is that I left the Jura in Port Glasgow on the 23rd March 1952 and must have gone home on leave in readiness for the Easter term at college, so I think this is a good place to end this chapter.

Chapter 15

The Clan Line

I started studying for my 2nd Mate's ticket at the Royal Technical College Glasgow at the beginning of the Easter term in 1952. Everyone knew the college as the RTC and it eventually metamorphosed into the Strathclyde University. It is not strictly true to say that I started to study then, as I had been studying hard for the last couple of years. This was to be the formal part of study and a tremendous amount of work had to be crammed into a three-month term. There were financial pressures, of course, as there was no pay available to me. For this reason I think we studied much harder than most undergraduates would. We attended lectures continuously from 9 a.m. until 5 p.m. and then crammed and revised for hours every evening.

Maybe not every evening as I seem to remember doing quite a lot of things that were definitely not on the curriculum. I went one night a week to try to learn ballroom dancing, but that was not a great success, so I gave that up and just went to dances. I also remember going to some of the numerous golf courses around Glasgow, but I did not get very good at that either.

I became quite friendly with John McLennan at this time. He worked at the British Linen Bank and that is where I opened my first bank account with his help. They were affiliated in a loose way with Barclays Bank, which was the reason I moved to Barclays when I came to live in England. John was the uncle of Duncan McLennan from Laide. I used to meet him and his fiancée for drinks in one of Glasgow's nicer pubs. I am not sure if they ever got married as I lost touch when I went back to sea.

While I was studying in Glasgow I stayed with Mr and Mrs Whiteman, Flora's parents, who lived in Ibrox. It was just like home from home for me, as Mrs Whiteman was a very kind and motherly lady. I became a follower of Glasgow Rangers at this time as well, and used to go to all the home matches with Mr Whiteman. It was only a ten-minute walk from their house to the ground.

After twelve weeks of very intensive study, the week of the dreaded exams arrived. The written part of the exam consisted of six papers, which were sat on the first three days of the week. On the Thursday we took the signalling exam, which was in three parts, and on the Friday we had the oral exam, which was the most feared part of the whole examination process.

The six written papers were, Celestial navigation, Terrestrial navigation, Mathematics, Astronomy, Physics and English. For a pass, 70% had to be achieved overall and within the mix one had to have 70% in the first two papers, and over 50% in maths and physics. To get the 70% overall we always aimed for close to 100% in the navigation papers. After all it is where anything less than 100% in real life could lead to something much worse than losing an exam.

The signalling consisted of being able to send and receive by Aldis lamp, in Morse code at the required speed, to send and receive by semaphore at the required speed, and to memorize all the most frequently used international coded signals in one, two, three and four flag hoists.

The oral examination lasted anything from an hour to an hour and a half. I found the most difficult part was memorizing the Articles, of which there were 29, if I remember correctly. People who were good at reciting poetry at school learned them off by heart and could recite them by just being given the number. I could never do that and so I had to concentrate on being very familiar with all the contents. Those of the articles that dealt with the lights and signals carried by various vessels did have to be learnt verbatim. One of those, which dealt with fishing vessels, was almost a whole page long. The ones that dealt with the 'rules of the road' tended to be shorter, but if you got one of those wrong you were out. The whole purpose of the exam was to find out if you were capable of taking charge of a watch with the safety and lives of all the ship's company in your hands.

You did not have to wait to find out if you had passed your orals and signals, but were told immediately. I had passed both, and only had to wait until Saturday to find out the results of the written papers. We had to go to the examination room outer office where all the results were pinned up on a notice board, with the marks achieved in each paper shown. I had passed with a fair amount to spare, but of greatest satisfaction to me was that I had got the highest marks in mathematics for that year. This was doubly satisfying as most of my fellow students had what would have been perceived as a much higher education than I had. Higher, but was it better?

I had forgotten to mention that at some point during my time at college I met Willie MacRobbie. He was also at college studying for his Chief Engineer's ticket at the same time. We met up for a while on Saturday evenings for a couple of pints and then go to a dance at Govan Town Hall. This was the dance that most of the girls from the West coast attended. I met Jessie Maciver. I also met Mary Cameron, who was later to become Danny's wife there.

The Royal Technical College
Glasgow.

School of Navigation
CERTIFICATE OF MERIT.

HECTOR GRANT

having attended satisfactorily the classes in

Navigation Senior Course I

involving attendance on full-time Day Classes

from 31st MARCH, *19* 52 *to* 3rd JUNE, *19*52 (216 *hours*)

has been awarded this Certificate of Merit on

the results of his work.

J.R. Corse { Superintendent School of Navigation.

D.S. Anderson .Director

Date 3rd June, *19* 52.

This Certificate is issued in respect of the syllabus of work stated on the back hereof, and is approved by the Scottish Education Department. It will be accepted by the Ministry of Transport under the Regulations relating to the Examination of Masters and Mates as equivalent to a period of the qualifying sea-service required from candidates for a certificate of competency as Second Mate. The maximum period allowed under this certificate will be one-half of the period as certified above but will in no case exceed three months sea-service.

Navigation course certificate

Willie asked me if I had any idea what I was going to do when I got my ticket. I told him that I had not, but as jobs for certificated officers were easy to find at that time I had no worries. He suggested that I could do a lot worse than join the company he was with, namely, the Clan Line. I agreed that this would be worth a try, and when the time came that I was proudly in possession of a 2nd Mate's ticket, I presented myself at the Glasgow offices of the Clan Line to be interviewed by the Chief Marine Superintendent, Captain Innes.

I don't remember anything about that interview, all I know is that I was accepted, and offered immediate employment. I think that I must have been given enough time only to get my uniform sorted. I probably had a uniform already but I had to have the braid changed. The Clan Line, for some reason, did not wear the traditional Merchant Navy braid, which had a diamond shape on the centre ring, but instead had a loop on the upper ring, much the same as the Royal Navy. The Clan Line was often referred to, jokingly, as the Scottish Navy, but I don't think that was because of the braid.

A brief history of the Clan Line would not come amiss at this point. The company was founded in 1877 and called C W Cayzer & Co. Mr Cayzer had worked for many years in India for a shipping company and had seen the growing potential for shipping goods to India. The following year Mr Irvine joined him, and the company was called Cayzer Irvine & Co henceforth until the 1970s. The company started with one ship but it very soon expanded until it became one of the biggest companies running to India. There was a story in the company that Mr Cayzer had vowed that for every funnel with two white bands in the Indian Ocean he would have a funnel with two red bands. The two white bands on the funnel were the company colours for the British India Company or BI, as they were known. Two red bands on a black funnel became the Clan Line company colours. Between 1907 and 1919 they bought three other companies, the Scottish Shire Line, the Houston Line and the British South American Steam Navigation Company. The Shires and the Houston Line, although fully integrated, kept their old names. The Houston Line had names such as Hesperides, Hermione, Hesperia etc. I actually served on the Hesperia at one time. In 1956 the Clan Line took over the King Line and Bullard and King, and at the same time amalgamated with the Union Castle Line and became the British and Commonwealth Company, finally coming to an end as shipowners in 1981.

Very soon after being accepted into the Clan Line I was told to join the Clan Brodie on the 21st of August 1952 as 4th officer. The 4th officer did not have his own watch, just acting as assistant to the chief officer on the 4–8 watch. I was less than happy with this arrangement as I felt that I had more watch-keeping experience than the 3rd officer, and possibly even the 2nd officer. I realized that it was because I was new to the company so I just swallowed my pride and got on with the job.

Fortunately it was quite a short voyage, just down to South Africa and back, probably one of the shortest voyages I made in the whole time that I was in the Clan Line. I say fortunately, partly for the reason given above, but more because of the poor relationship I had with the chief officer. I thought he was a pompous individual whom I just could not like. I don't know what he thought of me, but I left the ship with a good report from the captain. I see from my discharge book that I signed off in Liverpool on the 17th of November 1952.

I must have had some leave then, as the next entry in my discharge book is 13th of December 1952. This does not always tell the full story as we sometimes spent time on ships without being entered on articles, in which case there would be no discharge book entries. I joined the Clan Macbride as 3rd officer on the 13th December 1952.

I was on the Clan Macbride for just over a year, and this was a very happy time. As the discharge book tells me only when and where I joined and left different ships, I have to rely on memory to fill the bits in between. I think that it was on this trip that we loaded a part cargo of bagged sugar in Greenock for Port Sudan, and finished loading general cargo in Birkenhead for India.

The captain was a Yorkshireman from Dewsbury, Captain Dalley. I once saw him described as a human dynamo by a passenger who sailed on one of the ships that he was serving on. I think it was a very apt description. He was of a restless nature and could be found at all times of the day or night striding purposefully around on his own private section of bridge deck, or up on the navigating bridge. He was, maybe paradoxically, a very kind and considerate man for whom I developed a great respect.

On our first night at sea I was on the 8–12 watch after we had dropped the pilot and were proceeding down the Clyde Estuary. The captain, quite naturally, remained on the bridge as we were in restricted waters, and my competence was an unknown factor at that time. I ignored the fact that he was there and just got on with the business of navigation, taking frequent bearings to establish our position and adjusting the course as necessary. After an hour or two of this he just bade me goodnight, saying that I could call him at any time that I felt in need of assistance or guidance. I felt very happy at this, and my respect for his good judgement started then.

It is from this time onwards that memories of different voyages become less distinct. There is a tendency for things to merge together. Maybe it is the end of youthful wide-eyed wonder at the world, and I am now getting

Me as 3rd Officer on the Clan Macbride

a little bit blasé about all these foreign parts. I have strong recollections of discharging our cargo of sugar in Port Sudan. This was mainly because of my amazement at the strength and stamina of the native Sudanese workers who, in the days before political correctness, were known as fuzzy wuzzies, I think because of their unique hair style. The sugar bags weighed 140 pounds and they built them into a high pyramid on the wharf alongside our ship. A sling of bags would be landed on the quayside and a group of men took one bag each on the top of their heads and ran up the side of the pyramid which got progressively higher as the day went on. This was in temperatures in excess of 40°C. The only explanation I could offer for their stamina was the fact that they had broken into the first bag that was landed and were mixing the sugar with some water to make strong syrup, which they kept swigging constantly.

After leaving Port Sudan we must have gone on to India to complete discharging the rest of the cargo. After discharge our orders were to proceed in ballast to Chalna on the Pusser River in the Eastern part of Bangladesh, or East Pakistan as it was known then. Chalna is in the regional district of Khulna which has the city of Khulna as its capital, and Khulna is a further 30 miles or so upriver from Chalna. I cannot find Chalna on any map. It is not very surprising as it was a settlement that was occupied only during the jute-exporting season when I was there in 1953. Surely it will be of less importance now that man-made fibres have super-seded the use of jute.

When we arrived on the Pusser River we were told to anchor about five miles downstream from Chalna, as we were too early in the season. At this point I should explain some of the idiosyncrasies of navigation on the Pusser River at that time. There were two pilots, both of whom were Germans who had either been interned or had been taken as prisoners of war and had stayed on in Bangladesh and set up in business as pilots for the port of Chalna which had only just been opened a couple of years before I got there. To describe it as a port is probably magnifying its status. It was just a slightly wider part of the river with a couple of mooring buoys and a collection of shacks on the bank to house the stevedores. The jute arrived from farther inland in barges, carrying about 200 or 300 tons. The navigational aids in the river were almost non-existent, and amounted to the occasional lantern hanging from a tree, placed there by the pilots.

We did not know how long we were going to have to wait at anchor before moving up to a loading berth so we settled down to what we thought would be a nice, but short, restful interlude. In the end we were there for six weeks, by the end of which time we were totally bored. The captain had decided at the beginning that we would not keep sea watches. All that was required of us was to take turns being on the bridge for an hour or so at the turn of the tide, which happened only twice in every 24 hours. It was an extremely isolated place to spend such a long time. The river was only a few hundred yards wide, but all that could be seen in any direction were mangrove swamps, with the mangroves right down to the water's edge. We would frequently hear tigers growling at night.

One of the consequences of our long stay in this place was that we ran out of beer, and indeed all alcoholic drinks. This probably happened after about four weeks, and about that time another vessel arrived, and anchored quite close to us. We immediately launched one of our lifeboats and went across to buy a few cases of beer from them. We were rather coy about the length of time that they were likely to spend there in case they wanted to conserve their own stocks. I think it was a City Line vessel, which I cannot remember the name of, but I do remember how grateful we were.

You might think from the foregoing that we were a heavy-drinking lot but this would not be true. In normal sea-going mode one might have a beer or a G&T before dinner, but with no sea watches being kept there was much more leisure time that was taken up with a bit more drinking. Four of us set up a card school during this time and we used to play from about 8 p.m. until midnight. The four were the chief engineer, the chief steward, the 2nd officer and myself. Our game of choice was solo whist and we started off playing for cigarettes. We soon found that after handling the cigarettes across the table in placing our bets they rapidly became too soggy to smoke owing to the high humidity. Our solution to this problem was to "buy" a few hundred dried beans each to use as counters, each bean to represent a cigarette, to be cashed in, not at the end of each session, but at the end of our six-week stay.

We finally got our orders and moved up-river to the loading area where we tied up to a mooring buoy. The method of tying up to the mooring buoy was to hang the anchor off and use the anchor chain to shackle on to the buoy. As a further precaution we also shackled on our heaviest mooring wire. We had been warned that at this time of year, which must have been April, there was a risk of sudden violent storms. These were known locally as Northeasters, presumably because they came from that direction. We had been told that the only warning that you got was the appearance of a small black cloud in the NE about one hour before the storm hit.

Once we started loading the jute, work went on day and night. As was the usual practice, the 2nd and 3rd officers shared the cargo-loading duties by doing a 12-hour night and splitting the day into two 6-hour shifts, alternating each day. When we were about half loaded, I was on the foredeck one afternoon and saw Captain Dalley up on the bridge, peering anxiously towards the north east. He must have spotted the ominous black cloud, because he shouted to me to stop loading, get everyone out of the holds, and get all the hatches closed and secured. With five hatches working cargo I had a very busy hour. I am sure the other officers would have been out on deck by this time. We had two barges alongside with another two doubled up outside of those, waiting their turn in the queue. We were parallel to, and fairly close to, the west bank of the river where the small settlement stood. The barges, which were on our port side, were between the bank and us.

That was the position at, say, 3 p.m. At 3.05 p.m. we were aground on the riverbank. Within seconds of being hit by the strongest wind that I have ever experienced, the heavy wire and the anchor cable had both parted and we were driven on to the riverbank. We were saved from being totally stranded by the double-banked barges on our port side that were driven right up the bank, demolishing most of the dwellings in the settlement. When we let go of the lines holding the barges alongside us, we just slid off the bank, started the engines, and by executing a very delicate manoeuvre, got ourselves out into mid-river and dropped our one available anchor. When we brought the end of the anchor cable on board we found that the shackle pin, which was made of 2-inch diameter tempered steel, had sheered. This gives some indication of the ferocity of the storm. By the next morning, the barges, which had been so unceremoniously dumped in the middle of the village, had been towed off by the combined efforts of all the other barges. We moved back to the original buoy, which was still intact, and resumed loading.

In the world of hydrography it used to be common practice to name geographical features and new discoveries after reigning monarchs, or important personages, particularly if they had been sponsors of the voyages of discovery. It was also quite common to name places after the commander of the expedition or commanders of individual ships. Very occasionally they would use the name of the ship, as for instance HMS Erebus and Terror, vessels that were used in Arctic and Antarctic exploration and have each given their names to mountains on Ross Island in Antarctica. If the reader is wondering what any of this has to do with our stranding on the bank of the Pusser River, I can tell you that we were greatly honoured by the Port Authorities when they decided that the particular part of the river where we were stranded would henceforth be known as Macbride Point and that all subsequent admiralty charts of the region would be so marked.

We loaded a full cargo of jute, the greater part of which was destined for Dundee where the jute processing was the major industry in the city. Smaller parcels of about 500 tons would be delivered to various European ports from Genoa all the way round to Hamburg. The ports would vary from voyage to voyage but would seldom be less than three or four. I see that we arrived in Dundee on the 25th of June making it a six and a half month voyage.

I think I must have had about ten days leave before rejoining the Clan Macbride in Tilbury on the 16th of July 1953. Captain Dalley had left the ship by then and was replaced by Captain Bagnall. He was not as friendly or approachable as Captain Dalley. He once ordered me off the bridge for being improperly dressed when I arrived on watch in all the proper uniform, but with no socks. I have been ridiculed many times since then for wearing socks when wearing shorts and sandals. Maybe Freud would have an insight on this.

I don't remember much more about this voyage although I think we must have gone to Chalna again, as I see that the voyage ended in Dundee once more. It could have been Chittagong of course, as we still used to load some jute there. I finally left the Clan Macbride in Glasgow on the 22nd of December 1953 and I clearly had some leave then, because I did not join my next ship until mid January. In all my time at sea I did not get very many Christmases at home, but this must have been one of them. I think I should start a new chapter for the next ship, as something momentous happened during my time on her.

Chapter 16
Love and Marriage

I joined the Clan Cumming in Birkenhead on the 18th of January 1954 as 3rd officer. At this time the Clan Line was still operating with many of the ships it had acquired during the war. These were very utilitarian, having been built in the USA and designed for a short life, as the life expectancy of ships was very short in the war years. There were several classes, known collectively as Liberty ships. Some were known as Sam boats and some as Ocean boats. The Clan seemed to end up with Ocean boats mostly, as my previous ship had been. The Clan Cumming was a modern ship, custom built for the Clan Line, and was similar to the Clan Brodie. The reader might notice a trend here. As one gained seniority, so one moved up the scale into the better class of ship, only to slip back down again on getting promoted.

As was usual, we had loaded a full general cargo in Birkenhead for various ports in India, starting in Bombay (Mumbai) and completing in Calcutta. We probably loaded 2,000 or 3,000 tons of manganese ore in Visagapatnam on our way up the East coast. The greater part of the cargo loaded after that would have been tea. There would have been various other products, including one complete hold, which was loaded with hooves and horns bound for the glue factories. At least one hopes that it all went there, as some of the alternative uses don't bear thinking about. We always finished up loading Ceylon tea in Colombo before heading home.

Most of the tea was destined for Hay's Wharf so our first port would have been Tilbury. While there, Captain Booth, who had been our captain on the voyage, left, and was replaced by a Captain Forster for the coastal part of the voyage. We had cargo on board for some North European ports. I remember particularly going to Hamburg and marvelling at how much it had changed since the first time I had been there. Captain Forster had a tragic story to tell. He had gone to the USA with his wife for the holiday of a lifetime, and while there his wife became terminally ill with cancer. She was hospitalized there and was too ill to travel home. She eventually died leaving him with such high bills that he was forced to liquidate all his assets. The chief officer bought his house, and I bought his car. It was a pre-war model Morris 8 for which I paid £100. That does not

133

The Clan Cumming, on which I was serving when I met Anne

seem very much now, but it was about three months' pay for me, so in that context it would have cost around £6,000 today.

I don't think that the bureaucracy involved in buying and selling cars was quite as strict in those days as it is now. I had sold the car again within three weeks for £95, but some life-changing events had happened in the meantime. We had completed discharging our cargo around the continent and had arrived in Birkenhead to start loading for our next voyage. Captain Forster lived in Wallasey, and when I had paid over the money I was invited to collect the car from his brother's house, which was also in Wallasey. I must have taken someone with me to collect the car as I had no licence, or indeed any driving experience other than having taken the wheel of my father's car a few times with him sitting beside me. I think it was one of the Clan Line shore staff engineers who came with me, and after getting the car we went down to Harrison Drive, which was a favourite place for learner drivers. After an hour or so driving up and down Harrison Drive he pronounced me quite fit to drive.

It was customary when in Birkenhead, and indeed in many of the major ports, to have a telephone brought on board, which was connected to the GPO (now BT) system. It was also customary for one or more of the officers to arrange a party and try to find some nice ladies to invite along. They would sometimes be from the nurses' home at the local hospital, or sometimes the telephonists from the telephone exchange who needed to be contacted every time you had to make a call in those days. On this occasion it was the telephonists who were invited. I was quite unaware of this. I did not even know that there was going to be a party. I was far too excited about my new car.

The smoke room, which was in effect the lounge where off-duty officers met to socialize, was immediately below my cabin, and after returning from my early evening driving lesson on Harrison Drive I went to my cabin intending to have a quiet night in. After some time I became aware of muted party noises coming from the smoke room, so I grabbed a bottle from my locker, went down, and asked if anyone could join the party, and of course I was invited in.

I have related in earlier parts of this story how incidents and encounters, which at the time seem relatively insignificant, have a profound life-changing effect. Walking into that room was one of those times. Sitting on the other side of the room facing the door as I walked in was this gorgeous creature called Anne Caley. As far as I was concerned the room could have been empty as I only had eyes for the one person and I think that I knew then that this was the person with whom I wished to spend the rest of life.

These shipboard parties were quite decorous affairs with just a modest amount of drinking, some music, and some dancing in the rather confined space. When it became time to break up some people started making arrangements to get taxis. At this point I magnanimously pointed out that I had a car and would be glad to run everyone home. To this day I almost break into a sweat when I think of what happened next. I certainly would have imbibed far more than the law would permit now. The car was very small, I had no driving experience, or driving licence and there were at least six ladies. I somehow fitted them all in, but I don't think I ran many of them home. I think I must have dropped most of them off by a taxi rank. I did, however, take one of them all the way to her door, and that was Anne. That run to Heswall was not without incident. At some point I got a little confused about an instruction to turn right and mounted the pavement. A police motorcyclist pulled up and asked if I was OK. I still find it hard to believe that he accepted my assurances and let me drive away. When I dropped Anne off at her home, and having made arrangements to meet next day, she must have given me very good instructions for getting back to my ship, as I seem to have got there without serious mishap.

I believe that Anne and I met every night until it was time to sail, which was no more than a week. We ate out, went to the cinema, which was the regular form of pastime then, and just enjoyed being together. The week passed all too soon and I have tried many times since then to elicit from

Anne whether she wondered if she would ever see me again. I had no doubts in my mind. The last thing I did before sailing was to sell my car to one of the officers who were employed by the Clan Line to act as reliefs while the ships were in Birkenhead.

This was a fairly uneventful voyage with calls at all the usual ports: Port Said where we always received and sent mail, followed by Aden where we usually bunkered, then on to India, where we would call at many ports, finishing up in Calcutta. There we would start loading the usual mix of cargoes, but with the main part of the cargo being tea, where as usual we would finish the loading in Colombo. I had remembered Anne's 21st birthday, which had occurred when we were in the middle of the Indian Ocean, and by the good offices of wireless telegraphy and Interflora I was able to send her a large bouquet of flowers. I think this probably encouraged her to think that I was not just a roving sailor with a girl in every port.

I don't remember if it was on this voyage or the previous one that we went into the harbour of Trincomalee in Ceylon (Sri Lanka). We had gone there to load some large mooring buoys that had been cut lengthwise and were being sent back to the UK as scrap iron. This was not a normal loading port, so the labourers sent on board to do the loading were very inexperienced. We were loading into two holds and we found it necessary to have an officer down the hold constantly to organize the loading. We had to rig up some fancy gear to haul these awkward pieces of metal into the wings. My only purpose in telling this story is to convey to the reader my admiration for these happy young people. They were such willing and cheerful people and I thoroughly enjoyed the two long days I spent working with them. It was many years later that I came to recognize that they were quite likely to have been the fathers or even the grandfathers of the infamous Tamil Tigers. What turns a happy and apparently contented people into killers? The desire for freedom and independence must course strongly through the veins, but is the perception of persecution greater than the reality?

Anne and I corresponded regularly throughout the trip and when I signed off in Tilbury on the 2nd of October 1954 I made my way to Heswall. I think that I first booked into a hotel in Birkenhead before going to see Anne. She lived with her grandmother Mrs Caley, who was a lovely old lady. I had the necessary sea-time in by then to go back to college to study for my Mate's ticket. I had enrolled by letter at the RTC in Glasgow but had a week off before joining, so I decided to spend it in Anne's company rather than go home to Mellon Udrigle. I think I spent only one night at the Birkenhead hotel before Anne's grandmother invited me to check out and come to stay with them. I don't remember meeting her in the week that I had known Anne in May, so I must have made a very early good impression.

Anne was at work most days, so I decided, even although I did not own a car now, it would be a good idea to try to get a driving licence. I had six lessons with BSM and took a driving test, all within one week. Imagine trying to organize that now? I failed, as one might reasonably expect. After a week I had to leave to take up my studies at the RTC Glasgow. By this time Mr and Mrs Whiteman had moved to East Kilbride, so I stayed with Donald and Flora. I used to miss Friday afternoon lectures every other week and go down to Heswall to stay with Anne and her grandmother. I would catch a late train back from Liverpool on Sunday night. This was a slow, stopping train, which did not arrive in Glasgow until it was breakfast time, and then straight off to college again. The things we did for love.

I managed to fit in some more driving lessons during this time, but failed for a second time. The examiner had sneakily directed me into Kelvingrove Park where the speed limit was either 15 or 20 mile per hour. I had never driven in a park before and had not noticed the reduced speed limit, and as the roads were nice and quiet I breezed along at 30 mph. Quite understandably, I failed again. However, I did pass on my third attempt.

The Mate's Certificate included some of the same papers that were in the 2nd Mate's, mainly the navigation papers, celestial and terrestrial, and introduced some new subjects, including electricity and electronics. There was a paper on ship construction and stability, and one on the stowage and properties of cargo. The oral examination also introduced some new topics. In theory you were being examined to establish your competence to be the mate of a ship and there was a strong emphasis on rigging and spars, and on jury-rigging and repairs. One of the standard questions was on how you would go about shipping a jumbo derrick in to its operating position if it was lying on the side deck. As this was such a theoretical question – I never heard of anyone who had met the problem in real life – the answers suggested were various indeed. The real point of the question was to test your ability to talk your way out of a difficult situation. I had an advantage in that I was living with my brother Donald at the time, and he was then working for a company that had a national reputation as being the very best in the business of lifting or placing large, and/or heavy objects into difficult places. I put the question to him and he gave me a very convincing and plausible modus operandi. The question was not even asked at my examination, much to my annoyance, as I was looking forward to demonstrating my knowledge and ability to the examiner.

The week of the exams finally arrived. I did my six written papers by

Wednesday, passed the signals exam on Thursday, and took and passed my oral examination on Friday morning. I caught the train immediately after that and headed down to Heswall, having made an arrangement with one of the other students that I would call him at an agreed time and place so that he could tell me my results. I mentioned before that results were posted on a notice board on the Saturday in the same week as the exams took place. I was very happy and relieved to find that I had passed in all parts and would now be able to collect my Mate's certificate.

I don't remember how long I stayed at Greeba for this time. That by the way was the name of Anne's grandmother's house. I went back to Glasgow to attend a course at the Sperry Gyroscope works at the request of the Clan Line. At that time there were two principle suppliers of gyrocompasses, Sperry and Decca. Having done the course on Sperry I always favoured it thereafter.

I had forgotten that Christmas had occurred during my time at college and that I had gone down to spend it with Anne and her grandmother. Anne, at this time had not met my parents, but they knew all about her, and I think that she had written to them. My mother used to rear a couple of geese most years, which were always ready for the table around Christmas time. This year she had one killed and dressed, and sent by parcel post to Greeba for Christmas. Imagine being able to trust the post to deliver fresh food on time today.

Mrs Caley was a wonderful cook, and that Christmas dinner was a truly memorable one. I must have spent about a week with them before going home to Mellon Udrigle in time to enjoy the New Year celebrations. I cannot separate this Hogmanay from some of the others in my mind. By their very nature these celebrations brought on a form of amnesia. I do remember staying for a night with Anna and Bill Manson on my way back to Glasgow to resume my studies.

After finishing the Sperry course I went back down to stay with Anne for a few days before joining my next ship. This was the Clan Kennedy, which I joined as 2nd officer in Middlesborough on the 12th of February 1955. The captain was Jack Findlay from the island of Arran and the chief officer was Francis King, of whom more later on. It was a pleasant voyage to South and East Africa. I much preferred the Africa trips to the Subcontinent trips. The voyage from the UK to Cape Town in a 10-knot vessel took about 26 days with a short stopover in Dakar Senegal for bunkers. The run from the bulge of Africa down to Cape Town was long and fairly boring, as it was quite possible to do the whole run without seeing another vessel. As 2nd officer I would have used some of this time to do chart corrections while on the afternoon watch, but that was soon all done.

All navigators carried either Burton's or Norris's tables. These tables consisted of tables of logarithms and antilogarithms besides a mass of other tables that provided answers without having to go through laborious calculations. This was the pre-computer age, and pocket calculators had not even been dreamt of. There were tables that gave you the distance from an object of known height by entering with an angle as obtained by sextant. I thought it would be very useful to have tables that would give you the distance from an object of unknown height, say, a rock or a buoy that was between you and the horizon. Because you knew your own height of eye, you would also know the distance to the horizon. You could at the same time measure by sextant the angle subtended between the top of the object and the horizon. The formula required to solve the equation was so long that it could not be written on one line of A4. This was the point at which I called for the help of Francis King, who had an Extra Master's certificate. Only about 2% of people with Master's went on to take Extra Master's. It took all the elements of Master's to a higher level, and introduced some new elements. One of those was Oceanography, and it took mathematics to a very high level. This was the part that I made use of, as he was able to check that my formula was correct, but better still, he was able to reduce it to about half its length. It was still a laborious process, as it was necessary, if the table was to be of any value, to make calculations for every five minutes of angle, up to several degrees, and for every foot of height from 20 to 80. It had been my intention to have it published by Burton, but we had arrived in Cape Town before I was half way through the work, and somehow I never got round to resuming the labour.

At some time during this voyage I had come to the conclusion that I wanted to spend the rest of my life with Anne, and to this end I wrote to her asking if she would be my wife. In foreign ports there always had to be an officer on board in the evening even when there was no cargo being worked. It was my turn to be the officer on board one night in Durban and I was sitting in my cabin having a quiet drink when the captain came back from an evening ashore, and as he passed my cabin I asked him to join me for a drink. At this time I had not had an answer from Anne, but was feeling so confident of an affirmative answer that I told the captain that I was getting married at the end of the voyage. How arrogant can you be? The captain, for his part did his best to try and dissuade me from this venture. He said that I should wait until I had got my Master's before thinking of marriage. He painted a picture of me trying hard to study with little children running around. I don't think he had heard of family planning.

It was not very long before I got a letter from Anne accepting my proposal. I wrote back to tell her that I would be arriving back in the UK in early July and asked her to start making the arrangements. I see that in fact I signed off the Clan Kennedy in Avonmouth on the 4th of July and I must have come straight up to Heswall then. I don't know what happened to the rule about living in the parish for three weeks before being married in church; maybe it only applied to brides. Anne had already decided that she wanted to be married on her birthday, which is on the 16th of July, so that left me with eleven days to help Anne with the arrangements.

I mentioned before that Anne was living with her grandmother. Her mother had died in 1946, when Anne was only thirteen years old . Her father had not long been back from serving in the army during the war. She had seen very little of him as he had spent years on the African campaign. He had been wounded before then, I believe in Saint Nazaire. He had worked all his life as a telephone engineer, and in spite of the army's reputation for trying to fit square pegs in round holes he was actually in communications. I suppose his proudest moment was being introduced to Sir Winston Churchill at the Yalta conference where he was responsible for setting up the internal communications for the conference between Churchill, President Roosevelt of the USA and Joseph Stalin, premier of the Soviet Union.

When Anne was sixteen her father married Gladys, whom Anne had always thought of as her aunt. She was in fact the widow of Anne's uncle Eric, her mother's younger brother. This would have made Gladys her father's sister-in-law, but now his wife, and Anne's stepmother. Anne lived with them until she was eighteen, but left them then to go back and live with her grandmother. She had lived, along with her mother, at her grandmother's house for all of the time that her father was away at war. Her grandmother, Ethel Caley, was her father's mother, who had made a home for Anne and her mother, and indeed nursed her mother through the last year of her life. She had clearly loved her very much.

Anne had fallen out with her stepmother, which prompted the departure to her grandmother's home. Her father, who at that time was in charge of the Heswall Telephone Exchange, used to come and see her and his own mother quite regularly, and I met him for the first time in the week before we were married. I got on well with him. We both loved football so I think that was our first point of contact. When I came ashore a couple of years later he introduced me to the delights of watching football at Tranmere Rovers, and I have been a regular supporter ever since.

The day of our wedding finally arrived, Saturday 16th July 1955, and what a glorious, sunny, and hot day it was. Anne shocked her father, who was with her in the car on the way to the church, by declaring that she would rather be walking out over the sands to Hilbre Island. The only representatives of my family who came to the wedding were Anna and Bill Manson. Travel was not as easy then as it is now. My parents would have found it difficult to leave the croft and all the animals. Danny had only been in the police force for a few months then and would have found it difficult to get time off. I have just checked this with him and he says that not only would it have been difficult, but probably impossible to get time off. I cannot remember what the situation was with Donald and Flora. Francis King had agreed to be my best man. The Clan Kennedy had come to Manchester after I had left her in Avonmouth and I travelled to Manchester one day to meet up with Francis to tell him what the arrangements were, and what part he had to play. When I went to the Clan Kennedy in Manchester docks there was a Test Match taking place at Old Trafford. In later years when I had developed a greater interest in cricket I had fondly imagined that it was the famous test in which Jim Laker had taken 19 Australian wickets in a match. A recent Google search showed that I had been wrong for all these years. It happened in the following year, 1956.

As far as I can remember everything went very smoothly at the wedding and we all then repaired to the Devon Doorway for the wedding breakfast. Why do they call it that when it generally takes place in the middle of the afternoon? When we booked the reception we knew that the Devon Doorway at that time did not have a licence to sell alcohol but were told that we could bring our own wine. They would, however, charge us with corkage. I think that was the first time that I had come across that practice. I remember very little about the events of the afternoon. I have a vague recollection of my speech but I cannot remember anyone else's. We must have gone back to the house to change and collect our luggage. We took a taxi from there to Liverpool to get a train to Glasgow. Anne's Uncle Roly in his new car, carrying some of Anne's colleagues who had been at the wedding, chased us along the lanes, but never caught up with us.

We had always planned to spend our honeymoon in Mellon Udrigle but were spending the weekend in Glasgow where I wished to introduce Anne to some of my family. We were booked in to the North British Hotel, which was one of the classier places in those days. I don't know if it exists today. We did not have the easiest of journeys as the train broke down, or there was some trouble on the line, somewhere north of Lancaster. It was very hot and airless on the train, which had no buffet car and no means of getting a drink. We still hear all sorts of complaints about rail travel today, but when I look back over a long life I find that not too many things have changed.

We finally arrived in Glasgow and made our way to the hotel. I suppose we must have had dinner after we arrived, although I don't remember very much about that night. It was the culmination of the happiest day of our lives and the beginning of a long and loving relationship that is still as good today as it was 53 years ago.

At that time I thought of Glasgow as my city, and took pride in showing Anne around all the familiar sights the next morning. In the evening we went to see Donald and Flora. I don't think we saw Danny at this time. The journey from Glasgow to Wester Ross was not very easy at that time. One choice was to leave Glasgow Buchanan St at 9.15 p.m. on a very slow train, which arrived in Inverness around 5.30 a.m. The Station Hotel was open for breakfast then, and that took up some of the time until the shops opened. One then caught the Kyle of Lochalsh train at 10.30 a.m., getting off at Achnasheen around 1.00 p.m. The onward journey from there was by mail bus, all the way to Laide, stopping at every Post Office and hotel on the way. There was even the odd stop to deliver a newspaper. The bus journey took about three hours. The other choice was to leave Glasgow at around 4.30 a.m. and connect with the same 10.30 train in Inverness. Not many people chose that alternative. There was a third way that required you to make your own way from Achnasheen. That meant leaving Glasgow at about mid-day and getting the evening train from Inverness to Kyle of Lochalsh. This train got to Achnasheen around 7.00 p.m. We opted for the third way as we had arranged with my father to meet us at Achnasheen with his car.

I don't think that I realized at the time what a daunting experience this was for Anne. She would be meeting my parents for the first time, but was already married to me. My father at Achnasheen railway station was the first hurdle, and that went very well. They each had the greatest regard for the other, and maybe I am biased, but it would be difficult for it to be otherwise. As soon as the introductions were made, my father threw the keys to me and told me to drive so that he could get to know his new daughter-in-law. It was only some time afterwards that Anne told me that she found the journey interminably long. Not because of the company, or the scenery, which she found enthralling, but just the long winding miles in the slow old Ford 8. Don't forget that most of the road was single track with passing places back then in the mid-fifties.

As part of her going-away outfit Anne had a white coat, which was folded on her lap because it was a warm evening. My father, who would have known that rumours and speculation would have been rife among the neighbours about Hector's new wife, decided to have some fun at their expense. He took the white coat from Anne and folded it up so as to look very realistically like a babe in arms. He gave it back to Anne and told her to carry it in her arms when she got out of the car to walk into the house. We don't know if this was seen by anyone, but my father's sense of fun certainly endeared him to Anne.

My mother was Anne's next hurdle, and that also went very well. They had a very good relationship for the rest of my parents' lives. There could not have been a better introduction to Mellon Udrigle either, as the weather was perfect for the whole fortnight that we were there. Hot and sunny with clear blue skies. We did a lot of swimming in the sea, which is not the first entertainment one tends to think of in relation to Mellon Udrigle.

My father had put his boat on a running mooring in readiness for us, as he knew that I, at least, would be keen to get some fishing done. In the evening of our first full day at Mellon we decided to go fishing, so my father, Anne, and I set off for Geodha an Fhithich where the boat was moored. On arrival we found that the boat had sunk at the mooring, and only the top of the stem was showing. When we attempted to bring her in, we found that in and out hauls had got so twisted round the block that we could not move her. I decided that there was only one way to sort out this problem, as there were no other boats around. I stripped off, dived in, and swam out to the sunken boat and managed to pull up on the painter and untie it from the eye in the mooring rope. I then towed the semi-submerged boat to the rock where my father was waiting. Anne in the meantime had ran back to the house for a towel and while I dried myself and got dressed she and my father had bailed out the boat, after having tipped out most of the water. It was not unusual for wooden boat to leak badly enough to sink on their first day in the water after baking in the sun for months. My father, who was a very experienced seaman, was rather annoyed with himself for allowing it to happen, and put it down to the excitement of having a new daughter-in-law arriving. We were not deterred from our fishing trip but I cannot recall the size of the catch. In re-living that episode I realize that I must have been a much stronger swimmer then than I am now.

Like all good things, which tend to end quickly, our honeymoon came to an end after two glorious and happy weeks at Mellon Udrigle. We must have stopped for a night in Glasgow on the way back, as I distinctly remember Danny meeting us at the station. I don't remember anything else about that trip, or our stay in Glasgow, nor do I remember our arrival back in Heswall. We rented a flat over a chemists shop just down the road from Anne's home. I think we probably made these arrangements before going away, and came straight back to the flat. The owner of the chemists shop was a Mr Rider whose mother had the other half of the flat that we were in, and we shared the bathroom with her. She taped little notes with 'dos and don'ts' all over the place and made us feel a little bit uncomfortable. It was rather cramped in any case, and we decided that when I went back to sea we would give up the flat and move in with Anne's grandmother who very kindly offered us a room.

One of the promises that Anne had made to me was that she would never put undue pressure on me to leave the sea. I loved the life, and could see a good career path ahead. She kept her word, but was very happy when I made the decision to leave the sea, which was made for some very good reasons. However, there are quite a lot of oceans to cross before that happens as I will try and relate in the next chapter.

Chapter 17

Time for Change

I must have had rather a long leave after getting married. We must have returned from Mellon around the end of July, but I did not join my next ship for another three or four weeks. It is possible that I did some relief work on ships in Birkenhead without signing on. In any case I see that I joined the Hesperia as 2nd Officer in Dundee on the 25th of August 1955. I made two trips on the Hesperia and left her almost exactly one year later, on the 24th of August 1956. I have very few clear memories about that ship. I think that the first voyage was the usual India and Bangladesh round.

We had a 3rd officer on this voyage who had been cashiered out of the RAF for drunkenness. He was a little bit vague on details, but did tell me some of the story over a few drinks on one memorable occasion. He had been a fighter pilot and on one early morning flight after a heavy drinking binge he overdid the oxygen as a hangover cure and passed out at 30,000 feet. Plunging to the earth he was woken by the frantic radio calls of his wing commander, and was able to regain control and land safely. That, however, was the end of his RAF career.

The few drinks over which he told me this story took place in the port of Aden where we made a short stop on our way to India. We sailed at about 6 p.m. and unknown to me, and un-noticed by the chief officer when he passed the watch over to him at 8 p.m, the 3rd officer must have gone on drinking alone in his cabin, with the result that he eventually stretched out on the settee in the chartroom and had gone fast asleep. Fortunately for the safety of all concerned the captain had gone on to the bridge at some time during the 8 to 12 watch. He left him sleeping and kept the watch himself. When I came on watch at midnight the scene I was met with was that of the captain writing up the log for the watch and the 3rd officer fast asleep on the settee. The captain just said to "get it to its bed" which I accomplished with some difficulty. He was logged for this offence but completed the voyage with us. The 3rd officer might have been able to continue in the company employment if he had not had a similar fall from grace towards the end of the voyage when we were discharging cargo on the usual run of North European ports. For this he was finally discharged with ignominy from the company's service.

On the second voyage I remember that we loaded bagged cement at some wharf on the River Thames as part of our cargo. This was destined for East Africa, and on arrival in Mombasa we found that the discharge pipe from one of the toilets, which passed through the hold carrying the cement, had been leaking throughout the voyage. The cement was just one solid block, and the bags had to be levered apart with crowbars before they could be discharged. It reminded me of the incident on the Cranborne which I related in Chapter 13 where the pitch had solidified in the hold. I think the leaking pipe was from the toilet in the captain's quarters, not that that makes any difference; effluent is effluent.

It was in 1956 that the Clan Line amalgamated with Union Castle Group, which included King Line and Bullard King and Co. Some time after this the group became known as British and Commonwealth Shipping Limited. A certain amount of disillusionment started to spread among the younger officers in the Clan Line at this time. We found that 2nd Officers from Union Castle passenger ships were leapfrogging us to become 1st Officers in Clan Line cargo ships. We could not argue on the grounds of seniority, but considerable resentment was felt because the traffic was all one way. We would have liked sideways moves to the passenger ships. Furthermore, the officers who came from passenger ships did not come up to Clan Line standards in cargo work, and had to be carried to a great extent by the junior officers. Clan Line had, throughout its long history, prided itself on being the very best cargo company on the high seas, and rightly or wrongly its officers basked in this glory.

I see from my discharge book that I had signed on the Hesperia for a third voyage in Glasgow on the 7th of August but had signed off in Birkenhead on the 24th of August and signed on to the Clan Urquhart on the 25th of August 1956. This was a promotion as far as I was concerned in that she was a bigger and faster ship and as such was employed on a regular, and shorter, run. In fact, she was one of the older refrigerated ships and was employed in carrying citrus fruit from South Africa. We would carry general cargo on the outward voyage to all the usual ports in South Africa and Mozambique. The refrigeration plant would then be started, and when the temperatures were right we would load, mainly oranges and grapefruit in Durban and Cape Town. The stevedores always put a few cases of oranges in the Mate's office and we got so tired of eating oranges that we just used to make a hole in the side of the orange and squeeze the juice into our mouths. By modern standards the engines of the Clan Urquhart would have been considered very inefficient. When not carrying refrigerated cargo we steamed at an economical speed of 13.5 knots. At this speed she burned 50 tons of fuel oil per day. When loaded with fruit we had to steam at our top speed of 15 knots, but at that speed the consumption of fuel oil increased to 70 tons per day. At today's fuel prices the cost of running a ship like that would be prohibitive. There were other high costs that would not be tolerated today.

I described the manning of an ordinary cargo ship in an earlier chapter where the crew were all Europeans. In the Clan Line only the officers were European. There would be the captain, three deck officers, a radio officer, four engineers, a chief steward and a carpenter. There would also be two, three or four cadets. All the rest would be East Pakistanis or Indians. There would be far more of them than there would have been on a European crewed ship. There would be a serang (bosun), burra tindal and chota tindal who were his 1st and 2nd assistants. There would be four Seccunis (quartermasters) and at least twelve seamen. There was one other category among the deck crew, and that was the topaz. He was a lower-caste person who was generally ostracized by the rest of the crew, and whose only job was to go around from morning until night sweeping the deck. There was an equally large number employed in the engine room and in the catering department. The crew, who usually lived aft, had their own cook, who was known as the bhandari. Crews were usually changed whenever a vessel went to Chittagong, although occasionally some crew would be picked up in Calcutta. Otherwise, for vessels that did not visit these ports, a complete crew change would be organized with another of the Company's ships.

Crew changing in Chittagong was a very interesting affair. Several serangs would present themselves to the mate. There was a very good chance that among them there would be at least one that he would have known from a previous ship, although maybe not as a serang. Having made his choice of serang he would give him a fairly free hand in picking the rest of the crew, only intervening if there was someone whom he knew to be very good or someone to be avoided. The system worked very well as the serang usually picked men from his own village who were well known to him, and would be expected to show great loyalty. As a way of saying thanks for giving them all a job, which would probably be good for about twelve months, the bhandari would cook an especially hot curry just for the three mates. I imagine he did the same for the 2nd engineer who would have engaged the engine room crew.

The crew numbers I gave would hold good for a single screw vessel, but when it came to a twin screw vessel there would be eight engineers, and if it was a refrigerated vessel like the Clan Urquhart, there would be an extra couple of refrigeration engineers. I suppose that in total we are talking about something of the order of 60 people; compare this with, say, a large container ship today, we might be talking about a total crew of 20.

Life on the Clan Urquhart was very pleasant. She was a very well run ship with a happy crew. As 2nd Officer I was responsible for all matters relating to navigation, which would include working out the ETA for the next port. On the fruit run our last port of loading was Cape Town and our first port of discharge was Avonmouth. On our last night in Cape Town the captain, whose wife lived in Southport, would come to me and ask me which train from Liverpool I was suggesting that Anne would be catching. I would have already written to Anne giving her an indication of which train she should be getting from Liverpool and he would give this same information to his wife, so that they would both travel to Avonmouth on the same train. It was a risky prediction to make as it was a 17- or 18-day run from Cape Town to Avonmouth and many things could happen in that time to cause a delay. I cannot recall having got it wrong on any voyage. The Chief Engineer was very clever at concealing the true fuel consumption by overstating the amounts used in port, which were considerable. The result of this was that there was always more fuel on board than the record showed so that he was able to authorize an increase in consumption any time that we found ourselves falling behind on our ETA.

The same chief engineer had another claim to fame, or was it infamy. He was a confirmed alcoholic. I had joined the ship only about a couple of hours before she was due to sail and had hardly had time to become acquainted with any of the crew. My first duty was to go through the ritual of testing the gear, which always took place one hour before sailing. The 3rd officer did all the bridge controls, and my duty was to go into the steering flat with the chief engineer and observe the correct function of the steering engine while on an open telephone line with the 3rd officer on the bridge. When we had completed gear check I met the chief officer who asked me if I had met the chief engineer. I was surprised at the question, but replied that I had spent a little time with him doing the testing of the gear and that I thought that he had some difficulty in remaining upright. He laughed at this, and told me a little about some of the problems that were caused by him. One of the orders that the captain issued at the beginning of each voyage was that none of us were to offer a drink to the chief until after we left Dakar in Senegal where we always bunkered on the outward voyage. Taking about 3,000 or 4,000 tons of bunkers into six double bottom tanks was a very tricky operation that was the responsibility of the chief engineer, and required a clear head. When it was all done satisfactorily and we sailed away the captain relented and allowed the chief access to the bar. In spite of his fondness for the bottle he was a very good engineer and ran a very efficient department and was generally very well liked.

I made three voyages to South and East Africa on the Clan Urquhart, leaving her on the 9th of August 1957 to study for my Master's Certificate. It was going to make a change to attend college from my own home.

I had forgotten to mention that we had not stayed for very long at Greeba after giving up the flat. On our first wedding anniversary we moved in to a brand new semi-detached house in Meadowcroft. We called the house Carramore, which is the name that Alasdair has called his company. People from Mellon Udrigle and surrounding areas might recognize this as an Anglicized version of Carraig Mhor, the large skerry that guards the outer reaches of the bay at Mellon Udrigle. We were very proud of our new house. Before setting off on my first voyage in the Hesperia we ordered all the furniture for the house. The floors were polished maple blocks and I undertook to buy all the carpets in Bombay, having been instructed on the colours to get by Anne. I was just getting carpets for the lounge, dining room and one bedroom, but I got mixed up with the lounge carpet and got dark green instead of grey. I have continued to make this kind of mistake to this day. Anne sold the green carpet to a colleague at work and I got a grey carpet on the next voyage to India. I think it was in Calcutta this time. I only mention this to illustrate how much easier it was to conduct this kind of business then. Within three weeks of our returning from honeymoon we had selected a house when its foundations had not even been dug, and ordered all our furniture. Maybe we were just more decisive then.

I enrolled at the Liverpool College of Technology, which is now the John Moores University, soon after leaving the Clan Urquhart. I will always remember my first morning there. I must have been a little bit late, because all the desks in the lecture room were taken, with many of them having two people seated to a desk. I looked around to see if there was anyone there that I knew but did not see any. A certain John Parsons made space at his desk, and indicated that I could sit there. I am very glad to say that 51 years on we are still very best friends.

The time spent at college was the usual hard grind of lectures all day and cramming until late at night at home. Towards the end I used to get up early in the morning and get a couple of hours of study in before setting off for college. The subjects studied included some of those already done for earlier certificates and introduced some new ones: meteorology, commercial and business law as it related to shipmaster's business, deviation and the deviascope, and marine engineering. I think we all found deviation and the deviascope the hardest subject to grasp. It was one of those subjects that became quite easy after the penny dropped. The actual examination in this subject was a practical one where you were sent to a room that had large windows with views of distant buildings. It would have a standard compass mounted in a binnacle into which had been placed lots of magnets in various places that were all sealed. Your task was to swing the compass through 360 degrees, taking bearings of a fixed point in the distance and from those observations, calculate the adjustment to be made by way of the "good" magnets at your disposal. You made the adjustments and swung the compass again to show that it was properly adjusted.

The meteorology paper was always a race against time, as, in addition to three or four questions that required written answers, it always included a huge block of coded weather reports, ostensibly from ships all over the Atlantic Ocean. These had to be decoded, plotted on to a chart of the Atlantic Ocean, and from it you had to produce a weather forecast for the next few days for some particular part of the country.

At that time most of the liner companies offered some of their ships as weather reporting ships, and I was fortunate in having served in a couple of those. Having collected the data at each of the synoptic hours and decoded it for wireless transmission helped, insofar as some of the codes were sufficiently familiar for decoding without reference to the codebook.

I have my Master's Certificate in front of me as I write and I see that it was issued to me in December 1957 upon having passed all my examinations on the 25th of November 1957. This was followed by several days of partying.

My Master's Certificate

I had got used to the delights of home life during this time and decided that I was not going back to sea. I resigned from the Clan Line and thought that I would have no trouble getting a job, as the papers seemed to be full of vacancies. It did not prove to be as easy as I thought it might be, and the only employment that I got was a commission-only job selling deep freezers to shops. They were the latest "must have" gadgets of that time. Unfortunately I never found a customer who felt that he must have one, so I concluded after a few weeks that I was not cut out to be a salesman.

I had in the meantime made contact with the Mersey Docks and Harbour Board, as it was known then, following a recommendation by a neighbour of Mrs Caley. There were no vacancies at that time, but they agreed to put my application on file. At this point I swallowed my pride and went back to the Clan Line and asked if they would take me back on for coastal relief work. I need not have worried as they were desperately short of experienced officers and I was welcomed back with open arms.

I made nine coastal trips over the next four months on five different ships, which included multiple trips on some of them. Strangely enough the Clan Urquhart was the first of those. The others were Clan Macbride of old memories, Clan Malcolm, Clan McDougall and Clan Forbes.

The longest time that I spent on any of those ships was on the Clan Macbride, which I had joined in Immingham on the 20th of January 1958 and left in Poplar on the 21st of February having been to Antwerp and possibly one or two more North European ports. I remember this trip particularly well, for reasons that might have proved fairly serious for me. This was one of the winters where there was a serious 'flu epidemic. I think it was known as the Asian 'flu. While we were in Immingham the majority of the crew succumbed to the illness including the captain and the chief officer, which left me in charge of the deck. A doctor had been called in early, and visited every day. I used to do the rounds of all the invalids with him, and he showed me how to diagnose the onset of pneumonia when I did further rounds on my own. We would then go back to my cabin for a drink. On one of these occasions I asked him why I seemed to be immune, considering the time that I spent in the company of the 'flu victims. He suggested that as long as I kept taking the whisky I would be alright.

The biggest problem arose when we were nearing completion of loading and were due to sail to Antwerp. We had just about enough crew to do the sea passage but not enough for un-docking. The solution we arrived at was for the doctor to prescribe Dexedrine to all of the crew and that I would line them all up on deck about half an hour before we were due to sail and administer two tablets to each man. He said that this would make them hyperactive for an hour or two, but that they would then collapse again. To save the doctor having to write 25 prescriptions, he just wrote one prescription to me for 50 tablets. This all worked very successfully, and by the time we arrived at Antwerp sufficient numbers of the crew had recovered to work the ship normally. The captain and chief officer had not recovered in time and were replaced prior to sailing.

The sting in the tail of this episode came many weeks later when I received a letter from head office asking me to explain why the company should support my drug habit as they had just scrutinized the accounts from Immingham and seen that I had been provided with a fairly large amount of a class 2 drug. Needless to say I was somewhat less than well pleased about this. I thought that a pat on the back would have been more in order, as my action had enabled the ship to complete her contractual obligations with regard to her closing dates at the subsequent ports. I suppose it illustrates further the changes that have taken place over time. I think that in the 1950s we were more prepared to take responsibility for our own decisions without reference to higher authority than people are now. Communication is so easy now, that there is always someone available to pass the buck to. In Glasgow, Liverpool or London we would have had a Marine Superintendent available to make difficult decisions, but in all other ports we only had agents.

My time in the Clan Line finally came to an end on the 2nd of May 1958 in Glasgow while serving on the Clan Urquhart once again. It all happened rather suddenly. Anne must have had a letter from the MDHB asking me to call their office, as we did not have a telephone in the house at that time. She contacted the Glasgow office, and one of the assistant superintendents came down to the ship and told me to pack my bags and sign off and get down to Liverpool as fast as I could if I wanted to get a job with the MDHB. He was called Ian Cameron and was most helpful in getting me away in time. I got to know him quite well some years later when he became one of the stevedore superintendents for the company that the Clan Line employed in Liverpool.

Chapter 18
Docks, Coast Lines and Pilot Service

I don't remember much about joining the Mersey Docks and Harbour Board (MDHB). The Board became Company some years later. I do remember being told by the 2nd-in-command of the floating plant section, which I was joining, that nobody ever left the MDHB until retiring age, and that dismissals were very rare. I did not trouble to remind him of this when I, along with about twenty others were made redundant two and a half years later.

My first job was as mate of a motorized 1,000-ton hopper barge that was laid up in dock doing nothing. I found this very boring, just lazing around from 8.00 till 5.00. This went on for a week or two before the work that a lot of new recruits were engaged for started. This was the opening of a new entrance to the North Liverpool Docks at Langton Docks. The work involved dredging a shelf of hard rock in the river about 200 yards from the proposed entrance. This was done by a bucket-ladder dredger, with the spoil being discharged into hopper barges, which then carried it out to sea to be dumped seven miles west of the Bar Lightship. We worked 24-hour shifts with three hopper barges in attendance on one bucket dredger.

At the time that I joined the MDHB, the floating plant consisted of 3 bucket-ladder dredgers, 4 grab dredgers, 3 large suction-pipe dredgers, 10 or 12 hopper barges, 1 tug and 5 floating cranes including the Mammoth, which I believe was then the largest floating crane in the world. The 3 suction dredgers were Leviathan, Hoyle and Hilbre. The Leviathan was quite definitely then the largest dredger in the world, being capable of sucking up 10,000 tons of sand or silt in 90 minutes.

Mate of the Leviathan was my next job, joining her about three months into my time with MDHB. We worked one week on and one week off, with two crews on each shift, making it four crews to maintain a 24/7 service. We loaded and discharged four loads in each 24-hour period. Two loads were taken from the Pluckington Bank, off the South Liverpool Docks, and two loads from the outer channel.

A requirement of continued employment was to obtain a pilot's licence. There were three grades of licence, which determined the size of vessel you were allowed to pilot. These were for vessels up to 12 feet, 18 feet and

30 feet of draft. One could only get a licence for the grade of ship you were serving on, and as the Leviathan was the only ship in the fleet that had a draft of 30 feet I was lucky to be sent there, as having the top grade of licence would be a distinct advantage.

Being in the right place was one thing, getting the licence was something else again. It was less than a year since I sat for my Master's so the brain was still active and used to assimilating knowledge. Nevertheless, it was a hard slog. The Liverpool Pilotage area was quite extensive. It was the whole of the area of Liverpool Bay and East of a line taken from St Abbs Head in Cumbria to Point of Ayre on the Isle of Man, down the East side of the Isle of Man to the Calf of Man and a line from there to Point Lynas on Anglesey. All buoys, channel marks, lights, fog signals, shoals, banks and everything else that has any bearing on piloting a ship within that area had to be learnt by heart. This included, amongst other things, knowing the depth of water at any place within the area, and the bearing and distance between any buoy or seamark and any other.

A tip that I was given by someone who had taken the licence was to take a pack of 200 or so blank white cards and write a question on one side in one colour ink and the answer on the other side in a different colour. I would then shuffle the pack and Anne would deal them from the top, asking the questions as they appeared. After doing this for hours on end over a period of many weeks, it was a toss up for who should go to be examined, Anne or I. I was examined by the Chief Conservator for the port of Liverpool and by the senior Liverpool pilot and passed. I should point out that having this licence did not entitle me to pilot any vessel, only a vessel that I happened to be serving on. The Liverpool Pilotage was a closed shop to anyone who had not served his or her time in the service. The knowledge required of us, and the examination we had to take, were the same as that required and taken by the pilots; our certificates were deemed to be exemption from compulsory Pilotage only.

In my time with the MDHB I served in all the different types of vessel, but probably spent more time on floating cranes than any other. Apart from the Mammoth, which had to be moved around with tugs, the floating cranes all had engines, and were very manoeuvrable craft. This was far more interesting work. We were constantly on the move through the whole dock system in Liverpool and across the river to Birkenhead. This was in the days before containerization and there would be about 60 ocean-going vessels in dock on any particular day. There were 17,000 dockworkers on the River Mersey at that time. Any piece of cargo heavier than 5 tons generally had to be handled by floating crane, so we were kept very busy.

Some time during the summer of 1961 the MDHB made major policy changes in the way they were to continue dredging the port. They got rid of the 3 bucket-ladder dredgers and that meant there was no further need for hopper barges. They also got rid of the suction-pipe dredgers. Most of their work would in future be done by contractors using trailer suction dredgers. All of us, the latest recruits, could see this coming and were not surprised when given our redundancy notices.

They did try and find alternative employment for most of us. In most cases this was back to sea again. I was offered an interview with Coast Lines, which I thought might be better than going back deep sea again. Coast Lines was a very important company at that time. Besides having about 20 vessels employed on regular services to most of the ports in the UK and Eire, they owned and ran all the passenger ferries between Britain and Ireland at that time, except for the British Rail ferry between Holyhead and Dublin.

I was offered the 2nd mate's job on the Caledonian Coast, which was one of four vessels operating a service from Liverpool to London, via Falmouth, Plymouth and Southampton outward, and Cork and Dublin

---

No. **G/1888**

UNITED KINGDOM OF GREAT BRITAIN AND NORTHERN IRELAND.

RESTRICTED CERTIFICATE OF COMPETENCE IN RADIOTELEPHONY

This is to certify that, under the provisions of Section 7(1) of the Wireless Telegraphy Act, 1949, and the Radio Regulations annexed to the International Telecommunication Convention, Geneva, 1959,

Mr. *Hector Grant*

has been examined in Radiotelephony and has passed in :—

(a) Practical knowledge of the adjustment of radiotelephone apparatus.

(b) Practical knowledge of radiotelephone operation and procedure.

(c) Sending and receiving spoken messages correctly by telephone.

(d) General knowledge of the regulations applying to radiotelephone communications and particularly of that part of those regulations relating to the safety of life.

It is also certified hereby that the holder has made a declaration that he will preserve the secrecy of correspondence.

Signature of Examining Officer ....

K741   Date .... 31 OCT 1962 ....

Wireless Operator's certificate

homeward. I accepted the position and joined her on the 8th of September 1961. I was not particularly happy about going back to sea again, particularly as by this time Anne and I had become the proud parents of Alasdair, who had been born on the 14th of January that year. I did not mention that I bought my first car soon after joining the MDHB, at least the first car that I kept for a while. You might remember that I kept my very first one for only two weeks. This one was a second-hand Ford Prefect and on the night that Alasdair was born I drove Anne to the Royal Hospital in Liverpool in fairly dense fog. She had to go to that hospital because she had a rather rare blood group that meant there was a possibility that the baby would have to have a complete blood change. Fortunately this had not been necessary.

Alasdair was only eight months old when I went back to sea, but fortunately I was never away for very long. On this particular run we were only away for ten days, unless we were held up by bad weather. We sailed from Liverpool every other Saturday, returning ten days later on the Wednesday. This gave us three nights at home every other week. It did not always work out because of winter storms. I do remember that on one trip we did not get back to Liverpool until Saturday morning, but we still had to sail at noon again, so as to keep to our schedule. The Caledonian Coast carried 12 cruise passengers during the summer months, which added some interest to the humdrum life at sea.

I had been rather anxious to get home for Alasdair's first Christmas. We were due into Dublin on the Sunday morning, which was Christmas Eve, and I had planned to catch the BR ferry to Holyhead, and a train from there to Chester. Unfortunately we had encountered a SW gale coming down the English Channel and were running about eight hours late. You can imagine my utter disappointment on meeting the outward-bound ferry as we were entering Dublin harbour. I had to spend Christmas in Dublin with only the company of my shipmates. It was even more of a disappointment for Anne. On Christmas Day she pushed Alasdair in the pram through heavy snow all the way to Irby to spend the day with her father and Gladys.

I left the Caledonian Coast in January 1962 and joined the Atlantic Coast. This was not a good move because she, along with one more vessel, ran a service between London, Kirkcaldy and Aberdeen. We used to have a long weekend in Kirkcaldy every other week so that those of us who lived in the Merseyside area would take turns to go home for the weekend. It was a very long way and I think I only did it once. I did two weeks on the Leinster in March, presumably as a holiday relief, and then back to the Atlantic Coast. The Leinster and the Munster were the two passenger ferries that operated the Liverpool to Dublin service. There were two more on the Liverpool to Belfast service and two on the Glasgow to Belfast service.

I finally left the Atlantic Coast in Aberdeen on the 18th of May 1962 and joined the Hadrian Coast five days later in Liverpool as mate. Nobody could serve higher than 2nd mate in Coast Lines until they obtained the Liverpool pilot's licence. I don't know if the office forgot that I already had my pilot's licence, or was it just that there were no vacancies until then. The Hadrian Coast supplemented the four passenger/cargo vessels on the Liverpool to London service, so I was quite happy to get back on a more home-friendly run. I stayed on her until the 28th of August, and joined the Brookmount on the 20th of September 1962.

This was probably the best ship I was on, in terms of getting home frequently. She was a cattle-boat, and made two trips a week between Liverpool and Belfast. We were in Liverpool every weekend and one other night during the week. We carried cars on the cattle-deck on the outward trip from Liverpool, and cattle on the run back from Belfast. It was mostly cows and bullocks for slaughter that were carried, but occasionally we would carry pigs or sheep. I do remember on one occasion calling in at Douglas in the Isle of Man and loading a full cargo of sheep. I don't remember how many that would be. Something in the order of 1500 I would think. When we carried fully-grown cows it would be 350. They were secured in pens of four, all on one deck, with walkways in between. As chief officer I was responsible for their safe passage and for ensuring their well-being. We generally left Belfast around 6.00 p.m. and arrived at Woodside Stage in Birkenhead between 5.00 and 6.00 a.m. next morning. I used to walk through the cattle-deck twice during the night. I carried a humane killer that I was licensed to use. If any cow had fallen in the pen I was instructed to shoot it. I am glad to say that in the five late autumn and winter months that I served on the Brookmount we never lost a single animal. We had encountered many gales throughout that winter, and you could tell that the cows were suffering from seasickness.

There was a walkway linking Woodside Stage directly with the slaughterhouse to which all the cattle were driven, to have their lives ended that very morning. Ministry of Agriculture vets came on board as soon as we docked and walked through the cattle-deck with me to ensure that the cattle had been humanely treated throughout the passage, and then followed them into the slaughterhouse to see their lives ended. I cannot help feeling that there is a dichotomy here.

I left the Brookmount on the 26th of February 1963 and joined the Irish Coast on the 1st of March. The Irish Coast was a passenger ferry that was used as a relief for all the other ferries. Two operating the Liverpool to Belfast service, two on the Liverpool to Dublin service, two on the Glasgow to Belfast service and one on the Fishguard to Cork service. Each of these vessels had an annual service and dry-docking, so they were out of service for about one month. Including her own annual service that took up eight months of the year. The other four months were quite interesting, but I will come to that later. I was on the Irish Coast until the 16th of April. I think we did the Liverpool to Dublin service, and I have a very clear memory of doing the Glasgow to Belfast service.

Having left the Irish Coast in Glasgow on the 16th of April I see that I joined what was my first Coast Line ship, the Caledonian Coast, as chief officer, in London the next day. It was unusual to do crew changes in London on the regular Liverpool-based vessels, so I think there must have been some sort of emergency. There was a change from the last time that I was on this vessel. The summer cruising season had started so that we had passengers on board. We carried a maximum of only twelve, but I don't remember if we had that many on board. I do remember one family. They were an elderly couple with a daughter who was approaching middle age and another lady friend. We left London as usual on Friday night and when we arrived in Cork on a lovely Sunday morning the daughter and her lady friend expressed a desire to hire a car with the captain and have a long drive through the country. Neither of the women nor the captain could drive, so I was pressed into service. It did not require much pressure, as I was delighted to get the chance to see some of the country at the expense of someone else. We hired one of the nicest cars available, which I think was an Austin Cambridge, and set off for what turned out to be quite a memorable day's touring. It was memorable, in so much as the fact that we must have done about 250 miles and hardly met another vehicle. We went all around the Ring of Kerry and back along the south coast. As the women had paid for the car, and I had done the driving, the captain contributed to the day out by treating us all to dinner at a hotel in Skibbereen. We all had a great day. The car was kept and on the Monday I drove the women to Blarney, where we all kissed the Blarney stone.

The reader may recall that I wrote in Chapter 11 about the allied commission that was running the port of Hamburg for two or three years after the war and that Captain Mara had suggested the letter C from the international code of signals as the temporary national flag for Germany. This was the same Captain Mara who was captain of the Caledonian Coast at this time. I must have made five or six round trips on the Caledonian Coast this time before, apparently, having some leave before joining the Irish Coast again on the 11th of July 1963.

I joined the Irish Coast in Ardrossan this time as she was engaged in her alternative activity to humdrum ferry service. This was taking day trip passengers from Ardrossan to Belfast. We left Ardrossan at 8.00 a.m. each day, arriving in Belfast at 1.00 p.m. They had one hour ashore as we left again at 2.00 p.m., arriving back at Ardrossan at 7.00 p.m. We carried 1500 passengers, and were full every day. There were several bars and cafés on board but no restaurant where people could sit down to a meal.

Captain Angus Mackinnon from Colonsay was the captain for most of the time and he was quite a character. The course from Ardrossan to Belfast took you close to the Ailsa Craig, a high rock in the Clyde estuary and home to thousands of seabirds on its cliffs. He would station one of us at the radar, calling out the distance every minute while the ship headed straight for the cliffs at 18 knots. When about 300 yards from disaster he would order hard over on the helm and give a loud blast on the fog horn. By the time the ship answered to her helm we would all have our hearts in our mouths as we passed almost within touching distance of the cliffs, with the air full of screeching seabirds. The passengers thought that this was great fun. They did not appreciate that it needed only one little thing to go wrong, such as a hydraulic pipe to the steering engine to spring a leak thereby making the rudder ineffective, for a devastating shipwreck to occur.

There were three officers on board as well as the captain. We were all chief officers from various other ships from the fleet, and seniority was determined by your time of arrival on board. There was a fair amount of movement in and out, and one moved up each time someone left. It made little difference to our duties as we all spent most of our time on the bridge. Ordinarily, the bridge was out of bounds to passengers, but Captain Mackinnon used to invite about a dozen or so on to the bridge. Elaborate practical jokes would then be played. I remember on one occasion that one of us dressed up as a priest and came up on to the bridge to remonstrate loudly with the captain in front of these passengers for cruelty to seabirds on the Ailsa Craig. He used to put spoof messages out on the tannoy system as well. In spite of such idiosyncratic behaviour he was a first-class seaman, and one of the best ship handlers I ever sailed with. To see him berthing the ship in Ardrossan, where he had to go in stern first round a difficult bend, was seamanship of the highest order.

It was during this time on the Irish Coast that my father and mother came down to stay with us for a short holiday. Anna and Bill had gone down to Mellon Udrigle to look after the cattle while they were away. I managed to get some time off, and got home for about a few days. I don't know how we arranged this because there is no interruption in my time on articles. It must have been unofficial. I do remember that I left the Irish Coast in Belfast and hitched a lift on a spare bed in the officer's quarters of the Ulster Monarch on her night run to Liverpool. I also remember that I telephoned Captain Mackinnon the next night, presumably to find out if we could get away with this subterfuge. It was marvellous having my parents to stay with us. I only wish that they could have done it more often. In later years when they lived in Evanton, and had no animals to tie them down, they had reached an age when to travel to Glasgow and stay with Danny and Mary was the limit of their capability.

Having completed the summer cruising season the Irish Coast went for her annual service in Belfast on the 2nd of September where I left her for the last time. I joined the Ocean Coast on the 4th as chief officer and was there until the 2nd of October. She was a twelve-passenger ship like the Caledonian Coast and operated the same route, but leaving Liverpool on the Wednesday instead of Saturday. The captain on this ship, who shall remain nameless, was a very heavy drinker. I remember on one trip when we were sailing from Southampton, I realized as we were pulling away from the quay that he was very drunk. I ran up on to the bridge as soon as I was finished on the forecastle head and suggested that he went quietly to his cabin before the passengers noticed the state he was in. He complied with this request and I did not see him again until we had arrived off our berth in London. This meant that I had done the Pilotage in Southampton and London on the strength of his licences.

I mentioned before that to be a chief officer in Coast Lines you had to have a Liverpool pilot's licence. To be Master you had to have a licence for every port that you were likely to go to. Lots of the masters were confined to the Liverpool to Ireland services as they only had those licences, but if you wanted to be able to go to any ship in the company you had to have many more. Captain Mara, for instance, had studied for and obtained licences for the ports of Glasgow, Belfast, Dublin, Cork, Falmouth, Plymouth, Southampton and London as well as Liverpool. I was studying for, and almost ready to take the Belfast licence examination when I left the company.

When I left the Ocean Coast I must have had some leave, as I see that I joined the Caledonian Coast once again on the 24th of October but left on the 7th November to join the Ulster Pioneer on the 8th. This vessel ran a regular cargo service between Liverpool and Belfast, but as she had a mainly Irish crew we seemed to spend our weekends in Belfast. I was not too happy about that, but it was not to last for very long.

While I was away in Belfast one weekend an old friend from MDHB days called at our house and told Anne that if I got in touch with him when I returned he would have some interesting news for me. Some months prior to this a new Superintendent of Pilotage had been appointed in Liverpool. He wanted to change the system that had pertained for many years whereby a large group of pilots would be kept on the Pilot vessel out at the Liverpool Bar for boarding inward bound ships. They would some-times spend days out there before their turn came to board an inward-bound ship. Two high-speed launches were acquired that had accommodation to carry twelve pilots as well as a crew of four. Only one launch was used, the other being kept in reserve. These launches were called the Puffin and the Petrel, and were intended to shuttle pilots out to the Bar pilot vessel as required. The younger pilots welcomed the new system, but the older ones, who were in the majority, were very much against it. I think that they must have enjoyed being away from the cares of family life for a few days at a time, and it is quite probable that outward-bound pilots would get duty-free spirits from their ships, which would be shared with those already on the pilot vessel. In the old system pilots would be put aboard and taken off ships at the Bar by gig boat, oper-ating from the pilot vessel.

Because of the antipathy from the majority of pilots to the new system, the superintendent of pilotage decided that the captain of the pilot launch would have to have a 1st class pilot's licence and a foreign-going masters certificate, so that he would be more highly qualified than the pilots, who were only required to have a 2nd mate's certificate, which they obtained after a few years at sea, having served as apprentices on the pilot boat.

This was the interesting news that Jimmy Heald had for me. The service had only been operating for a few weeks at this time. There were four full crews required to operate a service around the clock for 365 days a year. I knew three of the captains, including Jimmy Heald, from MDHB days. The fourth one was not known to me and in any case was leaving, as he had just bought a hotel in the Lake District. This created a vacancy for which I successfully applied. I did a couple of shifts with one of the other captains to familiarize myself with the system and then took over my own watch.

This must rank as the very best job I ever had. Imagine being well paid to mess around in a high-speed launch. Messing around is a bit of an exag-geration as there was quite a lot of hard work involved. The system was designed initially to have the launch ferrying pilots from Liverpool landing stage to the bar pilot vessel. It soon evolved into something more. The pilot master on the pilot boat soon saw the advantage of letting the launch do the boarding direct. We generally picked up a full complement of pilots at 8.00 a.m. and again at 8.00 p.m. and if there were a lot of ships approaching the Bar we would be instructed by radio to put certain pilots on to certain ships. You might get rid of four or five this way, before depos-iting the remainder on the pilot boat. If there were no pilots to be taken ashore imminently we would tie up alongside the pilot boat, and do the boarding of ships as they arrived. Liverpool was a very busy port at this time, with as many as 30 ship movements in and out on each tide.

The shift system that we operated was very conducive to having a lot of prime time at home. We did 12 hours on, 8.00 a.m. to 8.00 p.m., followed by 24 hours off. Then a 12-hour shift from 8.00 p.m. to 8.00 a.m. next morning followed by 48 hours off. This averaged out at 42 hours a week over a two-week period. If someone was off sick or on holiday, this would be covered by doing extra shifts. Each shift had a crew of four. Captain, engineer and two ABs. I had a very good, efficient crew who enjoyed working with me. I think that this was because I gave them more responsi- bility than any of the other captains. When we were navigating in fog I would let them do the steering and take control of the engines, under my orders, while I could concentrate on the radar. We had to keep a log of all the pilot movements. If you did not know the pilot's name you had to ask him. This was OK the first time, but if you had to ask him for his name again in a couple of week's time he would be very annoyed. I have always been very good at remembering faces, but putting names to faces has always been a problem. For this reason I appointed one of the ABs as the keeper of the log, thereby avoiding any embarrassment to me, and I don't think he ever had to ask anyone for his name twice.

The launches were twin screwed, with the engine controls situated on the console in front of the wheel. When going alongside vessels I always took the wheel and controlled the engines. Because of our speed we created quite a big wave, which could cause problems when going along- side other vessels. As the other vessel would be underway we would be caught up by our own wash before we could do the transfer unless we were very quick. Putting pilots on to ships was not as bad, as we had control of the situation, but taking them off was a different matter, as the pilot might not be ready to disembark when we got alongside. If he was climbing down the pilot ladder as the wash arrived he stood the risk of being soaked, or at worst being crushed between the launch and the ship. In time we got very proficient at avoiding such risks. The problem was really confined to fine calm weather periods, as in rough seas your own wave was lost amongst all the other waves.

The navigating area was quite spacious and besides the crew of four we would sometimes have five or six pilots there as well. They did have a twelve-seater saloon aft for their use. The older, unfriendly ones always went there, but the younger ones preferred to join us. It was very tiring to do a twelve-hour night shift if you were boarding ships all night. This did happen some nights, and your shoulders would be aching by the time you were relieved at 8.00 a.m., after wrestling with the wheel all night. Other nights you would take a contingent of pilots out to the Bar and just hang around until 6.30 a.m. when you would take any pilots to be taken ashore off the pilot boat and head for Liverpool landing stage. I remember this happening once, when one pilot joined us in the wheelhouse while the rest went into the saloon. Almost as soon as we set off we ran into dense fog which stayed with us all the way to Liverpool. Once or twice on the way up I stopped the engines and crept our way right up to a channel buoy until we were almost touching it without ever seeing any of them. I just wanted to confirm our position. The first thing we saw was the landing stage when we were less than ten feet from it. The pilots who had been in the saloon just jumped ashore without a word but the pilot who had stayed in the wheelhouse with us, shook my hand and said that that was the finest piece of Pilotage that he had ever seen. Coming from a senior pilot, this was praise indeed, and I felt justifiably proud.

I did not mention earlier that my good friend John Parsons, whom I first met at college when we were both studying for our Masters, had alerted me to the possibility of employment with UML, the Unilever Company that operated Bromborough Dock. He had gone there as Assistant Dockmaster within a month of taking his Master's Certificate. This must have been while I was with MDHB. I got an interview with Jim Blair the Traffic Manager. Jim Blair was the father of Sir Ian Blair, the current Commissioner of the Metropolitan Police. Jim Blair took a liking to me, and being of the old school that had little time for HR (personnel) departments, he wanted to appoint me then. The job was Assistant Manager of the Cargo Handling Department. He was over-ruled by the board, who decided that the appointment should wait until the retirement of the supervisor who fulfilled part of the function then. This was to be in three or four years, so I think I forgot all about it. The job was advertised again during the winter that I was in the Pilotage Service, which was very convenient for me, as I was always on hand to attend for interviews. By this time HR had got their fingers in the pie and everything had to be done properly. I was joined on the final shortlist of three by two other master mariners who were still serving at sea. Jim Blair excluded himself from all the interviews, to avoid charges of favouritism, but I still won through and was offered the job, starting in March. I had to give a month's notice to the Pilot Service.

Something of even greater significance happened in the meantime while I was still on the Puffin/Petrel. To our great delight the lovely Lisa was born on the 28th of February 1964 in Clatterbridge Hospital. Our neighbours, and very good friends on one side in Meadowcroft, were the Millers. I still had the old Ford Prefect that had no heater, and Anne thought that it would be too cold to bring Lisa home in, so we got Geoff to bring them both home in his car on the Sunday, when Lisa was two days old. The neighbours on our other side were the Shaws. Mrs Shaw was like a mother to Anne. Her own children were grown up by then and she was marvellous with our children.

This brings to a close my sea-going career. Well, not quite, as my new career is very much connected to ships and shipping. Indeed at the end of my working life when I spent 12 years as a self-employed Supercargo I was even more intimately concerned with the sea.

Chapter 19

A Life in Port

I am fairly certain that Lisa was one month old when I joined UML, so it must have been near the end of March 1964. The staff at Bromborough Dock at this time was, Tom Blything, manager, to whom I was assistant, an office supervisor, two clerks and a typist. There were four other supervisors who looked after all the outside work. Two of those were stevedore supervisors, while the other two were master porterage supervisors. There were 25 dockworkers permanently employed. These included crane drivers and various other plant operators. The vast majority of dockworkers were at this time employed by the National Dock Labour Board (NDLB). We requisitioned the numbers we required on a daily or half-daily basis. There was a local NDLB mustering place just outside the dock where about 120 men gathered every day. The supervisors went there and picked the men they needed. Those not chosen went home until the next muster time, but were paid a small wage by the NDLB. We paid those chosen for work at a much better rate. If we required more men at any time, they could be bussed in from other areas. We could have as many as 500 men on some busy occasions.

Bromborough Dock was privately owned by Unilever, who built it on the west bank of the River Mersey to serve all their factories in Port Sunlight. It was opened in 1930 and had about 1500 linear feet of quay space. It was an impounded system with locks that would allow ships up to 65 feet beam to enter when the dock was levelled to the river, which happened for 90 minutes before high water. Small vessels up to about 180 feet in length could lock in for three or four hours each side of high water.

Raw materials for the factories were imported from all over the world: copra from the Pacific islands, vegetable oil and oil seeds from West Africa, lard and tallow from the USA, fish oil from South Africa, South America and Scandinavia and feldspar rock from Norway. We also exported a lot of finished products. The nature of the business was constantly changing. As the overseas companies owned by Unilever became more sophisticated, they produced ever more of their own finished products, so that the nature of our imports and exports was always changing. For one period of two years we were very much involved with exporting cattle food to Romania. This was during the time when communism reigned and at the end of a five-year plan we were told that the only way we could keep the contract was by accepting tractors in payment for the cattle food. That was not acceptable to the suppliers, so that was the end of that, and we just had to move on to the next phase.

In 1967 there was a huge change in working practices in the docks throughout the country. The government had set up an enquiry under Lord Devlin, which criticized the casual system of employment of dock labour, and attributed most of the unrest on the docks to this system. He was largely correct in his findings, although the changes, which were brought about as a result of his report, did not bring immediate peace.

My immediate boss, Tom Blything, had suffered a severe heart attack earlier in the year, and in fact he never worked full time again after this. Because of this I represented UML throughout the long negotiations between the Employers Association of the Port of Liverpool and TGWU. The final result was that each of the employers had to directly employ the number of dockworkers that they believed was correct for their on-going business. The corollary to this was that the whole pool of available labour, then employed by the NDLB, had to be absorbed by the registered employers. This caused a great deal of infighting among the employers. One concession agreed upon was that it would still be possible for employers to loan dockworkers between one another by mutual agreement. The number on which we finally settled at Bromborough Dock was 50.

The total number of dockworkers on Merseyside, which included Liverpool, Birkenhead and Bromborough, was 17,000 when I first started at Bromborough Dock. This figure had reduced to around 8,000 in 1967, owing to better working practices, and the increasing containerization of shipping. The figures kept on decreasing due to natural wastage, and our figure had finally decreased to 22. Initially, our 50 were often not enough, and we had to get men in on loan. I was never very happy with this situation, and when I assumed complete control of operations, I persuaded our men that it was not in their best interests to share the decreasing amount of work with the employees of other companies, and that if they would guarantee to me that they could handle all the work that we could bring in, they would be the best-paid dockworkers on Merseyside. This indeed happened, and not only were they the best-paid dockworkers on Merseyside, they were also the most productive by a long way. This made the company and me very happy, as the operations at Bromborough Dock were more profitable than they ever were in the days when we employed hundreds of men.

Tom Blything had taken early retirement around April or May 1972 and I became the Cargo Handling Manager. Jim Blair also retired about a month later and Kit Coward succeeded him as Traffic Manager. Kit and I had a most harmonious working relationship for 14 years, and we remained good friends until his death, sadly in 2007.

Some time in the late 70s, in addition to my cargo-handling duties I took control of a large warehouse from which Lever Industrial did their distribution. To enable me to act effectively in this new function I spent two weeks in an SPD depot in Woking in Surrey. I came home for the middle weekend and wrecked my company car. Lisa, who was fourteen or fifteen at the time, had gone to a youth club disco with three other girls on the Saturday night. I picked them up around 10.00 p.m. and had just arrived outside the home of the first girl to be dropped, when I noticed in my mirror that there was a car coming up behind us, being driven in a very erratic way. I shouted at the girl who was about to alight to hang on tight. It was just as well that I did, as the other car ran straight into the back of ours and pushed us along until we collided with a lamppost, making a total wreck of our car. I quickly ascertained that none of the girls was badly hurt and ran after the other car, which was travelling slowly due to having one of its wheels almost hanging off. By the time I reached it three men got out and ran off, abandoning their car. Lisa had in fact incurred a bad whiplash effect and spent the weekend in hospital. Instead of travelling down to Woking on Sunday evening as intended, I had to wait until Monday to get a new car. I had been due to get one in any case, and fortunately it was immediately available. We reported the incident to the police, who put a watch on the car. The owner reported the incident to the police 24 hours later, by which time it was not possible to accuse him of drink driving. I don't know what he was charged with, but Lisa was offered an out-of-court settlement of £100, which our solicitor advised her to accept.

A few years later I wrecked another of my company cars while doing a favour for another family member. This time it was Alasdair and his friend Hilary. They were living in Liverpool at the time, and I picked them up early on a Saturday morning to take them to Manchester Airport. On the slip road between two motorways my front tyre blew out. I lost control immediately, left the carriageway, turned over and we skidded on our roof for about a hundred yards. We all crawled out a little bit shaken and bruised, but otherwise not seriously hurt. Hilary was bleeding from a cut on her arm, so the police, who were on the scene very quickly, took all three of us to Warrington General Hospital. Hilary was dealt with quickly, and Alasdair and I declared ourselves fit. Alasdair then had the temerity to ask the police if they would run him and Hilary to the airport as they were going on holiday to Morocco and it was getting very close to their check-in time. To my amazement the police agreed and got them there on time at high speed with sirens blazing. Their only request to Alasdair was that he would not write to the Chief Constable thanking him for the courtesy extended to him. I then had the task of calling Anne to explain what had happened and to get her to come to Warrington in her car to pick me up. A few days later, when I found out where the car had been taken to, I went there to retrieve the radio, taking one of my work colleagues with me. It was just as well that I did, because I felt so sick when I saw the wrecked car that I could not go near it. It was so flattened that I don't know how we got out of it relatively unscathed. My only consolation was to learn later from the insurance engineer who viewed the wreck, that there was evidence of a serious fault with the tyre, which literally exploded, so it would have been quite impossible to control the car.

One of the most interesting contracts that we had at Bromborough Dock was the building of the tanker-loading facility at Sullom Voe in the Shetland Isles. It seems strange to get involved with something like that. A local company had won the contract to build all the loading arms and they rented a large area of open land from us. This was adjacent to the dock, so we had the contract for loading all these weird pieces of construction on to ships. This lasted for three years and we had one ship on charter for the whole of this time, making a round trip every two weeks.

The next major business that we became involved with was on behalf of Unilever Shipping, exporting mainly raw materials, but with some finished products to the Lever Brothers Nigeria (LBN) factory in Lagos. This was a very interesting and profitable business. The fact that we performed with great efficiency after they had had some bad experiences at other ports made us quite invaluable to them. As head of the department and the first point of contact, I personally benefited greatly in later years from the goodwill engendered, as you will see.

All the time that these things were happening in my career, family life was running along happily in parallel. Alasdair started at Calday Grange Grammar School in 1972, and Lisa started at West Kirby Grammar School for Girls in 1975. I seemed to have spent a lot of my time in evenings and weekends acting as unpaid chauffeur to both of them. Alasdair played rugby for the first team for his whole time at the school. Lisa, although quite a keen sportswoman, never got involved with travelling to events. She was very keen on earning money, and started taking waitressing jobs from the age of fifteen.

In 1967 my parents moved from Mellon Udrigle to live in Evanton, near my sister Anna. Until that time we had a two-week holiday with them every year, from the time that we were first married. We went there twice with Alasdair before Lisa was born, but the first time we took Lisa we had borrowed a caravan. Anne's stepmother's brother-in-law was Deputy

Head of an approved school in Hayton near Carlisle. He taught wood-work, and as a project he built a 15-foot caravan. As he was a very honour-able man I presume that he supplied all the materials, but the boys, under his supervision, did the construction. The caravan had everything that all caravans of that period had, by way of equipment and fittings. The main difference was in its weight, being made of good solid wood. I had a Hillman Minx at that time, and I had it fitted with a tow-bar and a lighting harness for connecting to the caravan.

We loaded the car on Saturday morning and headed for Hayton. We removed the body of the pram from its chassis and secured this on the back seat for Lisa to lie in. This left about ten inches for Alasdair to sit in. He sat there without complaint for the three days it took us to get to Mellon Udrigle, and also for the three days on the return journey. We transferred our clothes and food to the caravan on Saturday evening and set off after breakfast on Sunday morning. I had never towed a caravan before, but we were soon bowling along quite happily. This was in 1964 and the only motorway that we encountered on the entire route was the ten or eleven miles of the M6 which by-passed Preston. This was of course, the first section of motorway built in Great Britain. Our first stop for morning coffee was in a lay-by near Lockerbie and much to my consterna-tion I found that the five-pin plug connecting the car's electrics to the caravan had fallen out. Not only that, but in being dragged along the road for many miles, all five brass pins were worn down and useless. This was rather disconcerting as the caravan obscured the braking and turning indi-cators on the car. We had to resort to hand signals with arms at full stretch. We stopped for the Sunday night at Shotts, which was not a very long run, but made it all the way from there to Mellon Udrigle on the Monday. We had tried in various places on the way up to buy a new plug with no success. We finally got one from Alex Forbes at Aultbea.

We had one further mishap with the caravan on our way back home. We left Mellon Udrigle after lunch and stopped for the night at a small site by Loch Ness. We had taken some large juicy pork chops with us and were looking forward to our dinner. Halfway through cooking the gas ran out, and when we went to the site shop to get a replacement bottle of calor gas, we found out that the caravan had been fitted with a regulator that would not take calor gas. We had to resort to buying a new regulator as well as a new gas bottle, and by the time we had fitted all this I think that the half-cooked chops were probably consigned to the dustbin.

We hired caravans for each succeeding summer until my parents left Mellon Udrigle. I think that the only reason that they left then was because of my father's failing sight. In fact it had failed almost completely by then.

He still drove his car, but only with my mother sitting beside him as a second pilot. She could not drive, but was able to warn him of approaching vehicles, and where to pull into passing places etc. Anna and Bill were more aware of this than we were and they instigated the move. Danny was actually involved in helping them clear out the house. That must have been a very sad day. They were very happy in Evanton in their small modern house. My mother always had a nice garden and my father went on growing vegetables right up to the end of his life. For the first few years after they moved we just used to go up for a week at the Easter holidays, staying in a very nice B&B.

I think it must have been around 1971 that we bought a new caravan, which we used extensively for short breaks all over the country. We used to go to Evanton once a year and park it just beyond Anna's house. There are houses built there now. For some time after my parents had moved we lost the inclination to go to Mellon Udrigle, but eventually the pull to return became quite strong and we started to take our full two-week summer holiday there. We always parked at the bottom of Alice and Jessie's field, within yards of the beach. We had some marvellous holidays there. There was always a boat available, so we could go fishing whenever we wanted to. Haddock were still plentiful and we used to go around with the car after a day's fishing distributing fish to all our friends.

My cousin Minnie with her husband Donald and five children lived in Ormiscaig. They made us so welcome, and as washing facilities were fairly primitive in the caravan, Minnie always insisted that we had baths when we went there. I don't think that she was casting aspersions on our personal hygiene. Minnie just could not do enough for anyone, and really was kindness personified. Margaret, the eldest of the five children, still remembers with affection our annual visits. We never knew that we had made such an impression. I can still remember, with great sadness, the day that we heard that Minnie had died suddenly while working on hay with Donald.

For two or three of the years that we went up to Mellon Udrigle with the caravan, Duncan Mackenzie (the Governor or the Barla) was there as well, staying at Silverhills. Duncan had been born in Opinan, but the family had moved to Mellon Udrigle when he was a young man. At some point in his life he joined the Prison Service, eventually ending up as governor of Barlinnie Prison, from which he had retired by this time. He had kept the house at Silverhills, and spent a lot of time there during the summer. He always had his boat the Maggie on a mooring. We used to fish for lobsters with him. We also had the use of his boat whenever he was not using it. His daughter Margaret and her husband Murray would be there some of the times with their family, and the same arrangements applied then. We had some great holidays. Alasdair and Lisa learned to drive on the field by the caravans, and on the road to Opinan. I must have taught the clutch control part of driving very well, as I had the confidence to let Alasdair reverse the car on to the towing hitch of the caravan while I stood at the back ready to connect it, and this when he was only fifteen years old.

By the time Alasdair was seventeen, the novelty of going away in the caravan had began to pall except for going to Mellon Udrigle. We decided to sell it as it was hardly worth keeping it for one or two long-haul holidays. From that time onward until I retired we spent our Mellon Udrigle holidays at Silverhills. Duncan used to rent the house out to a few privileged friends. Our best friends, Joyce and George, with Tim and John Kelly spent quite a few holidays there with us. We had many more holidays with them abroad. Besides the fishing, which was the favourite pastime, we had great fun working on peats and haymaking with Alice and Jessie, and all their many friends who spent a lot of their summer in caravans on their field. Some of those had been coming for many years, and indeed some of them are still going up there to this day. We had got to know many of them over the years.

There were some sad interludes during these times. Bill Manson, Anna's husband, died in January 1975, followed by my father in November 1976. Having been married to my father for 56 years, life no longer held any zest for my mother and she followed him in April 1978. Danny will surely remember that date well, as he had just got the breakthrough in the investigation of the worst murder enquiry of his career as a detective in time to attend his mother's funeral.

Back to work again. I mentioned earlier that Bromborough Dock was privately owned. It was built to supply the Unilever factories in its immediate vicinity. It had required an Act of Parliament to get it built, and owing to its close proximity to the MDHB docks it was restricted by law to handling only Unilever goods. There was a small relaxation of the law that allowed us to handle up to 3% of 3rd-party goods, as it was felt unreasonable to make a ship move to another dock to discharge a small amount of cargo. There was a further concession that allowed us to handle a certain percentage of cargo for 3rd parties who had premises on the dock estate.

By the early 80s the amount of work that we were doing for Unilever companies was dwindling rapidly. To enable us to remain viable we took to stretching the law to its utter limits in handling cargo for 3rd parties. At this time John Parsons, who had been the dockmaster since 1965, was made marketing manager for the dock and I was made dockmaster along with all my other duties. This enabled us to keep going for another few years, but we could see the writing on the wall. Like all large companies that have changes of strategies, Unilever had entered a phase of getting back to its core business. We at the traffic department of UML clearly did not fit this profile, and the decision was taken in early 1985 to close the dock down sometime before the end of 1986, and at this point I would be given early retirement.

John Parsons and I put up a management takeover proposal to operate from the river wall as we had sufficient assurances from existing clients to make this viable. The proposal was well received by UML but the Unilever board turned it down because they could see an unacceptable ongoing responsibility for the fabric of the dock. At this point I started casting around for some form of employment, as I felt that I was too young to retire.

I decided that setting up as a freelance cargo and ship surveyor was something that I was well qualified for, and to this end I composed a short CV, which I then circulated to about fifty ship owners and agents with whom I had done business over the years. It might have been of some concern later that I only ever got two assignments out of all that, had it not been for my good friends in Unilever Shipping Department. Mike Rossington, who, in 1985 was shipping manager for Unilever, and was responsible among his other duties, for the shipping of raw materials to the Lever Brothers Nigeria factory in Lagos Nigeria. Because of congestion in the port of Lagos, this shipping was done by chartered vessels direct to a private jetty adjacent to the LBN factory. At Bromborough Dock we consolidated all the UK cargo and loaded it on to the chartered vessels. All cargo from Northern Europe was loaded at Antwerp.

As I mentioned earlier in this chapter, we had proved ourselves invaluable to Unilever Shipping Department, and when Mike Rossington heard that Bromborough Dock was going to close he expressed concern to me as to what might happen to the LBN operation. Much as I would like to claim that I had had an instant flash of inspiration, it was not quite so, as I had given some thought to the problem, with reference to my own position, and my answer to Mike was that he should contract me to find a suitable port to continue the LBN operation, and that when I retired I would be used as a Supercargo on all the charter vessels in the UK and in Antwerp. He agreed to this immediately, and asked me to catch the next shuttle to Heathrow, where he had his office, so that we could draw up an agreement.

Mike Rossington and I had a very good rapport, and I always found it easy to do business with him, although he could be pretty tough with other people. We very soon had an agreement that we were both happy with. I knew that my future was secure, and he knew that I could be relied upon to make sure that the LBN operation would continue to be performed efficiently.

I researched several ports and finally made my recommendation that the Port of Heysham was the best option. This was accepted, and in November 1985 the cargo-handling operation at Bromborough dock ceased after 55 years of continuous operation. I had the unenviable task of terminating the employment of all the dockworkers who had served me well over the years. I did manage to find employment for most of them with other operators within the Liverpool docks.

All the men knew that I was being given early retirement next year, but nevertheless I was very pleasantly surprised and astonished to be called to their mess room on their last day at work to be given a genuine present with accompanying speeches. There cannot be too many managers who get a present from those to whom they have just issued redundancy notices.

Bromborough Dock remained operational, as we still had tankers bringing in edible oils. The barges were still in operation so I still had some work to do, particularly as the assistant dockmaster had been made redundant by this time. I still had to attend at the dock at all hours of the day and night when ships were coming in or going out. When any of the charter ships were being loaded at Heysham I attended there, but used to travel up and down daily.

During my last nine months at Bromborough Dock I used to take a day off each week in recompense for all the nights and weekends that I had to work as dockmaster. Lisa was living with us at this time and we went for days out in North Wales, and tramped for miles over the hills. The final day eventually arrived on the 30th of June 1986, and after a very good party I had to be driven home by my good friend John Parsons. He was fortunate in having severed connections with the dock, and was able to continue for a few more years as marketing manager for UML.

Chapter 20

And Finally...

A new life has now begun. I believe that lots of people imagine that retirement brings one into the final phase of life. I did not see it that way, but was full of excitement for what lay ahead. In the first instance I had secured for myself a good income doing something that I really loved, but only working on average about one week in four. Secondly we were now able to fulfil the dream we both had nurtured for many years; namely to move back to Wester Ross to live.

At some time in late summer or early autumn of 1986 we chose a site at Laide where we wished the Macrae Brothers to build a house for us. I initially drew up plans for a four-bedroom bungalow, which I submitted, to John Macrae for his consideration. This was just a rough plan that went back and forth between Heswall and Gairloch many times before agreeing on a final plan to be submitted to the local authorities. We were determined to stick as close as possible to our original plan, and this we managed to do.

This had taken most of the winter, and in the spring we put our house in Lime Tree Grove on to the market and authorized the start on building our house at Laide. We had a choice of six sites adjacent to each other, and a great deal of thought had gone into choosing the exact spot. We even had Anne walking around the area until she found the very best position with regard to the views, and that is where the kitchen sink was to be situated. The rest of the house then fell naturally into place. That might sound sexist, but as I expected to spend just as much time there as Anne, it made a lot of sense.

The building of the house at Laide came to a stop in mid-summer when the sale of our house in Heswall stalled. We eventually sold our house, but had to be out in about six weeks, which did not allow sufficient time to get our house at Laide finished. Kate and Steve Macdonald, who lived just below our house, very kindly let us stay in their flat. We moved at the end of October 1987, and all our furniture and new carpets, which we had bought while in Heswall, arrived the next day. The deal that we had with Macraes was that we would do all our own decorating, and fortunately there were two bedrooms and a double garage ready to put all our furniture in.

We started immediately on decorating one room at a time, and getting the carpet laid professionally. Digging out the correct carpet for each room and the furniture to go in that room from the piled-up mass in either the bedroom or garage gave us some exciting moments. Lisa was staying with us and was a tremendous help. She used to draw up lists of daily tasks for me, and helped to keep the whole project on track so that we had enough rooms ready for us to move in to from the flat within a month. We had the whole house decorated and furnished in time for Christmas.

I had forgotten to mention that soon after I had retired, Alasdair had gone off to hitch-hike through Africa. He had first spent a month in Tunisia perfecting his French language, and then walked and hitched his way over the Atlas mountains and down through the Sahara desert. Kim joined him in Burkino Faso, from where they made their way to Tema in Ghana. As they were going to be there for Christmas, we filled a tea chest with all sorts of goodies for them, including about 20 rolls of film. We had arranged through our friend Geoff Morris to have this shipped out by an Elder Dempster ship to arrive in Tema in time for Christmas. Unfortunately, instead of being given to the chief officer, to be kept safely in a deck locker, it was stowed in the hold with all the other cargo. When Alasdair and Kim went to the dock to clear it through customs, they found the chest to be completely empty except for a few pieces of wrapping paper. Their disappointment was extreme, as was ours when they phoned us on Christmas day and told us.

Anne and Lisa had driven down to Liverpool with the chest as I was laid low with a severe bout of bursitis. It was so bad that I could not walk to the bathroom unaided. We were still in the flat, but by the time they had to go, to catch the ship before she sailed, I was sufficiently recovered to be able to look after myself. In fact, by the time they got back I was busy decorating. We had put Tabatha, our cat, into kennels when we moved, so Anne and Lisa brought her back with them. She did not enjoy car journeys, so a 450-mile journey must have been purgatory for her. We put her into her new home, and she had sole possession of it until we moved in about a week later. I don't think she went out of the house all that winter as it was all so strange for her, but by the spring when she ventured out, and discovered wide open fields with mice under every bush she started to enjoy life and finally gave us her approval of our move.

My part-time employment as a supercargo was on behalf of Unilever Shipping initially. Two years before this, two senior buyers from Unilever had left the company and formed a company of their own which they called ICSL. Around the same time, the company within Unilever that looked after shipping and forwarding was bought by an Irish company that diverted all its profits to the parent company, with the result that it was put into liquidation. At this point Mike Rossington joined ICSL as the director responsible for shipping, and with whom I collaborated happily for the next twelve years. Exporting to Nigeria was never easy, and at this time was particularly difficult. Smaller, independent companies, like ICSL, where decisions could be taken quickly, were far more effective than large companies, which seemed to work through committees, where it was difficult to get anyone to make a difficult decision.

Being a supercargo involves one in a variety of skills. Besides the obvious, technical knowledge of ship stability and the safe stowage of cargo a fair amount of diplomacy was required. There are many parties involved in the shipping of cargo. These include the shipper, the ship-owner, the stevedore, the inspection agencies, the forwarding agents and Customs and Excise. They each have their own agenda, and their interests are often in conflict. My job was to keep them all reasonably happy, while making the interest of the shippers – my paymasters – paramount.

My first indication of a job would be a faxed list of all the cargo to be loaded in Heysham and Antwerp on the next charter vessel. After studying this I would telephone Mike to make suggestions as to the size and type of vessel he should try and charter. From then on I would be in daily contact, and would be receiving faxes with details of vessels that may be available for charter. We would finally agree on a vessel and Mike would then conclude the charter at the most favourable terms that he could manage, and the loading date and port would be fixed.

If the first port was Heysham, I would commute daily from Heswall to Heysham. It took two or three days to sail from Heysham to Antwerp, so I would come home for this time and then fly over to Antwerp to meet the vessel there. The procedure would be reversed if Antwerp was the first port of loading. When we moved to Laide I was unable to commute daily to Heysham but just stayed in a hotel. I still went home between ports, and flew to Antwerp from Inverness via Heathrow and Brussels. On one occasion I had to go to the port of Huelva in Spain to complete the loading. I had to fly to Seville on Saturday and stay there until Monday morning when I hired a car and drove down to Huelva. It was my first visit to Seville, and I spent the whole of Sunday just wandering around the city. I was very favourably impressed, as were Anne and I when we visited it eighteen years later. This work pattern continued for five years, after which there was quite a major change, coinciding with our move back to live in Heswall. More about that later.

By Christmas 1987 we had almost finished the decorating of all the rooms in the house. I was fortunate in a way as there had been a quiet period in the Nigerian export operation. It was early in 1988 before I had my first job since moving. Lisa was working in Gairloch at this time.

Danny, although two years younger than me, had retired a year before me, and Mary and he had moved north very soon after that and had a new house built in Tighnafiline. They are still there so must have better sticking power than us. Before retiring, Danny and I always talked about having a decent-sized boat, and going back to lobster fishing. When we moved up this became a serious discussion, and in the spring of 1988 we bought the Mara from Murdo Macrae. The Mara had been built in 1919 as a sailing boat for the salmon fishing in the area. Murdo's father, Findlay, my first cousin, had converted her. She was seven metres long with a transom stern, an inboard diesel engine and a wheelhouse. She was not very fast, having a top speed of not much more than six knots, but was extremely manoeuvrable and well suited for what we wanted to do, which was just slightly exalted hobby fishing.

When we bought her she was sitting in Murdo's yard on an old lorry chassis which had a framework built on it to accommodate the boat. The lorry chassis still had a steering wheel, but you had to stand on a small platform in the open to use it. We spent most of the spring and early summer scraping and painting her, and then got a friend with a tractor to tow her down to the sands at the Boom base, from where we launched her. We did sea trials that first day, and then moored her off Ormiscaig. We used a small dinghy that Danny had as a tender. The next day was calm and sunny, and we enjoyed motoring round to Laide where we laid a good, permanent mooring which I believe is still there.

We realized that we needed something other than our cars for towing the trailer and for subsequent launching and bringing in for the winter of the boat. Also for moving around smelly fishing gear and fish, and to this end we bought a long-base land rover between us. We had great fun with the land rover. I used it to carry stones from an old ruin in Mellon Udrigle for a wall that I was building in the garden. It was excellent for going to Slaggan for picnics.

The first thing we did with it was to bring the trailer from Mellon Charles to its summer storage place up a track on the hill behind Laide. Because it had four wheels, and the front wheels were still free, it had to be steered when being towed. This job fell to me, while Danny had the warm job of driving the land rover. When taking the boat ashore at the end of the season, we would put the trailer down to the bottom of the jetty, and as the tide came in we would float the boat over it. By the time we could do that there was too much water to hook on to the tow bar, so we had a long rope attached to it and hauled it up with the land rover. This was quite tricky as the boat had to land perfectly on the trailer. I used to wear angling waders for this operation as I was nearly up to my waist in the sea. The launching procedure was much easier. We just backed the boat and trailer to the bottom of the jetty, and when the boat floated off we pulled the trailer up, again using a long rope.

We bought about 40 lobster pots, and fished for lobsters and velvet crabs every year, from July until about mid October. We never bought any bait, but relied on catching all our own. We found this a very pleasant occupation, especially when the mackerel were abundant. It was a great treat for people who might be staying with us, to go out in the boat fishing. We sold lobsters and velvet crabs to several different dealers, but latterly only to Elders of Gairloch. They were exported to Spain live, in tanks of constantly oxygenated seawater. Fortunately we did not depend on this to make our living, but made enough money to cover all expenses with a little left over.

In April 1988 Anne went back to Heswall where she joined up with our good friend, the late Margaret Mackenzie, for a month's holiday in Zimbabwe. Margaret's brother had been living there since the 1960s, and had always wanted her to go out to visit them. She would go only if Anne went with her, so I think that this had been arranged before we had even left Heswall. I remember well the day that Lisa and I took her to the train in Inverness as I was caught in a speed trap just after leaving the station, for which I received a fine and three points on my licence. Ironically, on our way to Inverness two weeks later I was caught again going through Contin, and was fined again and received a further three points. I don't think the policeman was very amused when I told him he would have to get my licence from his colleagues in Inverness as it had not been returned by then.

Anne and Margaret had a wonderful holiday in Zimbabwe and to Anne's great delight Alasdair and Kim had met them at the airport on their arrival. They had made their way slowly southward from Ghana, through Nigeria and down to French Cameroon. It was from there that they flew to Harare. They knew that Anne and Margaret were going there and had decided to surprise them. Alasdair must have been given some addresses at some point because they were staying with my cousin Anne from Kyle of Lochalsh, who had been living in Zimbabwe for most of her adult life. I think Alasdair and Kim had continued their trek northward up the east coast of Africa before Anne and Margaret had left for home.

Lisa was still working at Gairloch during the time that Anne was away in Zimbabwe, but soon after that she started working in a sports shop in Inverness. She had responsibility for organizing outside sports events, and was made a director of the company. She called on us to assist at one event, the 10K run through the town. I was a marshal at some point and Anne was the doorkeeper at the shop where some celebrities were to be entertained. She was told not to let anyone in, but had taken her instructions too literally as the first person she barred was the main celebrity. He was a well-known TV actor who was on a regular sitcom that we always watched, and liked. Her excuse was that he looked quite different in the flesh, but he took it all very well and they had a good laugh about it afterwards.

As well as getting the boat ready and sorting out fishing gear, work in the garden went on apace: building walls, digging over the whole garden, laying lawns and planting trees, shrubs and plants. We also laid a large patio at the back of the house. All this did not happen in that first year. I think we must have been in the house for about two years before everything was done to our satisfaction. I kept going away to Heysham and Antwerp fairly regularly, on average about ten times a year. I would drive down to Heysham and spend two or three days there, then drive home for a couple of days before driving to Inverness and flying to Brussels via Heathrow. I would spend one to three days in Antwerp before flying home. I think this contributed to Anne's growing dissatisfaction with life at Laide. We decided that we would eventually sell up and move on, but that we would give it some more time.

We still had some very happy times there and had many of our friends coming to stay with us. In the summer of 1988, a couple of months after Anne had come back from Zimbabwe we had a strange telephone call from Margaret Maclean in Inverness. Lisa was working in Inverness at this time, and used to come home most weekends. The call from Margaret was to say that she would call on that particular Saturday evening with her sister Joan, and for us to make sure that we would be in. We thought it rather strange as we would have been expecting Lisa and would be in anyway. Around 7.00 p.m. Anne was ironing in the kitchen and had not heard Lisa's car pull up, but happened to look up to see Alasdair and Kim with Lisa walking up the garden path. I was in the sitting room when I heard Anne scream, and came rushing through in time to participate in this joyous reunion.

It transpired that Alasdair and Kim had been staying with Margaret for the last few days, and it was only then that we realized the significance of a call that we had had from Mick Stacey the previous week, asking for Margaret's telephone number. They all thought that we were a bit slow on the uptake, but it is easy with hindsight to be clever. As far as we were aware Alasdair and Kim were still wandering around Africa. They had in fact decided to head home from Malawi, and came via Malta, where they both took it in turn to be quite ill with malaria. They had already been to Mick and Audrey's – Kim's parents – before coming to Inverness.

They stayed with us for the rest of that summer. I think it was some time in late August that Kim left to take up a post in Barnsley, although I think she must have lived in Holmfirth. Her grandmother was still alive then. Alasdair left later, maybe early October. It was marvellous having them with us for such a long time. We did some nice trips in the Mara, round Priest Island, and around Gruinard Island to admire the seals. They also helped with some of the digging in the garden.

Kit and Barbara Coward came to stay with us once when they were doing a rail trip around Britain. We picked them up at Achnasheen, and took them back to Garve thereby giving them a sight of some of the finest scenery in the Highlands. Kit came out with Danny and I in the boat each day, and also insisted that he was going to have fish at least once a day while they were with us. We had already had wild salmon and lobsters, and so as to keep to his promise of a fish a day, we had to have mackerel for breakfast on the last day. Kit had taken it upon himself to mix the drinks each night, and we still call his favourite tipple a Kit Coward. It consisted of gin, Cinzano bianca and tonic. On the day that they left we had tickets for a concert in Inverness being given by a Peruvian Pan Pipe band. It was a lovely summer evening, and as we were going to be too early for the concert we drove quite slowly. When we were within a mile or two from Garve, Kit reminded me that their train was due in a couple of minutes. We speeded up then, and just got past the level crossing as the gates were coming down. They caught their train and we thoroughly enjoyed our concert.

We had many other people come to stay with us for a few days at a time. Pam and John Parsons, Edna and Norman Mylchreest, Joyce and George Wilkinson, Molly and Geoff Miller several times, Mick and Audrey Stacey and the Morris family from Meadowcroft who came every year for a week at Easter. We enjoyed having all of them. Mick came out with Danny and I in the boat fishing for lobsters and made a video recording of some of the trip. I wonder if he still has that tape. That reminds me of something strange that happened with my camera. We had been on holiday some-where abroad where I had taken photographs in a fruit market. I then double-exposed that film when taking a photograph of the deck of our boat, which, when developed, showed the boat as being full of baskets of fruit instead of lobsters, crabs and fish.

When I had to go away to Heysham, Anne would sometimes come with me and stay with Margaret Mackenzie. When this happened I would fly from Manchester to Brussels without going home and come back the same way to pick Anne up. On one occasion we went over by car. Anne loved Antwerp as much as I did. It was summertime and there was a lot of Parisian-style pavement eating. One evening we could hear beautiful music in the distance, and on making our way towards it, we found that there was a classical concert taking place in the Groot Market of the old town. The area was roped off, but we were close enough to enjoy it as much as those inside the rope, who must have paid for the privilege. We told the concierge at the hotel the next morning about it and she told us it was an annual event to celebrate a battle of long ago where the Flemish people had beaten the Walloons. There is still a lot of enmity between these two distinct peoples of Belgium.

We left Antwerp that morning as I had finished my work, and made our way leisurely southward through Belgium enjoying the beautiful scenery along the River Meuse. We crossed the border into France where we spent the night. We decided next morning that we would use country roads to make our way to Calais, as we had about five hours to catch our ferry. We got hopelessly lost somewhere on the outskirts of Arras and were in a lay-by studying our map when a French car drew up with a lone driver. When we told him our problem he said that it was now too late to go by the scenic route, but that he would guide us to the toll road. This happened to be twelve miles away, and when we got there we realized that he had come out of his way to help us. We thanked him effusively and he told us that he had been waiting for years to find some British people that he could help as he had once been helped in a similar way in London, by someone walking with him for a mile or two to show him the way to where he wanted to go.

I think that it was in the winter of 1989/90 that we put our house on the market. This was with our solicitors, which was still the standard way of doing things in the Highlands at that time. It was rather ineffective as I think we got only about three enquiries in eighteen months. The solicitor finally decided that we had better put the sale in the hands of a new estate agent that had just opened up in Inverness. We did this and a sale was completed within six weeks. I was in Antwerp on business when the agent got in touch with me to tell me that a conditional offer had been made, but that I had only an hour in which to give my response. After a brief telephone conversation with Anne, who was down in Heswall at the time, we agreed to proceed with the sale. I celebrated by going out to dinner that night with our agent in Antwerp. It was a very memorable meal in a Vietnamese restaurant where we had opted to use chopsticks. By the time we had finished the meal the tablecloth was covered in rice and particles of food. This was made worse by being on an outside table with a good breeze of wind and the consumption of copious quantities of good Belgian beer.

The day that we left Laide finally arrived and we were rather sad to be leaving. It must have been early November 1991 because I can remember that we had snow showers driving south. I had to be in Heysham for the next morning, so in the end we had to leave the house before all the furniture had been loaded up. Danny and Mary had kindly offered to stay at the house until it was all done, as the hotel that we were heading for closed its doors at midnight.

We had not found a house to buy in Heswall at this time, but fortunately Lisa had moved to West Kirby a year earlier, and was renting a two bedroom flat, which she was happy to share with us until we found a place of our own. As soon as I finished the job in Antwerp we started house hunting in earnest. We finally settled on the delightful 200-year-old cottage, which is still our abode. A lot of work was required on the cottage and, as our furniture was in store, we got it all done before finally moving in on the 8th of January 1992.

Our move back to Heswall coincided with some rather big changes in the ICSL/Nigeria operation. The European end of the operation would be conducted from Vlissingen in the Netherlands, and the British end from Grimsby. I had accompanied Mike Rossington to both ports before we signed them up. The main reason for the switch from Belgium to Holland was to escape from the problems that were being caused by Cotecna, the inspection agency for Nigeria. Bureau Veritas, with whom we had a very good relationship, carried out inspections in Holland. It made sense to move from Heysham to Grimsby at the same time, as this cut the passage time between ports from three days to eighteen hours.

At the same time as these changes had taken place I took on the task of attending the pre-shipment inspections by Cotecna at Grimsby. This was a very long day for me as I drove over early in the morning, and it was usually late evening before I got home, and as it took place a few days before loading started, I would have found this very difficult to do if we had still been living at Laide. The successful completion of the inspection was critical to the whole operation. The inspector would be checking for quantity, quality and weight. There was one product, which we shipped in large quantities, where the weight varied marginally from pallet to pallet, although the total weight was never in doubt. If the inspector pulled out three or four pallets at random for weighing, and he found the average to be, maybe half a kilo short, he would reduce the whole consignment pro rata. This represented a considerable amount of money in a consignment of 2,000 tonnes. I developed a subterfuge to deal with this problem. During the morning inspections I would steer him away from this product and spend as much time as possible counting drums etc until lunchtime. I would then take him to his favourite pub for lunch where he usually managed to drink at least three pints of strong cider while I slowly sipped a pint of beer. The happy result of this was, that he signed everything off without any trouble. I had no qualms about what I was doing as we had no interest in cheating LBN and had our own quality control. It was just a bureaucratic nuisance as far as we were concerned.

I was very happy with my involvement in the whole operation. It kept me in touch with shipping/seafaring people that I had always worked with. I made some very good friends in Grimsby and particularly in Holland. Some of these friendships were extended to Anne as well. The first time she came to Holland with me we took our car across on the ship from Grimsby and travelled on the ship from Grimsby ourselves. The chief engineer had given his cabin up to us. On arrival at Vlissingen the agent from Vertom took Anne back to his home where she stayed for a couple of days while I got on with my business. When the loading was finished and the ship sailed we went to Delft for three or four days and had a very enjoyable time. We came back by ferry from Vlissingen to Sheerness. That service stopped soon after that.

The next time that Anne went over to Holland with me we went by ferry from Hull to Rotterdam. We had our own car but were met at the terminal in Rotterdam by Aad, a good friend from Vertom, who acted as our pilot, whereby we just followed his car wherever he wanted to go. We visited various places of interest and ended up in Scheveningen where his daughter was at university. We met her for lunch at an open air standing-up fish bar where one of the most popular dishes was the raw herring, this being the season of the "nieuw hierring". This was a very memorable lunch. We went from there to Aad's home in Roosendaal where we met up with his wife and made our way from there to Berg Haamstede, the home of John and Yvette Ouwens who were having a barbecue to celebrate John's 40th birthday. John was the Bureau Veritas representative with whom I had become particularly friendly over the years of meeting regularly. Anne was going to stay with them all the time that I was working at Vlissingen. Having my car with me I took the opportunity of going there to sleep each night. It was somewhat less than 30 miles from Vlissingen.

I forgot to mention that when we moved the operation from Heysham/Antwerp I had an arrangement with each ship as soon as it was chartered, that I would have full bed and board on the ship and sail on it between ports. I would leave my car at Humberside Airport. The standard of accommodation varied, but was generally OK. The best food generally was on Danish or Dutch ships. I spent over a week on one Ukrainian ship where I shed five pounds in weight due to the poor food. Apart from the quality of food I found the people most kind and hospitable. This was one of the largest ships we had ever chartered and when we left Grimsby for Vlissingen there was a Westerly gale blowing. When we were approaching the pilot station off the Dutch coast the captain sent for me to come on to the bridge. His radio officer who spoke only Russian and French, was trying to contact the River Schelte pilot via a radio station in the south of France. I used their VHF radio to call the pilot boat direct, only to find that she was off station due to the weather. I had been up and down the sea channels leading to the Schelte often enough to feel quite confident in piloting the ship myself. I got permission from the pilots to do this provided I kept the radio channel open and that they would meet us just outside Flushing. This was in the late evening and I knew that we had gangs of men waiting to start work as soon as we arrived, and I was anxious that this expense would not go to waste. I was also anxious to get this particular job finished before I lost any more weight.

While Anne was staying with John and Yvette she met up with Aad's wife and they went to the great flower show at Kirkenhof. When the ship sailed we left Berg Haamstede and went north to Volendam for a few days, which we thoroughly enjoyed. We drove all round the Zuider Zee and marvelled at the number of sailing boats of all sizes to be seen. We went back home on the Rotterdam to Hull ferry.

I went out to Lagos, Nigeria on two separate occasions. I went out with Mike the first time with the object of observing the operation at that end and hopefully making recommendations that might improve the woefully poor turnaround time of the ships at Lagos. I made my recommendations to the board of LBN, which consisted mainly of different pieces of equipment that they should acquire. It was agreed that I would negotiate the purchase of these items, second hand, from the stevedores at Vlissingen. This I did and sent them out by the next ship. Several ships later I went out again on my own to Lagos. This ship had a very large cargo, including several hundred tons of deck cargo. When I arrived on the quayside they had started discharging but were making a hard job of it. The equipment that I had sent out to them was ideally suited for this work, but when I asked them where it was, I was told that it did not work. I asked them to bring it out and show me. It did not work because they were using it incorrectly. When I showed them the correct way to use it they were delighted, as it made their work so much easier and quicker. I saw this as an indictment on management, who had never questioned why this piece of useful equipment had lain idle for the best part of a year. We were always well looked after by LBN when we went to Lagos. We had a company house complete with housekeeper/cook and a car with driver for our exclusive use. We generally got invited to dinner at the home of the vice chairman at least once during our visit. The vice chairman at that time was a Dutchman. On one occasion when we had been to the vice chairman's house and were being driven back through the centre of Lagos to Apapa where we were staying, we asked our driver why he was driving through the city streets late at night at such very high speed. He told us that there were gangs on the lookout for what might appear to be affluent foreigners, and that going at normal speed would make it quite easy for them to ambush us. We did not question his reckless driving after that, as we thought that a road crash might be preferable to an ambush.

Lisa had moved back to Scotland within a year of our moving in to our cottage. She spent a couple of years living in her friend Hilary's house while she went off to do a second degree. After that she moved over to the Scoraig peninsula where eventually she was granted a plot of land on which to build a house. Lisa herself did a lot of the foundation work with some help from her good friend William. Two local joiners put up the framework of the house and put on the roof. From then on Lisa did the rest of the building with a lot of help from Anne and I and various friends. We used to spend weeks at a time staying with Lisa and working on the house. Initially we stayed in various places locally, but once the house became liveable it was much easier.

I was still working while this was going on, but by the time that I was 70 years old I thought it was about time that I fully retired. The problem was that ICSL did not want me to. They felt that there was nobody else that they would want doing that job. I suppose that I became a victim of my own efficiency. However, relief was at hand, as the whole operation changed. LBN decided that in future they would have all their supplies sent by container vessel into the port of Lagos instead of by charter vessel into their own private wharf. I did my last vessel at Easter 1998 after twelve happy years, and was then able to think of myself as being fully retired.

Not having to think about the next job and all the pre-planning that went into it gave us a lot of freedom to come and go as we pleased, which meant in effect that we spent even more time helping Lisa finish her house. Soon after this our third grandson arrived and each in turn had brought a lot of joy into our lives. Calum was born in 1993, Niall in 1996 and Rohan in 1998. They live in West Yorkshire, which puts them within easy reach, so we are able to see them quite frequently. Alasdair established his own company round about the time that Calum was born and we have had the pleasure of seeing it expand into what is now a highly-respected international company. Kim has gone from being almost a full time member of the team in the company to establishing a new career for herself, although she is still one of the company directors. That is when she can find the time between work and ferrying the boys to tennis and rugby.

Lisa's house was finally finished just in time for her to leave it and set up home with her partner Bill in his house. We still go there regularly, and help Bill with building work, and Lisa with her market garden. We find it easier to take holidays that require forward booking than we did when I was working, as I never knew when the next job would arrive. We still managed to go to Australia and New Zealand for a holiday when I was still at work. I think there had been a Presidential coup in Nigeria at the time and we knew that there would be no commercial activity for some time.

Life goes on a little more quietly now in the slow lane, although we still do a fair amount of travelling. We get to visit our beloved Scotland three or four times a year and will continue to do so as long as we are fit enough. I still think of my life as a work in progress and that is as good a place to end as any other.

Epilogue

I hope that I will be forgiven for going on so far beyond my original intention of recording something of my early life. It occurred to me quite early on that going away to sea in the 1940s was almost as different from what it is now as going to sea in the days of sail was to the time that I went away. That gave me the incentive to carry on, and to be perfectly honest I found that I was really enjoying reliving my life. If it all seems to be about me I can only claim that what had begun as a description of a time and place soon became my autobiography, which by definition has to have me at its centre. If those who read this book get even one quarter of the pleasure out of reading it as I got out of writing it, I will feel well satisfied.